Legacies of the Occult

Legacies of the Occult

Psychoanalysis, Religion, and
Unconscious Communication

Marsha Aileen Hewitt

SHEFFIELD UK   BRISTOL CT

Published by Equinox Publishing Ltd.

UK: Office 415, The Workstation, 15 Paternoster Row, Sheffield, South Yorkshire S1 2BX

USA: ISD, 70 Enterprise Drive, Bristol, CT 06010

www.equinoxpub.com

First published 2020

© Marsha Aileen Hewitt 2020

All rights reserved. No part of this publication may be reproduced or transmitted in any form or by any means, electronic or mechanical, including photocopying, recording or any information storage or retrieval system, without prior permission in writing from the publishers.

ISBN-13 978 1 78179 278 0 (hardback)
         978 1 78179 279 7 (paperback)
         978 1 78179 947 5 (ePDF)

British Library Cataloguing-in-Publication Data
A catalogue record for this book is available from the British Library.

Library of Congress Cataloging-in-Publication Data

Names: Hewitt, Marsha, 1948- author.
Title: Legacies of the occult : psychoanalysis, religion, and unconscious communication / Marsha Aileen Hewitt.
Description: Bristol : Equinox Publishing Ltd, 2020. | Includes bibliographical references and index. | Summary: "Telepathy, thought transference, unconscious communication. While some important early psychological theorists such as William James, Frederic W. H. Myers and Sigmund Freud all agreed that the phenomenon exists, their theoretical approaches to it were very different. James's and Myers's interpretations of and experimental investigations into telepathy or thought transference were an inextricable part of their psychical researches. Freud's insistence on the reality of thought transference had nothing to do with psychical research or paranormal phenomena, which he largely repudiated. Thought transference for Freud was located in a theory of the unconscious that was radically different from the subliminal mind embraced by James and Myers. Today thought transference is most commonly described as unconscious communication but was largely ignored by subsequent generations of psychoanalysts until most recently. Nonetheless, the recognition of unconscious communication has persisted as a subterranean, quasi-spiritual presence in psychoanalysis to this day. As psychoanalysis becomes more interested in unconscious communication and develops theories of loosely boundaried subjectivities that open up to transcendent dimensions of reality, it begins to assume the features of a religious psychology. Thus, a fuller understanding of how unconscious communication resonates with mystical overtones may be more deeply clarified, articulated and elaborated in contemporary psychoanalysis in an explicit dialogue with psychoanalytically literate scholars of religion. In Legacies of the Occult Marsha Aileen Hewitt argues that some of the leading theorists of unconscious communication represent a 'mystical turn' that is infused with both a spirituality and a revitalized interest in paranormal experience that is far closer to James and Myers than to Freud"—Provided by publisher.
Identifiers: LCCN 2019033527 (print) | LCCN 2019033528 (ebook) | ISBN 9781781792780 (hardback) | ISBN 9781781792797 (paperback) | ISBN 9781781799475 (ebook)
Subjects: LCSH: Telepathy. | Psychoanalysis.
Classification: LCC BF1171 .H415 2020 (print) | LCC BF1171 (ebook) | DDC 133.8/2—dc23
LC record available at https://lccn.loc.gov/2019033527
LC ebook record available at https://lccn.loc.gov/2019033528

Typeset by JS Typesetting Ltd, Porthcawl, Mid Glamorgan

In memory of
Albert Hewitt (1914-2001)
"In whose mind the electric current of belief never closed."

Contents

	Preface	ix
	Acknowledgements	xv
1	Freud, the Unconscious, and the "Irreligious" Psychoanalysis of Religion	1
2	Fluid Subjectivities, Extended Minds, and Unseen Worlds: Mystical Psychologies of Frederic W. H. Myers and William James	22
3	Telepathic "Presencing" in the Analytic Relationship	58
4	What Is the "This" that Changes Everything?	88
5	Psychoanalytic Hierophanies: The Sacred in Transit	118
6	Concluding Thoughts on the Psychoanalytic Psychology of Religion	153
	Notes	159
	References	164
	Index	179

Preface

> God loves man because He loves stories.
> (Elie Wiesel)

I am a scholar in the study of religions, with a particular interest in psychoanalytic theory. Whether or not one agrees with his views, Sigmund Freud offers a powerful critical hermeneutic framework for understanding the psychological forces that give rise to and shape that infinite variety of human experiences that scholars call "religious". Psychoanalysis has come a long way since Freud in theoretical and clinical knowledge. Unfortunately, there is in some areas of academic psychology and religious studies an assumption as widespread as it is erroneous that psychoanalysis means Freud. Related to that is an equally distorted view found throughout the secondary scholarly literature that Freud's theory of religion is reducible to a single text – *The Future of an Illusion*. In *Freud on Religion* (2014), I outlined the serious inadequacies of this myopic approach to Freud's critical theory of religion. Despite their significant differences, authors such as Carl Jung, Melford E. Spiro, Gananath Obeyesekere, Robert Paul, and Jeffrey J. Kripal have, along with Freud, made important contributions to the psychoanalytic/psychological study of religions. Simply put, psychoanalysis is fascinated by the internal worlds, unconscious fantasies and subjective experiences of human beings. The late historian of religions Jonathan Z. Smith joked that religious studies scholars and anthropologists are "gossips" ([1978] 1993, 298). So, too, are psychoanalysts "gossips", in the original Greek sense of the word – people who enjoy talking about other people. Smith also thought that Freud's 1907 essay, "Obsessive Actions and Religious Practices", which compares the ritual practices of both neurotics and religious actors, offered one of the most telling descriptions of a distinctive feature of religious activity he knew of. What was so important for Smith about the essay was Freud's use of *comparison* for illuminating and understanding patterns of human behavior within religious and non-religious contexts (Smith [1982] 1988, 38).

My research, graduate and undergraduate teaching, and writing in religious studies and psychoanalysis eventually included clinical training, which continues to enrich my academic work in many ways. When I write about trauma and its connection with multiple forms of visionary experiences, I do so from my years of witnessing the impact of trauma on *actual patients,* as well as from the scholarly literature in psychoanalysis. Clinical work has helped me to see with greater depth and clarity the kernel of existential truth that inevitably lies at the core of the most seemingly "crazy" stories that people tell. It has also contributed to a refinement of the comparativist perspective that is methodologically important in the study of religions, and which reveals how the similarities of human psychologies *also* illuminate their important differences in specific contexts. Very much like the study of religions, psychoanalysis helps to construct meaning out of the incredible, irrational, and strange narratives and texts that scholars struggle to interpret. The contribution of the hermeneutic power of psychoanalysis should not be underestimated or devalued, *especially* with respect to the study of religions. And to be clear: the psychoanalytic study of religions does not set out to *psychoanalyze* religious experiences or the people who have them. Rather, it strives *to think psychoanalytically* about these experiences in order to gain increased depth and complexity in formulating explanatory frameworks in the service of knowledge and understanding. Thus, comparison of obsessive, repeated patterns that are seen in both the private rituals of so-called neurotics and those of religious actors in communal contexts need *not* collapse into simplistic and vulgar conclusions dismissing religious individuals as merely neurotic, even if some may well be. Rather, a *comparison* of ritual actions in both individual and communal contexts provides insight into the ways in which human beings attempt to make sense of, influence, control, negotiate and position themselves within their worlds.

While psychoanalysis and the study of religions can work well together in formulating theoretical, interpretive, and, yes, explanatory frameworks for understanding religious actions, experiences and beliefs, they are also distinct and different. One thing the study of religions and psychoanalysis share is curiosity about the vast diversity of ways that human beings struggle to organize, articulate, and negotiate the contents of their minds. Both psychoanalytic theory and the study of religions are, again to cite Smith, "second order" discourses that scholars fashion in *their* efforts to make sense of and find meaning in human experiences (2004, 179). These theories may be understood as translation activities through which we attempt to connect with each other across our infinitely diverse differences. I want to stress that for me, threaded through the spectrum of diverse historical, cultural, social, ethnic and personal identities, is a stubbornly constant universal: *the human. Human beings. Humanity.* The study of religions and psychoanalysis are powerful intellectual technologies for interpreting and understanding our shared humanity. Psychoanalysis contributes to our efforts to build bridges between human beings in their sometimes astounding, often confusing, manifold differences. Everybody knows what it is like to have visions of other dimensions of reality because everybody has had a dream of some kind, at some point. Powerful affects and startling fantasies can sometimes cause us to wonder "who else" resides in the depths of our minds? "Why did I do or say what I did? It is so unlike me." "Whatever *possessed* me to do that?" Psychoanalysis begins with curiosity about ourselves and others. It struggles to understand the incongruities, the surprises, the things that don't fit on the surface, the realms outside conscious awareness that, while hidden, exert power over our lives. These are some of the reasons why psychoanalysis is a crucial dialogue partner for the study of religions.

Clinical practice has taught me that the mind of every individual is a unique, and uniquely human, internal universe containing astonishing capacities for creating meaning and coherence out of chaotic personal and social experiences. One of the most important means through which we all do this is by telling stories of our lives, our families, communities, and ancestors. These are our personal mythologies, culturally shaped and mediated in much the same way as are our social, communal and religious mythologies. Our personal and collective myths are sometimes regarded as sources of knowledge about the world and our relationship with it, and with each other. I agree with Smith and Freud that religions are distinctive expressions of human creativity that help us to map, construct, explain and inhabit the worlds in which we are located. For many people, these worlds lead to apprehensions, intimations or glimpses of transcendent, unseen worlds that are accessible only through dreams, visions, and a wide array of ritually induced (or spontaneous) alternative states of consciousness. The study of religions, psychoanalysis, and anthropology share a common interest in exploring the minds of others, their beliefs, experiences, feelings, fantasies, desires, fears, and ways of life that tell us not only about them, but also about ourselves. Our shared humanity.

When a distressed, perfectly sane patient told me that while fully awake he was visited by a spectral mother who wordlessly communicated to him that life would get better, that he would be alright, who imparted to him a blissful sense of peace he had never before known, I believed him. Not, "I believe that he believes he saw the woman." No. Do I believe that if I had been present, I too would have seen the spectral visitation, or that if a recording device had been operating in the room, it would have captured her image? No, I do not. Did he see her? I believe he did. Do I believe that there was a spirit presence in the room, with its own independent ontological reality, that took the form of a woman dressed in white? I do not. However, I do know that *something* happened, because from the moment he told me about his vision, his therapy turned a corner. From a psychoanalytic perspective, my patient's vision represented an expansion of his latent emotional potential. It told me that he had been slowly connecting with emotional resources he had not previously been able to experience. As a lapsed Catholic who was raised by an emotionally absent mother, he was now able to dream a mother (or more accurately, a *kind of mother*) he never had, a mother who could soothe and reassure him in ways his own mother never could. His Catholic background provided him with a rich cultural resource that, along with his own hidden emotional potential, allowed him to reimagine the comfort of loving maternal care derived from the particular cultural symbol of the Holy Mother of God. He was finally able to connect with emotional resources that had been slowly emerging during the analytic treatment.

This is a small illustration of how psychoanalysis helps to explain and understand a vision such as my patient had in all its culturally postulated spirituality *without having to accept or deny the ontological reality of his vision*. Psychoanalysis doesn't need to accept or deny the independent existence of the Holy Mother. It is *beside the point*. What my patient saw in his vision was his own future possibility and promise that life would get better, that he was not condemned to a loveless existence of isolation and failure. According to Christian biblical and theological traditions, some of Jesus's companions saw him after he died. Some didn't. Maybe those who did see him saw a culturally encoded vision of future promise and hope in the midst of their despair. Whatever happened with my patient or the followers of Jesus and their visions, *both* perspectives must be held as true. This is not "crypto-theology". Far from it. One of the most difficult challenges for scholars that is posed by both the study of religions and psychoanalysis is to be able to hold the tension, the unfilled mental space, as it were, that exists between different and seemingly contradictory perspectives. Such anomalous incongruities force us to think, to formulate provisional theories and explanatory frameworks of understanding, not to dismiss. We must hold all of our theories lightly in order to make room for new theories that are the result of the ongoing accumulations of knowledge. Freud would heartily agree.

Psychoanalysis continues to struggle in its efforts to explain the anomalous experiences of patients and analysts. Their central focus has been on telepathy, or those uncanny instances of unconscious communication in clinical contexts that psychoanalysts continue to report with increasing frequency. Although he did speculate about it, in his published work Freud appears uninterested in trying to fully explain the mechanics of unconscious communication. He was confident that science would one day figure it out. Freud's critique of religion, which is an integral part of his larger psychoanalytic theory, would not accept any form of religious, mystical or spiritual explanations of unconscious communication. As far as he was concerned, telepathic capacities were thoroughly human and natural, having nothing whatsoever to do with any form of transcendent reality. However, the psychoanalysts of subsequent generations are not so sure about this. My contention in this book is that in their efforts to explain the anomalous experiences they and their patients report, psychoanalysts are fashioning forms of spirituality that *for them* are fully compatible with both psychoanalysis and modern science.

This book offers a critical analysis of what I call contemporary spiritual or mystical psychoanalysis and the efforts it makes to explain unconscious communication by grounding it in paranormal sciences. In this way, a number of the psychoanalytic writers I discuss in this book are moving towards constructing what I call a "parapsychoanalysis". Psychoanalytic theory is often troubled by its own (and others') efforts to define it. Is psychoanalysis a science, a hermeneutic, a philosophy, a critical theory, or all of the above? In many respects, it may be said that it was all of these for Freud, as I argued in *Freud on Religion*. What it clearly was *not* for him was a religion or secular spirituality or parapsychoanalysis of any kind. Freud was adamant that psychoanalysis and religion remain utterly separate on the grounds that psychoanalysis must align itself with science, the antithesis of religion. Psychoanalysis has never been fully at ease with Freud's uncompromising critique of religion, even during his lifetime. However, Freud's acceptance of telepathy, or unconscious communication, may well be the unintended breach in his theorizing that has permitted psychoanalysis to double back on itself and become a modern psychological spirituality.

It may be argued that with his acceptance of telepathy, Freud opened a portal for later analysts to walk through and radically transform his most important concept, the crux of all psychoanalysis: the unconscious. Although I do not necessarily agree, I think there is nonetheless a reasonable argument to be made that with telepathy, Freud may have attenuated his own critique of religion. He was certainly aware of this risk, and said so. However, as I make clear in the pages that follow, I think there are some serious theoretical problems with the ways in which contemporary psychoanalysts attempt to justify their embrace of spirituality, most significantly through superficial readings of contested, unresolved and enormously complex theories in modern science. My argument is that a more robust psychoanalytic theorizing of anomalous experience is to be located in an explicit dialogue with the study of religions, which is where it belongs. Psychoanalysis needs to take a step back from its rush to proclaim the "scientific" proof for its spiritual intuitions and think instead about where it stands in the history of the *religious psychology* of religion. As Barbara Ehrenreich said in a published interview about her own mystical experience at Lone Pine, "if something has happened that you don't have words for, keep thinking" (*New York Times Sunday Magazine*, 30 March 2014).

Toronto, Canada
June 2019

Acknowledgements

I am grateful to my friends and colleagues who discussed many of the ideas presented in this book with me over the years and who read portions of the manuscript. In particular I thank Ann Baranowski, Stuart Pizer, Joel Ruimy and Donald Wiebe. I especially want to thank Jeffrey J. Kripal, not only for his insightful comments, but for our many conversations over the years that continue to challenge my own thinking. May they continue. Although I take full responsibility for the arguments and interpretations advanced here, the thoughtful, critical comments of my colleagues helped me clarify and deepen my own thinking along the way.

I also want to thank the undergraduate and graduate students in the Department for the Study of Religion at the University of Toronto whose interest in psychoanalysis and religion has been more gratifying and helpful to me in developing these ideas than they will ever know. Teaching is very much a two-way street, and I continue to learn from my students. My gratitude also to the patients with whom I have worked in clinical practice over the years. Psychoanalysis is truly alive when working with human beings, whose life experiences contribute to tempering scholarship with humility and intellectual honesty.

And again, to Joel Ruimy, my heartfelt thanks for your editorial skills and your commitment to supporting this work.

Thank you all.

1

Freud, the Unconscious, and the "Irreligious" Psychoanalysis of Religion

> Culture fantasies protect men from clear knowledge of their predicament at all times. But that is the function of sacred culture.
>
> (La Barre [1970] 2010, 207)

> [Freud] did not anticipate the close relationship that psychology now shares with spirituality in the transitional space that is the world of illusion.
>
> (Hill and Hood 1999, 1037)

Sigmund Freud remarked on more than one occasion that psychoanalysis was his creation. While this is certainly true, he cannot be considered to own the field. Much has changed in the development of psychoanalytic theory and clinical practice since his death. What has not changed in psychoanalysis is the centrality of its defining concept, the unconscious, which distinguishes psychoanalysis from all other forms of psychology. However, there are different interpretations and approaches to the unconscious within psychoanalysis that I will explore throughout this book. The basic fault line that most clearly divides Freud's concept of the unconscious from that of the analytic writers I discuss later concerns the role and meaning of religion within psychoanalysis. Freud's unsparing critique of religion, which includes mystical spirituality, is well known. Religion in any form, as far as he was concerned, has no legitimate place in psychoanalysis. Religion, which privileges faith and the heteronomous authority of tradition, is the antithesis of evidence-based reason and the moral autonomy of human beings. In contrast to religion, Freud believed that psychoanalysis belonged within scientifically based epistemological frameworks. In a previous study I examined what I described as Freud's critical theory of religion and scholarly receptions of it, many of which distort and misunderstand the nuances of his complex and differentiated critique (Hewitt 2014a). His critical theory of religion deliberately went against the religious tendencies that dominated the emerging field of psychology in the late nineteenth and early twentieth centuries. As G. Stanley Hall, one of the founders of the field of psychology of religion stated in 1885:

> The new psychology ... is I believe Christian to its roots and centre; and its final mission in the world is not merely to trace petty harmonies and small adjustments between science and religion, but to flood and transfuse the new and vaster conceptions of the universe and man's place in it ... with the old Scriptural sense of unity, rationality, and love beneath and above all, with all its wide consequences.
>
> (In Fuller 2001, 128)

Hall is unequivocal that psychology's task is to preserve religious intuitions and spirituality in a context where the credibility and appeal of traditional religion, seriously undermined by the discoveries of science and technology, was being rejected throughout society. As Graham Richards notes, North American psychology prior to the First World War was "deeply infused with the need to reconcile" psychology and religion (2000, 207). Nonetheless, religious psychology incorporated a number of psychoanalytic concepts, most notably, the unconscious.

The Uncanny and the Unconscious

While Freud cannot be said to have "discovered" the unconscious, he was certainly the first to theorize it as a dynamic mental agency or psychic system that is made up of somatically based instinctual energies, repressed ideas, the conflicts of forbidden desire, and non-repressed phylogenetic inheritances. The major portion of mental life is made up of unconscious forces that are directly related to individual life circumstances and a realm of accumulated psychic inheritances that are "other" to specific autobiographical experiences. Sometimes individuals experience feelings that diverge so strongly from the context of their lives that a "phylogenetic" model is helpful for understanding their "innate dispositions" (Freud 1939, 99, 98). Depending on the historical and cultural context, the stirring of the phylogenetic unconscious may be experienced as an invasion of spirits, or any number of nameless, inchoate forces that seem to operate beyond or in spite of our conscious will. "Whatever possessed me to do such-and-such?" or "I don't know what came over me" or "the devil made me do it" are common, colloquial acknowledgments of self-experience that occasionally feels alien or "other". Such experiences need not be so dramatic. Intersubjectivity is "an essential aspect of human relatedness" (Brown 2011, 9), and as such cannot be claimed by any specific brand of psychoanalysis. Freud recognized that we are intersubjective beings whose internal mental models develop through countless interactions with our social environment. Intersubjectivity is also composed of unconscious processes of multiple internalized identifications with parents, social authorities, traditions, religious teachings and moral codes that all contribute to the constitution of individual identity. In cases of traumatic experience, these internalized others can often feel like uncanny presences that haunt our psyches if they cannot be fully integrated.

The uncanny sense that forces exist beyond our control and impact our lives in important ways include extra-sensory perception (ESP) experiences or "psi" phenomena. There is a growing, and widespread belief in the existence of various forms of paranormal phenomena, including and especially telepathy, which is a major theme of this book. It is a mistake to trivialize or dismiss belief in telepathy as appealing only to the uneducated and the superstitious, or to consider it as an atavistic relic of premodern cultures. As I argue throughout this book, belief in the paranormal belongs within the study of religion because it is a form of non-traditional religiosity, or spirituality, and in that sense, needs to be taken as seriously as any other area of religious belief. For many people, belief in some form of paranormal phenomena is part of the modern pursuit of deeper levels of self-understanding, personal authenticity, and spiritual wisdom (Wuthnow 1998, 152). As both Egil Asprem and Robert Wuthnow point out, telepathy is positively correlated with levels of higher education and negatively correlated with traditional religion (Asprem 2014a, 338; Wuthnow 1998, 134). Of even greater importance for the subject of this book, belief in telepathy especially correlates positively to attitudes to science and modern rationality. For people who believe in telepathy and other forms of paranormal phenomena, naturalistic frameworks of meaning are central for establishing a scientific basis and validation for these otherwise inexplicable phenomena (Asprem 2014a, 348). It is important to bear in mind that belief (or disbelief) in God is *not a requirement* for belief in the existence of the paranormal (ibid., 335). My argument throughout this book is that paranormal beliefs must be considered as a legitimate form of a secular, non-theological or traditionally religious spirituality. Psychology and psychoanalysis are an important part of modern, non-religious spirituality in so far as they offer assistance in exploring the inner self and its inherent connection with the sacred. In this way, the beliefs and intuitions associated with spirituality can be seen as compatible with science.

Older mythological and traditional religious explanations of non-material, occult or hidden dimensions of transcendent reality have by now been largely displaced by an increasing reliance on the promise that science can reveal the mysteries inherent within the natural world. This is not a new development. Nineteenth-century Anglo-American spiritualism turned to science, not religion, in order to explain telepathic communication between the living and the dead that were believed to have occurred in séances. As I will discuss in more detail in the next chapter, William James tried to explain how a discarnate spirit might possibly communicate with the living in a way that would not contradict the laws of nature. He was a psychologist, not a spiritualist. Yet scientists and spiritualists alike agreed that science had to expand its borders of inquiry and rational methodology in order to explain paranormal or "psi" phenomena, which they regarded as naturally occurring events. The rationality associated with Newtonian laws of causality were deemed as insufficient to explain the invisible but no less natural hidden dimensions of reality that operate according to their own laws and become manifest in the external world. Phenomena such as premonitions or telepathy were viewed as *super* natural capacities latent in human beings. Psychology was championed by some of the most important intellectuals of the nineteenth and early twentieth centuries as offering a new and promising scientific basis that could transform traditional religious beliefs such as human beings are made in the image of a remote, anthropomorphic God, by providing evidence for the divine nature of the self.

Freud and the Unconscious

A neuroscientist for the first two decades of his professional career, Freud did not believe that consciousness was simply reducible to brain functioning. He was an Enlightenment intellectual who nonetheless severely challenged the Enlightenment notion that human beings possessed the capacity for completely subjugating their affects and bodily impulses to the dictates of reason. As far as Freud was concerned, this was a dangerous myth. Under optimal social and material conditions the darker forces within the self were certainly capable of sublimation into higher forms of cultural productivity such as art, morality and scientific achievement, but they could not be extirpated. Freud unsettled and destabilized these Enlightenment ideals. Clinical experience with neurotic and hysterical patients, a knowledge of history, Darwin's evolutionary theories, the anthropological and religious studies scholarship of his day, and the devastations of the First World War alone provided more than enough evidence for him to conclude that the rational ego is by no means master in its own house. To think otherwise is to succumb to an arrogance of consciousness from which we need to free ourselves (Freud 1915b, 193). As far as Freud was concerned, human beings would do well to bear in mind that they are neither different from nor superior to animals, from whom they are descended (Freud 1917a, 143, 141).

The impulses and desires residing deep within the unconscious, a chaotic reservoir of internal conflict and strife, play out in the world of history in tragic and savage ways. In his meditations on the barbarity and carnage of the First World War, Freud bluntly acknowledged the impossibility of putting an end to evil because of the nature of instinctual life that ruthlessly fights for the satisfaction of primal needs. The oft-cited question posed by Horkheimer and Adorno in the immediate aftermath of the Second World War, as to why "humanity, instead of entering a truly human state, is sinking into a new kind of barbarism" (2002, xiv), speaks to a preoccupation of Freud's that lasted until the end of his life. Like Horkheimer and Adorno, whom he influenced, Freud also recognized the grim "dialectic" existing within the heart of the Enlightenment. He would have agreed with the assessment of Horkheimer and Adorno (2002) that, in its inexorable quest to conquer the universe and every living thing in it through increasingly sophisticated and lethal technical means, enlightenment consumes itself in a heartless expansion of instrumental reason driven by fantasies of mastery over nature and freedom from irrationality. In this way the Enlightenment not only collapses back into myth, it generates a mass psychotic delusion that increased domination and thanatological reason hold the promise of freedom. If he were alive today, Freud would not be surprised that humanity is methodically destroying the planet. Human beings have a long evolutionary history as primarily irrational creatures who are driven by the imperative to survive. An enduring premise of Freud's psychoanalytic anthropology is that human beings pass down archaic legacies originating in the primordial dawn of the species (Freud 1915a, 281, 283). According to contemporary neuroscience, we share the same neural "soil" as our mammalian ancestors (Panksepp 1998, 302). The unconscious preserves traces from every stage of evolutionary development, according to Freud.

Grim as this picture may be, it should not be regarded as merely the result of idiosyncratic moral judgments borne of solipsistic disillusion or despair. There is also a strong sense of hope that permeates Freudian psychoanalysis that is quite different, though far less satisfying, from consolations offered by religion. Freud investigated the irrational in the hopes of strengthening Enlightenment goals of individual autonomy and emancipation, social and individual justice, and contributing to the advancement of science (Hewitt 2018a). Freud also believed that the conflicts between culture and human nature reflected the dynamic conflicts within the mind, which he attempted to explore in his writings on culture, and on religion in particular. While Freud was a neuroscientific researcher and a clinician in private practice, he was also a critical theorist (Hewitt 2014a) who never lost sight of the interactions between the individual mind and its cultural context, and the ways in which they shape each other. Freud not only used his extensive knowledge of the anthropological and evolutionary scholarship of his day in forming his cultural and social analyses, he also drew upon clinical work to gain deeper insights into the ways in which unconscious fantasy and psychic life are reflected in art, myth, religions and moral codes.

A Psycho-mythology: *Oedipus Rex*

The tragic family drama of Sophocles's play *Oedipus Rex* was not invoked by Freud to argue for a simplistic and vulgar "truth" that sons want to have sex with their mothers. For Freud, the power of the play was demonstrated in its ongoing appeal to audiences over the millennia who responded to Sophocles's depiction of the human condition, familiar to them all, that despite one's best intentions and knowledge, and against one's will, horrific consequences may nonetheless result. The human condition is a complex web threaded through by will and fate that together comprise a "daimonic" force that we can only partly direct. "Daimon and Tyche [Endowment and Chance] determine a man's fate – rarely or never one of these powers alone" (Freud 1912a, 99n2). The daimonic is a force that lies somewhere between the personal and the impersonal, however the latter is conceived, as gods, demons or alien spirits (Loewald 2000, 537). Freud goes on to observe that the human constitution is "a precipitate from the accidental effects produced on the endlessly long chain of our ancestors" (1912a 99n2; Hewitt 2014a, 101–102).

The tragedy of the Oedipal drama is further augmented in its portrayal of the *inevitable* conflict between the generations and the *inevitable* guilt associated with the "primal crime" of the annihilation of parental authority that is inherent in the maturation process. The freedom and autonomy achieved by the mature adult are bought with the currency of guilt, loss and shame that inheres in the course of psychological development. The degree to which this process is attenuated by loving attachment experiences is largely, although not entirely, environment-dependent. For psychoanalyst and anthropologist Robert Paul, the Greek play dramatizes a "collective, publicly constituted fantasy that corresponds to the unconscious incestuous and rivalrous fantasies" that audiences the world over will recognize as resonating with the "repressed residues of childhood" (1991, 268). It is a "public text" that both reflects and helps us understand who we are (ibid., 269). Human beings are born within contexts of an already existing "social imaginary" that constitutes and powerfully shapes subjectivity. As psychoanalyst and critical theorist Cornelius Castoriadis observes, the individual subject is "traversed through and through by the world and by others" (1998, 106). Despite all this, individuals strive to develop a measure of freedom and autonomy that can end in tragic consequences far removed from what they imagine or consciously plan. Like all cultural productions, including religion, *Oedipus Rex* gives meaning and emotional power to the hidden yet active archaic dimensions of human existence through symbol and mythic narrative. As Freud wrote to Wilhelm Fliess on 12 December 1897, the "dim inner perception of one's own psychical apparatus stimulates illusions of thought, which are naturally projected outwards and characteristically into the future and the world beyond. Immortality, retribution, life after death, are all reflections of our inner psyche ... psycho-mythology" (1954, 237).

Archaic Inheritance: Psychobiological Tracks in the Collective Unconscious

For Freud, archaic inheritance refers to a vast reservoir of unconscious accumulated memory traces laid down and transmitted through an infinite repetition of experiences made up of biological and cultural interactional influences. Freud understood archaic inheritance as the legacy of psychical dispositions, any one or more of which may become operative in the life of an individual due to specific experiences (Paul 1991, 282). Unconscious ideas, derived from biologically mediated, endlessly repeated human experiences that are encoded within cultural symbolic structures, create "mode[s] of information storage that, like genetic information but independent of it, [are] transmitted across generations" (ibid., 282). Freud's efforts to trace the connections between biologically based drives and culture are compatible with ideas that surface in some later theories of religion. In a later effort to explain the ubiquity of religions across cultures and historical periods, classicist Walter Burkert argues for a theory that connects biology and culture as mutually informative or bidirectional. Like Paul, Burkert maintains that:

> This does not mean that genes prescribe culture – clearly, they do not. But it could be said that they give recommendations that become manifest in the repetition of like patterns, "the kinds of memories most easily recalled, the emotions they are most likely to evoke".
>
> (Burkert [1996] 2001, 22)

Religions, in all their infinite cultural and historical diversity and ubiquitous persistence, reflect "the hard rocks of the biological landscape, the dangers, limits, and the drive for the preservation of life, all of which are internalized and encoded in them" (ibid., 32). In his own conceptualization of the archaic heritage of human beings and the transmission of the memory-traces of earlier generations, Freud advances remarkably similar ideas to Burkert in formulating speculative parallels with the instinctual life of animals:

> it can only be that [animals] bring the experiences of their species with them into their own new existence – that is, that they have preserved memories of what was experienced by their ancestors. The position in the human animal would not at bottom be different. His own archaic heritage corresponds to the instincts[1] of animals even though it is different in its compass and contents.
> (Freud 1939, 100)

The point here is not to evaluate the merits or deficiencies of any particular version of evolutionary theory by attempting to adjudicate the ideas of Freud, Burkert, or Paul. Rather, my interest in introducing these ideas is to bring attention to Freud's insistence that we are embodied creatures with a long evolutionary history within which what we call civilization is a relatively recent development. His two most controversial cultural works, *Totem and Taboo* (1913) and *Moses and Monotheism* (1939) outline an evolutionary anthropology that situates the origins of religion and morality in the traumatic transgressions of patricide and incest. Briefly, Freud postulates that prehistoric humans lived in small tribal bands dominated by an alpha male. Frustrated and angry with their subjugated position and lack of access to the women in the tribe, the "sons" murdered the tyrannical father and then scattered as a result of the horror, terror and, later, the guilt associated with their patricidal action. Eventually the sons, having become exogenous, agreed that survival was far better ensured through the establishment of cooperative relationships rather than tyrannical rule. As Freud sees it, the "brothers" erected taboos against incest and patricide over eons of evolutionary development in order to ensure social cooperation and egalitarian relationships. These taboos constitute for Freud the universal foundation of moral norms, ethics and religious systems of later civilizations.

Freud's narrative of the primal horde is his interpretive, imaginative account of the transition from small hunter-gatherer tribal bands of the Upper Palaeolithic era to the formation of the more populous complex agrarian settlements of the Neolithic period. Freud argues throughout this time the memory of the brothers' ambivalent relationship with the father whom they loved, hated, feared and idealized persisted in their collective unconscious. Motivated by unconscious guilt, they eventually devised ways to memorialize and worship the father, now represented by a totem animal, in re-enactments of the original crime through ritual sacrifice that allowed for both reparation for the crime and the release of controlled aggression away from the community. Thus morality and religions, essential elements in the bedrock of civilizations, emerged out of countlessly repeated acts of violence, transgression, and trauma. For Paul, the value of Freud's myth of the primal horde does not lie in trying to establish its literal truth, since there is no evidence to support it. At the same time, he cautions that: "We lose more than we gain if we allow the dated and objectionable aspects of the work to blind us to its positive contribution" (Paul 1991, 271) as a rich resource of psychoanalytic insights into individual minds and the cultural contexts within which they are formed. Freud himself insisted that the primal crime was not a unique historical event, but rather likely occurred "countless times in countless social groups over eons of evolutionary time" (Paul 2010, 239). In this way the myth of the primal horde may be seen to symbolically encode the existence of psychological dispositions that both support and counter the "dominance hierarchy" that is a part of our "evolved psychological propensities" (239). As Freud remarked to his colleague Ludwig Binswanger, psychoanalysis as a theory of the human mind and culture rarely ventures "beyond the ground floor and basement of the building" (in Hewitt 2014a, 1).

Psychoanalysis and the Critique of Religion

As I have argued in greater depth and detail elsewhere (Hewitt 2014a), Freud's critical theory of religion cannot be separated from psychoanalysis *as he conceived of it*. This is an important point, because there is a large and significant body of psychoanalytic literature that argues the opposite, as I will show in the following chapters. Yet it is not the case that Freud's writings on religion can somehow be hived off from the rest of his psychoanalytic theory. As his most recent biographer, Joel Whitebook, rightly observes, it is a mistake to interpret them as representing a form of "applied" psychoanalysis; nor should they be regarded as "cultural supplements to his fundamental theory" (Whitebook 2017, 377). The centrality of Freud's critiques of religion in particular are inextricably entwined with his theory of the unconscious, which for him could not be associated with religion in any form, including spirituality or mysticism. Freud's theory of the unconscious is the watershed that divides what I call throughout this book spiritual or mystical psychoanalysis, from what he understood as a scientific or natural theory of psychoanalysis. Freud's attitude towards science is probably as egregiously misrepresented as are his views on religion. Freud is typically represented as adhering to a crude "positivist" scientism often associated with mechanistic rationality. Yet a careful reading of texts such as *The Question of a Weltanschauung* (1933), or the even more maligned and misread *The Future of an Illusion* (1927), show Freud's deep concern with both the intellectual values of evidence-based theorizing and the ethical and political values of human autonomy and critical, independent thought. In Freud's view, organized religions with their insistence on hegemonic doctrinal orthodoxy, conformity of thought, and demands for unreflective obedience to ecclesiastical authority are antithetical to critical thinking, mature independence and humane politics. Religions have their origins in the unconscious fantasies of early childhood. In other words, they are the creations of universal psychological capacities that are shaped and articulated through a diversity of expressions through the work of culture.

Freud's critical analyses of religion are directly opposed to the far more religiously oriented psychoanalytic traditions discussed in this book, which are mostly represented by the work of American psychoanalysts. While the intellectual trajectory of American psychoanalysis both preserves and transforms religion along the lines of a spiritual psychology, Freud rejects religion as antithetical to psychoanalysis. The radical difference between Freudian and American psychoanalysis with respect to religion is most clearly seen in their different approaches to the unconscious. While the Freudian unconscious is characterized by conflict and repression, the more religiously and spiritually compatible American approach "has an enduring tendency to symbolize harmony, restoration, and revitalization" (Fuller 1986, 5). As I argue in the chapters that follow, there are significant strains within American psychoanalysis that are highly compatible not only with spiritual and mystical forms of religiosity, but with belief in the paranormal. Freud was not a mystic in any sense of the term. While he is most often described as atheistic, I prefer the term "irreligious" because it is less cathected with emotional charge and clichéd baggage. Unlike Richard Dawkins or Christopher Hitchens, Freud took human religiosity seriously, which should be self-evident given the amount of careful attention he paid to it. It cannot be overemphasized that like every other mental phenomenon, Freud explored religion and spirituality *psychoanalytically*. He explored questions concerning the ubiquity of culturally produced religious beliefs and experiences by locating their origins in the human mind.

The concept of the unconscious, however, is not immune to spiritualistic or mystical interpretations, as Freud knew full well. Nor is it resistant to paranormal associations either, as he also knew from his association with Carl Jung. As I argue throughout this book, especially with reference to William James and Frederic Myers, (who were major influences on Jung) it is a Romantic version of a *spiritual* unconscious that is an important part of the legacy that has helped to shape contemporary mystical psychoanalysis in its most important aspects. American psychoanalysis, as most notably (but not exclusively) represented in contemporary relational[2] psychoanalytic writers, re-envisions the spiritual nature and potential of the unconscious as a key pathway to internal harmony and self-authenticity. The "I–Thou" relationship between God and humanity provides a model for unalienated intersubjective human relations of mutual recognition (Aron 2004, 447–448). This in part has to do with the assimilation of object relations theory, which generally emphasizes that the infant is motivated from birth primarily to seek an intimate, loving relationship with the mother, rather than satisfying bodily needs such as hunger. The emphasis on love as the prime motivator in seeking a relationship with the mother/world is often connected with an inherent need for connection with a loving God. A significant number of early object relations theorists, including those credited as its founders, explicitly use Jesus as the model for loving human relationships (Hewitt 2018a). As psychologists of religion Ralph Hood and Peter Hill rightly observe, of all the previously established psychoanalytical frameworks, object relations theory appears to be most compatible with spirituality and mysticism (Hill and Hood 1999, 1032).

Freud and Jung

The differences between mystical[3] ideas about the nature of the unconscious in these forms of contemporary psychoanalysis and Freud's could not be clearer. In part this is because a number of implicitly Jungian tropes have also found their way into contemporary American psychoanalysis. While Jung insisted that he was a "strictly empirical scholar" whose theory of mind was compatible with the natural sciences, he also insisted that the "occult" was "central" to his conception of psychology (Hanegraaff 2012, 285, 286). Jung's interest in the occult,[4] and the strong association of his mother and other relatives with spiritualism, need not be explored here (Jung 1963). The importance of Jung for this study is largely connected with the psychological theories that influenced him and continue to resonate within contemporary psychoanalysis, which I discuss in much greater depth in the next chapter. At first blush, Jung's notion that the unconscious represents what the German Romantics called the "nightshade of nature" that contains gnostic secrets of the "hidden powers" of the "soul" (Hanegraaff 2012, 287) may appear to correspond with Freud's idea of the "darkness" of the mind. However, nothing could be further from the truth. Jungian psychology is sometimes associated with a "new occultism" or "new spirituality" that emerged at the turn of the twentieth century and promoted "the self-conscious exploration of personal interiority" or modern striving towards "self-realization" through theoretical and clinical psychologies (Owen 2004, 11, 13), all of which remain important themes in spiritual psychoanalysis.

A brief discussion of Jung is relevant here primarily because it helps to clarify further the contours of what I mean by mystical or spiritual psychology. It is also relevant because identifiable Jungian tropes that can be detected within American psychological and psychoanalytic intellectual traditions were heavily shaped by the influence of William James, who is more important to this study. However, a brief consideration of Jung helps to bring out further the differences between mystical psychoanalysis and Freud, his erstwhile collaborator, on a few key points. To this end, I will juxtapose Freud's paper "Formulations on the Two Principles of Mental Functioning" (1911) with Jung's "Two Kinds of Thinking" ([1956] 1990) in order to further illustrate their diametrically opposed views of the unconscious. This will also help to illuminate the kind of spirituality that is embraced by the writers discussed later on. Whitebook's claim that Freud's paper is an implicit rejoinder to Jung (Whitebook 2017, 296) shows how concerned Freud was to establish clear boundaries between psychoanalysis, religion, and the occult. While Freud's psychoanalytic theory in general and notion of the unconscious in particular is based upon an uncompromising commitment to naturalism, freedom from religious bias and "de-occultization" and disenchantment (ibid., 275), Jung shows an equally uncompromising commitment to aligning psychology and the unconscious with the realm of spirituality and myth.

In a view with which we shall become very familiar in the course of this book, Jung explicitly subordinates "directed" thinking that privileges speech, science, and technology to "dreaming or fantasy thinking", which is spontaneous (Jung [1956] 1990, 18–19). Progress in science and technology, he writes, have made humanity "rich in knowledge, but poor in wisdom" (ibid., 20). He deploys a fairly typical modern strategy that has become associated with later New Age thought by elevating mythic, religious or spiritual knowledge above the "dead, cold" materialism of science (ibid., 25). As far as Jung is concerned, Freud represents the "outmoded rationalism and scientific materialism of the late nineteenth century" (ibid., xxiii). In sharp contrast to Freud's theory of archaic inheritance discussed above, Jung's version holds that there is an objective, collective mythic substructure or universal psychic reservoir that generates every manifestation of the individual unconscious. Myths are humanity's dreams, comprising the "oldest layers of the human mind, long buried beneath the threshold of consciousness" (ibid., 29). The "archaic basis of the mind is a matter of objective fact", he writes (ibid.). It is not dependent on individual experience or personal choice. Jung goes so far as to paint an idealized portrait of psychotic regression as leading to the deepest archaic strata of undifferentiated mind, the universal substratum of the raw unconscious. This undifferentiated unconscious is the universal source of all cross-cultural and transhistorical mythologies. In Jung's view, psychosis can represent emancipation from the constraints of harsh reality, a freeing-up of subjective tendencies that inhibit or block access to gnostic, elemental truths of the inner world. We will encounter traces of this idea in some of the psychoanalytic writers to be discussed later. Jung also believed that the psychotic delusions of the present are actually expressions of our collective, mythic past. As he said in his 1935 Tavistock lectures, the deepest level of the unconscious mind "is the layer where man is no longer a distinct individual, but where mind widens out and merges into the mind of mankind. ... On this collective level we are no longer separate individuals, we are all one" (in Addison 2016, 575). As we shall see in the next chapter, the influence of William James and Frederic Myers could not be clearer.

In his "Formulations on the Two Principles of Mental Functioning" (1911), Freud takes a very different approach to psychotic regression than Jung. Freud viewed mental illness, either in its neurotic or psychotic forms, as the individual's experience of alienation from "unbearable" reality (ibid., 218). Freud writes that dreams are an escape from reality and the painful conflicts between desire, the pleasure principle, and the unforgiving demands of the reality principle. In sleep and in dreams, the pleasure principle strives to achieve the fulfilment of wishes. However, human survival depends upon the capacity to embrace and adjust to the reality principle. Human psychological development is a process where the hallucinatory wish-fulfilments of infancy are superseded by the gradually unfolding capacity for affect and impulse regulation, reflective thought, the toleration of tension and the delay of immediate gratification in favour of more enduring individual and social benefits. An inevitable part of this developmental process leading to the ascendancy of the reality principle relocates phantasy mentation to play, "phantasying" and dreaming (ibid., 222). The tension between the wishing "pleasure-ego" and the "reality-ego" that is directed to adaptation and survival is attenuated by the compensations offered by religious myths. In Freud's view, the "doctrine of reward in the after-life for the – voluntary or enforced – renunciation of earthly pleasures is nothing other than a mythical projection of this revolution in the mind. Following consistently along these lines, *religions* have been able to effect absolute renunciation of pleasure in this life by means of the promise of compensation in a future existence; but they have not by this means achieved a conquest of the pleasure principle. It is *science* which comes nearest to succeeding in that conquest" (ibid., 223). Freud and Jung could not be further apart in their evaluations of myth, religions and, most important, what constitutes mental health. There is nothing romantic or idealized about the Freudian unconscious; for Jung, it is an entirely different story.

Nonetheless, albeit again in very different ways, both Freud and Jung acknowledged the existence of an archaic inheritance that is part of a collective unconscious. While Freud begs the question of the nature of the collective unconscious with his dismissive comment that it is "in any case a collective, universal property of mankind" (1939, 132), it clearly did not have the spiritualized, mystical quality that it did for Jung. While Freud did not have access to contemporary theories of "dual inheritance" and epigenetics (Paul 2015), his work makes it very clear that he would have been inclined to agree that human beings are "hybrid creature[s]" whose evolutionary development is "completely dependent on two different channels of information, one genetic and one cultural" (ibid., 5). As Freud comments:

> The experiences of the ego seem at first to be lost for inheritance; but, when they have been repeated often enough and with sufficient strength in many individuals in successive generations, they transform themselves, so to say, into experiences of the id, the impressions of which are preserved by heredity. Thus in the id, which is capable of being inherited, are harboured residues of the existences of countless egos.
>
> (Freud 1923a, 38)

Freud's ideas of a collective unconscious and archaic inheritance, however incompletely formed or disputed they may be within contemporary evolutionary theories, cannot in any way be linked to Jung's ideas of a trans-historical source of universal myths or primitive "thought-forms" of a "half-shadow" unconscious (Jung [1956] 1990, 29). Jung's psychological theories are interwoven with occult themes, which he readily acknowledged. His theory of synchronicity for example, "the occurrence of a *meaningful coincidence in time*" (Jung [1955] 2008, 144) is based on the idea of acausal reasoning that is also strongly implied in his descriptions of dreams and intuition in his "Two Kinds of Thinking". Synchronicity is closely linked to telepathy and the "numinosity" of meaningful "chance happenings" (ibid., 14n11) as illustrated in Jung's story of a beetle that appeared in his consulting room at the exact moment that his patient was telling him about her dream of a golden scarab (ibid., 31). Freud also wrote about telepathy, and he admitted that telepathy, or thought-transference (*Gedankenübertragung*), occurs in clinical contexts. Jung connected the idea of synchronicity to early quantum science as part of his effort to establish a naturalistic basis for psychic phenomena. Jung also included astrology, alchemy and magic within his own version of depth psychology in an effort to "unmask positivism as 'superstition' and announce the return of 'magic' as science!" (Hanegraaff 2012, 294).

As for religion, Jung regarded the established Western monotheisms as little more than alienating, historical veneers concealing the "universal substratum" (Hanegraaff 2012, 295) or fount of gnostic truth of the objective unconscious. Jung, who came to believe in the survival of bodily death and reincarnation (Shamdasani 2015, 299), represents a "depth psychology that emphasized multiple realities, psychic phenomena, supernatural powers, the mythopoetic function of the unconscious, and transformative mystical experiences" (Taylor 1996a, 554). It is especially relevant for this study to point out the "major epistemological differences" (ibid.) between Freud and the legacy of spiritual psychology that continues on in psychoanalysis. As I discuss in greater detail in the following chapter, William James remains by far the most important and relevant influence that continues to shape the spiritual trajectory of mystical psychoanalytic psychology in the American cultural context. As Fuller observes, "[i]f any one individual has ever personified what it means to be 'spiritual but not religious', it was William James. ... James casts a long shadow over American intellectual and religious thought" (2001, 130, 134).

It is important to reiterate as well that "Jung credited James with showing him how the horizons of the unconscious stretched off into the illimitable" (Taylor 1996a, 556). This also accounts for the greater emphasis I place on James rather than Jung throughout the book because of the importance of James's influence on contemporary American psychoanalysis. Fuller astutely observes that the "intellectual dispositions" inherited primarily from James "ultimately forced American psychoanalysts to modify their account of unconscious mental forces to accommodate to the prevailing cultural climate" that embraced an individualist, spiritual and mystical belief in the inner divine nature of all human beings. Mystical or spiritual psychoanalysis – I use the terms interchangeably – preserves and extends the central Jamesian idea that the unconscious is intimately connected with a cosmic, "transindividual spiritual force" (Fuller 1986, 74). Finally, it is worth noting in passing that Jung referred to his psychology, as his followers do to this day, as analytical psychology, *not* psychoanalysis. He wanted to distinguish himself from Freud as much as Freud did from him.

It is with the elements interwoven within the hermeneutic framework established above that I discuss the ways in which key representatives of contemporary, spiritual American psychoanalysis seek to explain telepathic phenomena and other psychic, paranormal or anomalous experiences that clinicians have reported with varying degrees of openness for decades. In identifying the important differences between Freud's concept of the psychoanalytic unconscious and the spiritual unconscious of contemporary psychoanalysis, I attempt to bring further coherence and clarity to the contradictory and overlapping meanings of the unconscious by situating my discussion with respect to the study of religion. In other words, I interpret this important strand of psychoanalysis as a religious phenomenon because it blends diverse elements of modern, secular, New Age spiritual/mystical psychology. As we shall see in the following chapters, exploration of the unconscious in non-traditional or non-Freudian psychoanalytic therapeutic settings is an integral part of a "psychologically regenerative" (Fuller 1986, 95) process directed towards the spiritual transformation of the whole personality. Thus psychological integration is gained through a clinical process whose goal is to realize or access the divine nature within the self that interconnects human beings and all reality. For psychoanalysts committed to this understanding of therapeutic action, psychoanalysis is a "sacred task" (Aron 2004, 449).

"New Prints of the Clichés we Bear within us"

Freud's friendly debate with Roman Rolland, the French literary figure, mystic and Nobel Prize winner, on the question of the "oceanic feeling" as the source of religions is well known.[5] Although I discuss Freud's treatment of the oceanic feeling in greater detail later, a few preliminary comments are in order. I am probably one of the few scholars who does not interpret Freud's disagreement with Rolland about the oceanic feeling as indicative of some form of a personality disorder. One writer portrays Freud's response to Rolland as that of a "controlled man who feared such feelings" (Farber 2017, 720). While Freud may well have been a "controlled man", it wasn't the oceanic *feeling* he had difficulty with but, rather, Rolland's argument that this feeling is the *source* of religion. Freud's effort to explain the oceanic feeling in terms of his theory of primary narcissism of early infancy could only go so far, and Freud admitted this. Whitebook draws a plausible connection between what he calls Freud's "tone-deaf" attitude to the *unio mystica* and his uneasiness with the "*unio maternalis*" (2017, 410), or sense of originary oneness the infant experiences with the mother. Freud certainly hints at the possibility that such a unitary sense of connectedness with an obscure, maternal essence lies "further behind" the helplessness (Freud 1930, 72) of early infancy that he argued was the source of religion. Thus, Freud's disagreement with Rolland is not about the neonatal basis of the *unio mystica* that is associated with different traditions and forms of spirituality. He admits as much with his reference to the "limitless narcissism" (ibid.) of the undifferentiated ego. What Freud disagrees with is Rolland's contention that the *unio mystica* constitutes the psychological *origins* of religion. In this study I explore how Freud attempts to formulate *psychoanalytic* explanations not only for the unitary feeling associated with mystical experience, but *all* inner experience, *including* anomalous, extraordinary or paranormal *subjective experience*. As he told Rolland, his interest was to interpret the oceanic feeling "from the point of view of our psychology" (E. L. Freud 1961, 388).

Freud has at times paid dearly in the scholarly literature for disclosing his personal unfamiliarity with the oceanic feeling, along with his inability to explain it fully in psychoanalytic terms. While he did not dispute that many people experience a sense of unitary oneness with all reality, it was more important for him to investigate what it revealed about the human mind. For example, he argued that the memory traces of the archaic, unformulated ego boundaries of early infancy may also be reactivated in adult experiences such as falling in love (Freud 1930, 66). Freud accepts that "originally the ego includes everything, later it separates off an external world from itself. Our present ego-feeling is, therefore, only a shrunken residue of a much more inclusive – indeed, an all-embracing – feeling which corresponded to a more intimate bond between the ego and the world about it" (ibid., 68). This sense of intimate connection is sublimated in linguistic and symbolic cultural productions in the course of psychological development. Memory traces of real experiences, such as the neonatal sense of unitary oneness with the mother, are preserved in the unconscious. They may, he avers, "in suitable circumstances" such as regression "once more be brought to light" (ibid., 69). For Freud, the achievement of the state of *unio mystica*, the apex of spiritual experience, occurs because the sensibility it expresses originates in the *real* experiences of early infancy which become culturally encoded in the vast diversity of the world's religious discourses. In other words, feelings of unitary oneness are manifestations of inherent psychological capacities and mental structures that become organized as expressions of cultural and personal meaning.

Freud, Rolland, and Love for the World

In one of his most telling letters to Rolland, Freud expresses his deep admiration for him as someone associated with "the most precious of beautiful illusions, that of love extended to all mankind" (in E. L. Freud 1961, 346). Unfortunately, Freud cannot share Rolland's attitude, and he goes on to explain why. He tells Rolland that the "sobering" effects of racial prejudice have blocked any temptation he may have felt to embrace all sentimental illusions. The experience of centuries of murderous anti-Semitism and repeated accusations that the Jews are responsible for historical catastrophes such as the "disintegration of the Austrian Empire and the German defeat" (ibid.) in the First World War seriously curtailed any inclination Freud may have had for an optimistic assessment of his fellow humans. In another letter, Freud tells Rolland that the "intention" of his life's work was to "explore, solve riddles, uncover a little of the truth", which he knows full well has garnered him little love from the public (ibid., 371). Like Karl Marx, Freud was also committed to ruthless, uncompromising critique. His refusal to "put the truth aside" (1939, 7) even extended to his critical view of the curative potential of psychoanalysis. In the conclusion to an early essay, "The Psychotherapy of Hysteria", Freud expresses satisfaction with the modest but not insignificant therapeutic goal that is sometimes achieved when "hysterical misery" is transformed and settles into "common unhappiness" (in Freud and Breuer 1893–1895, 305). He gave no credence to the still-lingering, smug psychoanalytic cliché that the post-therapeutic persistence of neurotic conflicts or the formation of new ones is the result of an incomplete analysis.

No analysis can possibly be complete or finished, and Freud knew this. He also knew that analysts are as flawed as all other human beings, which is why he astutely advises that they "should periodically – at intervals of five years or so – submit ... to analysis once more" (Freud 1937a, 249). While a psychoanalytic "cure" for Freud could only at best help the patient become a better version of himself, he nonetheless regarded such an outcome as "a very great deal" (1917b, 435). Freud's modest description of his therapeutic goals to his patient Bruno Goetz perhaps sums up this view best:

> [M]ainly I am a physician and I would like to help the many people who live in an inner hell as well as I can. Not in any kind of beyond but here on earth most people live in hell: Schopenhauer saw that quite correctly. My insights, my theories and methods have the purpose to make men aware of this hell so that they can free themselves of it.
>
> (Goetz, Grotjahn, and Wolf 1982, 290)

Given Freud's view of the human condition outlined at the beginning of this chapter, one may well conclude that even this therapeutic objective is a tall order. Freud's refusal to compromise his efforts to relieve human suffering in this world stands in stark opposition to what he regarded as the illusory compensations offered by religion. Freud was well aware of the multiple ways that poverty, violence, social injustice, domestic violence, excessively restrictive moral codes and authoritarian ideologies produce debilitating mental illnesses (Freud 1908, 1919a, 1927, 1930). As we have seen in his counterpoint paper to Jung, salvation of both the human species and the individual for him lies in successful adaptation to the reality principle. In response to Goetz's outburst that Freud could not possibly be an atheist after all, Freud (according to Goetz) protested that, "As for my part, I shall remain what one may call an old honest atheist, and I shall try to help people to their own insight. That is *my* good conscience. ... Man stands naked in front of his God: that is the only prayer which is still allowed us" (Goetz, Grotjahn, and Wolf 1982, 290). Goetz left this last meeting with Freud deeply moved by "the loving, melancholy kindness of his gaze" (ibid., 291). It is important to point out that, for Freud, the repudiation of religious illusions in no way entailed rejection of the ethical values they stood for or a diminished commitment to alleviating suffering (Di Censo 1999). Rather, Freud shifts morality to an irreligious footing grounded in modern rationality and independent critical thought that is free of blind compliance to the commands of a remote deity championed by traditional religious doctrines and institutional authority.

"Shovelling Fog": a Further Note on Spirituality and Mystical Psychoanalysis

It should by now be clear – as I will argue throughout the following chapters – that Freudian psychoanalytic theory cannot be accommodated without serious distortion within any form of mystical or "spirit" (Albanese 2007, 423) psychologies. My use of the terms "spiritual" and "mystical" are not connected with any specific theological or religious tradition. In using the terms mystical and spiritual as applied particularly to the living legacy of William James for the contemporary psychoanalytic writers under discussion here, I am referring to a loose confluence of cultural streams that some scholars associate with a category broadly understood as New Age religions. As I point out in the next chapter, the terms mysticism and spirituality are not only widely contested in the study of religion, they have assumed a variety of meanings well beyond their theological origins. According to Leigh Schmidt, some scholars describe these terms as "essentialist illusion[s]" strategically deployed to protect religious feeling and experience from "reductionistic explanation". "Mysticism", "beleaguered" a term as it is, is understood here as a "modern artifact" that covers the "catchall term spirituality" (Schmidt 2003, 273, 274–276).

As modern cultural and theoretical constructs, mysticism and spirituality are also constantly shifting terms that cover a wide variety of noetic, ineffable experiences of transpersonal, transcendent dimensions of reality that are *both* religious *and* secular. In New Age contexts, one does not necessarily exclude the other; nor does one necessarily entail the other. An important New Age theme that is especially relevant to mystical psychoanalysis postulates the existence of a limitless self and its interconnectedness with all reality. Modern spirituality in this sense draws upon a wide variety of cultural discourses and practices, including psychology and psychoanalysis, that make it compatible with "a secularizing culture" (Owen 2004, 11). However, the effort to bring coherent shape, consistency and conceptual clarity to a spirituality that is "free floating" across multiple cultural currents and yet deeply individualistic is often, to borrow an apt phrase from Courtney Bender, "akin to shovelling fog" (2010, 182). At the same time it is important to identify and locate some of the basic features of spirituality and mysticism in modern cultural and historical contexts in order to bring to light the important ways in which they shape contemporary psychoanalytic discourses.

My approach to mystical or spiritual psychoanalysis includes a number of features associated with New Age religiosity that are identified by Wouter Hanegraaff, whose work I follow here. The term "New Age", which emerged in the 1980s, is strongly associated with "religiously oriented" (Hanegraaff 1998, 363) psychologies such as alternative and transpersonal therapies. This psychological dimension of New Age religiosity regards the human psyche in terms of its potential for "transpersonal" mystical, paranormal or anomalous experiences and altered states of consciousness, all of which are seen to provide pathways to revelatory insight into the interconnected nature of reality. New Age spirituality appeals to people across all levels of society irrespective of their economic or educational status. Unsurprisingly, the psychological and psychoanalytic theories I too associate with New Age religiosity tend to see themselves as thoroughly secular and naturalistic. Both New Age thought and mystical psychoanalytic psychology embrace quantum mechanics, and its implications for the existence of what they see as a holistic and holographic universe that is "mirrored in each of its smallest parts" (ibid., 367, 368). Common themes in New Age religiosity and psychology criticize what they identify as the distorting and limiting epistemologies, dominant values and worldviews of Western modernity and science. Recurring criticisms of Newtonian mechanics based on charges of its woeful inadequacy for apprehending the true unitary nature of reality are widespread and common in New Age psychological and psychoanalytic discourses. Hanegraaff points out that New Age thought relies heavily on the term "gnosis" because of its potential to provide "profound insight into the wholeness of reality, which overcomes alienation by reuniting the human individual with the All, or God" (ibid., 371).

Along with these ideas, New Age religiosity rejects the binary thinking of Western hegemonic dualistic and reductionistic worldviews (Hanegraaff 1998, 372). Like the traditional gnostic ideas it appeals to, New Age gnosis embraces the view that all "human beings are in their deepest essence one with divine reality" (ibid., 373). For New Age thinkers, including psychoanalysts, "divine" is *not* synonymous with traditional theological beliefs in an anthropomorphic God of Biblical revelation as expounded in doctrinal orthodoxies, which they roundly oppose. New Age religiosity should *not* be confused with the idea of a distinctly identifiable New Age religion, although New Age religious groups and cults do exist (Hanegraaff 2000, 296). Oxymoronic as it may sound, New Age religiosity is secular and naturalistic in its understanding of reality as part of a living, organic, "spiritual force" (ibid., 291) or "cosmic Consciousness" (Barnard 2002, 311) that animates and is instantiated in the depths of every self. It offers a clear illustration of the ways in which spirituality and mystical ideas do not require connections with traditional religion for their legitimacy. In fact, the case is quite the opposite. New Age thought finds validation for its secular spirituality in science, particularly quantum mechanics, and in contemporary paranormal research, such as experiments in telepathic communication. The boundaries between spirituality, mysticism and psychoanalysis, like individual minds, are considered as porous and fluid, so that the psychoanalytic clinical space becomes the site of healing encounters with the sacred self and the sacred cosmos that both contains and flows through it. As we shall see in the chapters that follow, these New Age ideas are not so new after all.

2

Fluid Subjectivities, Extended Minds, and Unseen Worlds: Mystical Psychologies of Frederic W. H. Myers and William James

> For psychoanalysis is my creation ... no one can know better than I do what psychoanalysis is, how it differs from other ways of investigating the life of the mind, and precisely what should be called psychoanalysis and what would better be described by some other name.
>
> (Sigmund Freud 1914, 14:7)

> At the same time the electric current called *belief* has not yet closed in my mind.
>
> (William James in a letter to Charles Lewis Slattery, 21 April 1907, in McDermott 1986, xxiv)

There is significant confusion both within and outside the psychoanalytic literature about the meaning of the term "unconscious" (*Das Unbewusste*) and how it should be conceptualized. It is often invoked as a blanket term to cover almost any form of non-conscious experience represented by a diversity of mental states, from simple dissociative day-dreaming to the truly unconscious conflicts that manifest across a range of neurotic symptomologies. A number of important questions need to be raised in order to clarify what is meant by the concept "unconscious" – is it a psychic system, mental agency, or an ontological reality? Is it located solely within the confines of individual minds or does it have a collective, transpersonal nature (Jung [1953] 1977)? Does it transmit across generations and cultures, leaving archaic residues or psychic inheritances that shape individual and cultural trajectories of development (Freud 1913, 1939)? Should it be regarded as a noun or an adjective? Does it have an identifiable physiological location in the brain? Does it exist in the way Sigmund Freud conceptualized it, as a conflict zone of unseen, warring impulses, or is it an unreflective reservoir of affects (Solms 2013)? Does it belong to the category of metaphor or existent reality (Gargiulo 2006, 461–462)? Is it to be regarded as a universal aspect of human mentation that inevitably calls into question the nature of subjective identity by undermining assumptions about rational motivation? There are potentially as many different answers to these questions about the nature of the unconscious as there are psychoanalytic and even philosophical perspectives. A thorough investigation and adjudication of these questions would take this study too far afield from its major focus. Instead, my aim is to delineate the way in which Freud conceptualized the unconscious in contradistinction to religious psychological and psychoanalytic interpretations. This will help to clarify the ways in which Freud's irreligious view of the unconscious is a key feature that clearly delineates it from notions of the unconscious that underpin spiritual and mystical psychoanalysis.

The term "unconscious" is often used interchangeably and erroneously with the more popular notion of the "subconscious" (*Das Unterbewusste*). It is necessary to distinguish between the "unconscious" and the "subconscious" because they refer to different dynamics and operations of non-conscious mentation. While "subconscious" suggests the existence of a retrievable reservoir of awareness that exists "below" the threshold of waking, ordinary consciousness, the "unconscious" of Freud's psychoanalysis refers to a region of the mind that, due to repression, resists transformations into consciousness. However, contrary to many widespread assumptions,[1] not all contents of the unconscious are the result of repression. Some areas of the unconscious will never become conscious because they represent what Freud described as phylogenic, "archaic inheritances", as discussed in Chapter 1. Thus the psychoanalytic unconscious is constituted on the one hand by contents that are both inherited and innate, along with those that are repressed and acquired, on the other (Laplanche and Pontalis 1973, 197).

A full discussion of the complex and contested history of the term "unconscious" (Bishop 2010, 27) cannot be undertaken here. Prior to Freud the term "unconscious" referred to phenomena such as perceptions too weak to be noted until they became conscious when combined with similar stronger perceptions (Gödde 2010, 262). The Romantic tradition regarded the unconscious as representing the depths of the soul's darkness, and as the source of the dangerous and destructive impulses lurking within human nature (ibid., 262–263). It was also the source of creativity and insight into deeper dimensions of reality. Some of these ideas found their way into psychoanalysis. Although Freud was by no means the inventor or discoverer of what Immanuel Kant referred to as "the dark map of the mind" (*dunkele Vorstellungen*) (in ibid., 12–13), he is the first to conceptualize it *psychoanalytically* as a *dynamic* unconscious. This specific innovation with respect to the unconscious postulates it as a dark "chaos" (Freud 1933a, 73) of frustrated, conflicted and repressed forces that exert powerful influence on the individual personality.

Freud's clinical experience led him to conclude that it is "untenable" (1915b, 167) to claim that consciousness accounts for all of mental life, and that human motivation is solely the product of autonomous rationality. "In psycho-analysis", he writes, "there is no choice for us but to assert that mental processes are in themselves unconscious" (ibid., 171). He was adamant that the "unconscious" is a property of psychoanalysis in ways that clearly demarcate it from all other understandings of non-conscious mental activity. Although Freud's formulation of the unconscious became sharper and more subtly refined over the course of his writings, culminating in *The Ego and the Id* (1923a) and "The Dissection of the Psychical Personality" (1933a), he unequivocally clarified as early as *The Interpretation of Dreams* (1900) that the "unconscious" and the "subconscious" refer to *different* psychic categories. As will be argued below, the differences between Freud's concept of the unconscious, and the subconscious of Frederic W. H. Myers and William James, are closely interconnected with his non-religious naturalistic approach on the one hand, and their metaphysical-naturalist approach to the nature of mind and consciousness, on the other. Any adequate effort to understand not only Freud's concept of the unconscious, but his psychoanalytic theory in general, must include his critique of religion (Mack 2003, 17; Hewitt 2014a). Similarly, James's and Myers's metaphysical concept of the subconscious or subliminal mind cannot be fully appreciated without including their investigations in the field of psychical research and the implications for psychology they took from it.

The Psychoanalytic Unconscious and the Irreligious Mind

In 1912, Freud published one of his most important theoretical papers, "A Note on the Unconscious in Psycho-analysis", a preview to his more fully elaborated and famous metapsychological paper, "The Unconscious" (*Das Unbewusste*), published three years later. The 1912 paper is a tersely written, condensed description of the unconscious. However, two issues regarding this paper bear closer scrutiny. The first concerns the fact that Freud wrote it in response to an invitation from the Society for Psychical Research (SPR) to contribute to its journal, *Proceedings of the Society for Psychical Research*.[2] Given Freud's long-standing worry that psychoanalysis might be associated with any of the occult movements that had captured the popular imagination on both sides of the Atlantic in the late nineteenth and early twentieth centuries, it seems curious that he would have accepted the SPR's invitation. By 1912 there had already been a ferocious and continuing battle over what constituted not only legitimate science, but also the science of psychology. In this struggle to capture the banner of epistemological hegemony, the study of psychic phenomena was regarded as dangerous, nonsensical occultism (Treitel

2004; Wolffram 2009). Freud knew this, of course, and was well aware of SPR's theories, represented in particular by Frederic Myers, concerning the nature of consciousness and its implications for psychic phenomena. He had met William James, whom he admired. James had a well-known and long-standing involvement with the SPR's research. He was a founder of its American counterpart, the American Society for Psychical Research (ASPR) in 1885. He also served as President of the SPR for two years.

Freud would also have been aware of the early, positive reception of his and Josef Breuer's work on hysteria (1893–1895) by key members of the SPR, such as William James and, particularly, Frederic Myers. In fact Myers, a founding member of the SPR and its most important psychological theorist, not only presented Freud and Breuer's "Preliminary Communication" (Freud and Breuer 1893, 3–17) at a general meeting of the Society in London very shortly after its publication; he subsequently published it in the society's *Proceedings*. Myers was the first person to introduce Breuer's and Freud's *Studies in Hysteria* to the British public, seeing in it confirmation of aspects of his own thinking about the nature of consciousness. In Myers's view, hysterical symptomology demonstrated the mind's capacity for splitting and dissociation that revealed multiple personalities or "second consciousnesses" existing beyond the boundaries of ordinary waking consciousness. Myers, like many of his contemporaries in the emerging field of psychology, valued hypnotic trance as the "*via regia*" of access to non-conscious realms of the mind (Ellenberger 1970, 111).

In the early days of Freud's clinical career, he too relied on hypnotism as a clinical tool of access to the dissociated mental states expressed in the hysterical symptoms that caused varying degrees of debilitating physical and mental impairment in his patients. In the years immediately following publication of *Studies in Hysteria*, the initial similarities between Myers's psychology and Freud's emerging psychoanalytic theory quickly faded as Freud refined his concept of the unconscious. Freud, never fully at ease using hypnosis, was well aware of both its limitations and his own hypnotic skills (Freud 1925a, 17; Schimmel 2014, 39). He also realized that temporary alleviation of pathological symptoms through hypnotic suggestion was less valuable therapeutically than discovering the traumas that produced the symptoms in the first place (Freud 1925a, 19). Freud soon realized there was a better way to investigate the traumatic causes of hysteria that could be effective in the treatment of other pathologies, such as phobias and obsessions. He abandoned hypnosis in favour of what he considered for the rest of his professional life to be the far better clinical method of free association. Therapeutic success with hypnosis was based upon the subjugation of the patient to the doctor's will and direction, thus compromising both her autonomy and potential for genuine, lasting change. Freud believed that fostering the patient's autonomy rather than the doctor's authority was a crucial part of the analytic process. He committed himself to encouraging patients to speak freely, since it exerted "the least possible amount of compulsion" that in turn allowed the patient "in all essentials to determine the course of the analysis" (ibid., 41). Freud eventually discarded hypnosis outright as the physician's "mystical ally" (1910a, 22), dismissing it as mere "hackwork and not a scientific activity … [that] recalled magic, incantations and hocus-pocus". He emphasized that if the clinical success of hypnotism relied on the patient's submission to the authority of the doctor (Freud 1917b, 449, 450), it could not provide lasting therapeutic benefit. These radically different attitudes towards the use and efficacy of hypnosis help illuminate the complex nature of the differences between Myers's and Freud's conceptualizations of non-conscious mentation.

Trance and Telepathy

As with James, Myers's psychological theories of human consciousness cannot be considered apart from his psychical research. He was especially interested in the nature of dissociated states as providing evidence of a term he coined in 1885 as "supernormal" capacities (Kripal 2007a, 408) such as telepathic communication. Freud's own long-standing public ambivalence towards telepathy or thought-transference (*Gedankenübertragung*) is well documented[3] (Freud 1921, 184; 1922, 197; Jones 1957, 375–407; Gay 1988, 443–445; Hewitt 2014a, 85–108; 2014b). While Freud often expressed far less scepticism about telepathy than everything else associated with the "occult" (1921, 193), he was also sceptical about his own scepticism. "[I]f one regards oneself as a sceptic, it is a good plan to have occasional doubts about one's scepticism too. It may be that I too have a secret inclination towards the miraculous which thus goes half way to meet the creation of occult facts", he wrote with tongue-in-cheek self-deprecation (1933b, 53). It was not until more than twenty years *after* his publication with the SPR that Freud could bring himself to unequivocally acknowledge in print that thought-transference sometimes did occur. He had experienced it in his own clinical work. Nonetheless, the question still lingers: why did he accept the invitation to write an article *specifically* for the journal of the SPR in 1912?

Before proceeding further, it must be borne in mind that despite his ambivalence, Freud consistently treated telepathy as a *psychoanalytic* phenomenon to be explained, however incompletely, as such (Hewitt 2014a, 2014b). He was not uncomfortable with theoretical uncertainty. He accepted that scientific knowledge is provisional and incomplete. He also stressed the importance of the willingness to change one's mind in the light of accumulating evidence. For Freud, these attitudes were a crucial part of a scientific mentality. One of his major criticisms of religion was that it deliberately impaired development of the psychological capacity to tolerate uncertainty by offering faith-based illusions of absolute, incontestable truth. At no point did Freud turn to religion in its doctrinal, spiritual or mystical forms to provide answers to questions that were as of yet beyond the reach of science. He regarded religion as the "enemy" of science" (Freud 1933c, 160) and of independent, critical thought (Freud 1927, 28, 49). There are no "sources of knowledge of the universe", he wrote, "derived from revelation, intuition or divination" (Freud 1933c, 159). At the same time, because of his direct clinical experience, he accepted that telepathic or unconscious communication exists as a natural capacity. Theory, no matter how inconvenient, was always subservient to observation (Freud 1915b, 190). Freud "never tired of repeating" his teacher Jean-Martin Charcot's quip, "*La théorie, c'est bon, mais ça n'empêche pas d'exister*" – "theory is all very well, but that does not prevent facts from existing" (Gay 1988, 51). His own commitment to science forced Freud to accept the existence of telepathy.

Freud *encouraged* analysts to cultivate unconscious communication in clinical work, famously urging the analyst to "turn his own unconscious like a receptive organ towards the transmitting unconscious of the patient" (Freud 1912c, 115). Like the newly invented telephone, which "converts back into soundwaves the electric oscillations in the telephone line which were set up by sound waves, so the doctor's unconscious is able, from the derivatives of the unconscious which are communicated to him, to reconstruct that unconscious, which has determined the patient's free associations" (ibid., 116). Freud was never in doubt about the importance of unconscious communication in facilitating therapeutic action. As remains the case in psychoanalysis to this day, Freud did not understand how unconscious communication worked. Although he occasionally speculated about how it might occur, he mostly focused his attention on closely tracking its "derivatives" that surface in the patient's free associations. He wondered if the capacity for unconscious communication may have originated in an "archaic method of communication between individuals ... that in the course of phylogenetic evolution ... has been replaced by the better method of giving information with the help of signals which are picked up by the sense organs" (Freud 1933b, 55). However, the best analogy he could formulate and upon which he relied frequently was the telephone, the newly invented instrument that allowed for instantaneous communication between people over vast geographical distances.

What is especially noteworthy about Freud's use of the telephone analogy in the context of the discussion here is its materiality, which was crucial to his thinking about telepathy. The (pre-cellular) telephone is a physical medium of transmission along cables and wires through which human voices, broken down into electrical signals, pass and are reconstituted. "And only think", he wrote, "*if one could get hold of this physical equivalent of the psychical act!*" (ibid., 55, italics added[4]).

Although Freud was not a neurological determinist, his repeated references to the physical medium of the telephone suggest that he understood that unconscious communication both originated in and was transmitted through the body and its affects. Unconscious or telepathic communications are affectively charged, non-verbal communications that tend to occur most often between people who are or have been close, such as analyst and patient. In Freud's view, as internal mental systems rooted in somatically based "instinctual activity" communicate with one another via a shift from the unconscious towards higher levels of conscious reflection within an individual, so too does the unconscious of "one human being ... react upon that of another, without passing through" consciousness (Freud 1915b, 194). By the time Freud's "Note on the Unconscious in Psycho-analysis" appeared in the *Proceedings* of the SPR, he had already established the basic elements of a theory of the psychoanalytic unconscious that was significantly different from the concept of the "subconscious" theorized by Myers and James. A plausible reason explaining Freud's motivation to publish in *Proceedings*, then, holds that he wanted its readers to understand the *psychoanalytic* concept of the unconscious as *he* formulated it in terms of conflict and repression (Keely 2001; Gyimesi 2009; Hamilton 2009, 190–192). The significance for psychoanalysis of clarifying the differences between the nature of the subconscious and unconscious dimensions of the human mind, *especially in the context of psychical research*, would have important implications for psychoanalysis, and Freud knew it.

The Psychoanalytic Unconscious

In the opening sentence of "A Note on the Unconscious in Psycho-analysis" (1912b), Freud wastes no time in unequivocally declaring his intent "to expound in a few words and *as plainly as possible* what the term 'unconscious' has come to mean in Psycho-analysis and *in Psycho-analysis alone*" (ibid., 260, italics added). Although Freud doesn't name Myers or the SPR directly, he nonetheless follows up his opening statement by outlining the decisive differences between the psychological theory of the mind promoted by Myers and the SPR and his own psychoanalytic approach. Years before the publication of the *Studies in Hysteria*, both Myers and, as we shall see, William James, had outlined their theories of consciousness[5] structured in terms of "subconscious" and "supraconscious" areas of mind. Freud explicitly rejected this formulation by the time he wrote *The Interpretation of Dreams:*

> [T]he unconscious (that is, the psychical) is found as a function of two separate systems ... there are two kinds of unconscious ... both of them are unconscious ... but in our sense one of them, which we term the *Ucs.*, is also *inadmissible to consciousness*, while we term the other the *Pcs.* Because its excitations – after observing certain rules ... are able to reach consciousness. ...
>
> We have described the relations of the two systems to each other and to consciousness by saying that the system Pcs. stands like a screen between the system Ucs. and consciousness. ...
>
> We must avoid, too, the distinction between "supraconscious" and "subconscious", which has become so popular in the more recent literature of the psychoneuroses, for such a distinction seems precisely calculated to stress the equivalence of what is psychical to what is conscious.
>
> (Freud 1900, 614–615)

In his paper for the SPR's *Proceedings*, Freud uses the term "foreconscious" synonymously with his notion of the "preconscious" (*Pcs.*), which he settles on in his 1915 topographical model[6] of the mind. For Freud, the *dynamic* unconscious contains impulses and ideas excluded from consciousness by "living forces which oppose themselves to its reception" (Freud 1912b, 263), which three years later he called "repression". While the latent ideas in the unconscious cannot – and may never – "penetrate into consciousness" (ibid., 262) they nonetheless exert a strong influence within the mind, manifesting themselves in disguised forms of distortion in dreams and neurotic symptoms. While "foreconscious activity" may pass into consciousness "with no difficulty" (ibid., 263), unconscious ideas may either remain unconscious or "pierce into consciousness" (ibid., 264) only as the result of hard therapeutic work. Freud's novel contribution to the notion of the unconscious is his insistence on its dynamic nature as a psychical system containing repressed ideas whose energy originates in somatically based impulses, known as drives (*Triebe*) that strive for expression or discharge in thought and motor activity. The foreconscious or preconscious corresponds most closely to what Myers and James meant by the term "subconscious".[7] Three years later, in his important metapsychological paper "The Unconscious", Freud is even more adamant that the idea of "subconscious" is "incorrect and misleading" (1915b, 170) as far as psychoanalysis is concerned. Freud wanted the readers of *Proceedings* to know precisely that.

The Eternal Life of the Eternal Mind: the Psychology of Frederic W. H. Myers

Despite Freud's insistence both on clarifying the notion of the unconscious and claiming it for psychoanalysis, he certainly had no cause for concern that Myers or his colleagues in the SPR were confused about the distinctions between his psychoanalytic unconscious and the notion of the subconscious mind that was precursor to Myers's "subliminal" self. Myers's initial positive reception to Breuer's and Freud's *Studies in Hysteria* was perfectly understandable given the similarities of their research agendas focusing on the dissociated mental states of patients diagnosed with hysteria. Frederic Myers (1843–1901) was a Cambridge-educated classicist, theoretical psychologist and psychical researcher whose intellectual interests were driven primarily by his "passionate desire to learn whether or not individual consciousness survives death" (Kelly 2007, 72). Myers believed that the question of the soul's survival "most profoundly concerns" all human beings ([1903] 2005, 21). The son of a clergyman, Myers grew up in a Christian familial and cultural context. The impact of nineteenth-century materialist, mechanistic and physicalist approaches to science that reduced "spiritual facts to physiological phenomena" (Hamilton 2009, 81) did not necessarily extinguish the religious longings and sensibilities of Myers or many of his educated Victorian contemporaries. Rather, the loss of faith was personally "devastating" for Myers and many of his SPR colleagues (ibid., 80). In Myers's case, it is partly what motivated him to champion a scientific methodology that would provide what he intended to be a naturalistic basis for reality expanded to include exploration of the "unseen world" ([1903] 2005, 403).

Myers's involvement in the SPR and the psychological theories of human consciousness he formulated to explain paranormal[8] phenomena such as telepathy, clairvoyance and medium spirit channelling served his need to demonstrate the reality of an "inner transcendental core or individuality that would survive bodily death" (Hamilton 2009, 4; Kelly 2007, 61). Freud, on the other hand, dismissed claims of post-mortem communication, flatly asserting that "the appearance and utterances of spirits are merely the products" of the medium's "mental activity" (1927, 28). The notion of the survival of the human soul was a religious belief at odds with reason, the highest court of appeal in the adjudication of all contested truth claims (ibid.). But Myers's passionate and desperate efforts to prove that the soul "survives the grave" (cited in Hamilton 2009, 159) was driven by the grief of personal loss and need for consolation. In 1876, the "great love" (ibid., 40) of Myers's life, Annie Marshall, committed suicide. Myers believed not only that her spirit survived, but that its presence was accessible to him through mediumistic channelling (Blum 2006, 210). He attended a number of séances in the hopes of reaching her, and indeed believed that he had occasional glimpses of her, especially in séances conducted by the Boston medium, Leonora Piper, whose psychic powers both Myers and James regarded as genuine. Myers believed that his experiences in the sittings with Mrs Piper in 1893 provided him with "powerful evidence that the spirit of Annie Marshall had survived and wished to communicate with him" (Hamilton 2009, 212). For Myers, the emerging fields of psychology and psychical research promised to provide a scientific basis compatible with a generally Christian theological belief in the immortality of the soul that preoccupied him for the rest of his life (ibid., 75).

Frederic Myers was not a mere naive or gullible spiritualist, and should not be dismissed as such. In fact, his and the SPR's commitment to rigorous scientific investigation of psychic phenomena accompanied by an unquestionable willingness to expose fraudulent claims aroused the ire of a number of spiritualists. One of the most compelling appeals of spiritualism in nineteenth-century America and England lay in the consoling power for the bereaved of its reassurances not only of survival of the spirit, but the also the possibility of communication with the dead (Carroll 1997). The pain of loss could be mitigated by the belief in the possibility of a continued connection with loved ones who existed in another dimension. In this way, séances can be regarded as forerunners of group therapy or support groups led by medium-therapists for people struggling with the emotionally shattering impact of personal grief (Hewitt 2018b). Myers himself believed that departed spirits watched over the living with loving care ([1903] 2005, 405), and, as has been pointed out, could be contacted. At the same time, he was not content to accept immortality and spirit communication as simple matters of blind belief and scientifically unsupported faith. For Myers, establishing the credibility of post-mortem survival required scientific rather than theological justification. In order to place the survival of the spirit on a rational, scientific footing, he devoted himself to gathering empirical data that would provide naturalistic and evolutionary explanations of immortality based upon investigations of the mind/body relationship. The multiple consciousnesses that exist simultaneously below the threshold of ordinary waking states are manifested in a wide range of altered or hypnoid states and could therefore be studied. These hypnoid states included mediumistic trances, telepathy, automatic writing, and crystal gazing (Kelly 2007, 60) that provided access to the world beyond, which was for Myers evidence of supernormal potential. Myers's notion of the "multiplex" mind ([1903] 2005, 55) revealed in the trance states of mediums or "sensitives" (ibid., 120–121) thus provided him with naturalistic explanations of spirit possession. As the medium entered a trance state, her normal personality somehow decentred itself, so that the internal boundaries delineating her personal subjectivity became highly permeable and therefore vulnerable to occupation by a "disembodied spirit" (ibid., 346) taking up temporary residence in her brain.

For Myers, "spirit possession" in the form of a discarnate spirit temporarily occupying an individual mind should not be regarded as phenomena belonging to the categories of supernaturalism and superstition. Rather, it is most properly understood and studied as a *natural, psychological* event. Psychoanalysts from Freud to the present would tend to agree that spirit possession is indeed a psychological phenomenon pertaining to a person who *experiences herself as possessed*. However, in no way is it understood as an independent, ontological phenomenon of an objectively existing spirit invading a living person. For Myers, however, spirit possession combines both dimensions of subjective experience and ontological reality. Discarnate spirits *do exist* and, on occasion, are able to find their way into the mind of a living person who has a particular sensitivity, vulnerability, or supernormal capacity for extreme dissociation. At the same time, Myers adamantly refused to accept vulgar supernaturalist interpretations of such phenomena and the natural/supernatural, science/superstition antagonisms they were based upon. For Myers and the SPR, the *supernormal* character of genuine psychic phenomena[9] such as telepathy offered evidentiary glimpses of human evolutionary potential yet to be reached by the majority of human beings. Psychological investigations into abnormal or pathological mental states of hysteria and dissociation were instrumental for gaining insight into supernormal human potential that is closed to ordinary waking consciousness. The personal self of the quotidian, material world for Myers represented little more than a "fragment of a larger Self" ([1903] 2005, 27).

For all his sincere commitment to reconciling science and religion, and to scientific methodology, most of Myers's work centres around his preoccupation with the immortality of the soul. He fashioned the theological legacy of his Christian background into his own particular blend of faith and psychology that included distinct touches of spiritualism. These threads comprised for Myers "the basic elements of an entire mystical psychology of religion" (Kripal 2007a, 407). He believed that traces of the "deceased psyche's subliminal substance" could continue to exist in a real, if nonmaterial, way and interact with other human psyches (ibid., 409). These spiritual, disincarnate remnants of subliminal selves had to find a way, through trial and error, to smoothly ensconce themselves in receptive individuals. Some "unaccustomed" spirits, "new" to a particular brain, had to "learn more of the conditions necessary for perfect control of the brain and nervous system of intermediaries" for their communications to gain coherent expression through a living being (Myers [1903] 2005, 402). Myers believed that spirits were also willing moral educators of the living. Jesus and other spiritual beings "voluntarily" incarnated themselves in order to instruct humanity into the mysteries of the eternal, "spiritual world from which they came" (ibid., 405).

As Myers's biographer, Trevor Hamilton, observes, "Every fibre in him cried out for continuing existence, experience and growth. The idea of his extinction, that he would not go on, was for him, from childhood, the most intolerable, the most unsupportable concept" (Hamilton 2009, 86). While traditional Christian theological doctrines in themselves were no longer credible to him or his SPR colleagues, expanding the range of scientific inquiry into all aspects of extraordinary human experiences held the promise of reconciling the inherent spiritual or mystical *essence* of religious beliefs with science-based empirical knowledge. This is what Myers longed for (Kelly 2007, 113). For him, scientific study of psychic phenomena was best approached by establishing a coherent psychology of consciousness derived from a systematic analysis of dissociated and pathological states. In this way, Myers believed that deeper layers of consciousness extending beyond the boundaries of the individual personality could be illuminated for further study. Careful study of the trance states of mediums offered the most promising avenues of investigation of the unseen world and access to the discarnate spirits that inhabit it. In particular, Myers had high hopes for telepathy. If living human beings could communicate with each other telepathically, then it was entirely possible that telepathic communications could occur between the living and the dead.

The emerging field of psychology in the latter half of the nineteenth and early twentieth centuries offered Myers a way of preserving some of the spiritual precipitates of Christianity by grounding them in science. In this sense, Myers's approach was a later instalment of similar efforts to reconcile science and religion that was a major concern for many nineteenth-century American spiritualists. Bret Carroll described spiritualists as "rational people in search of a religion that answered their religious questions and satisfied their spiritual needs" (Carroll 1997, 2), and this assessment can be applied equally well to Myers and many of his colleagues in the SPR. No longer able to accept the traditional theological teaching and institutional authority of Christianity, the dehumanizing impact of nineteenth-century commercial materialism, cold Enlightenment science with its calculating rationality and a remote Deity uninterested in human affairs, Victorian society on both sides of the Atlantic opted for a spirituality that was also compatible with contemporary science. Many of those who joined the SPR were physicists[10] who shared this dissatisfaction with what they regarded as excessively materialist science. They too were seeking new ways of empirically validating the core Christian ideals they most valued, such as the existence of an immortal soul (Noakes 2008, 325, 328). The discoveries of electricity and X-rays, along with technological inventions such as the telegraph, the telephone, and the Marconi wireless, lent scientific credibility to the existence of unseen worlds as part of natural reality. If people could communicate with each other across oceans via submerged transatlantic cables and invisible radio signals, it was not beyond the realm of possibility for many that human minds could reach each other through telepathic means that included communication with the dead. (Hewitt 2014a; Noakes 1999, 2008; Luckhurst 2002). The sprawling religious culture of nineteenth-century American spiritualism and its beliefs in immortality and the permeability of minds that facilitated telepathic communication between the living and the dead made an important contribution to shaping the metaphysical contours of American psychology that are evident to this day.

Like many scientists of his time, Myers also believed in the existence of invisible "ether waves", or magnetic fluid, that provided a conduit for telepathic communication between living individuals as well as between discarnate and earthly spirits. The idea of such a fluid that "pervades all space and vivifies all nature" (Crabtree 1993, 49), dates back to the theory of animal magnetism of Franz Anton Mesmer (1734–1815) and his most important disciple, the Marquis de Puységur (1751–1825), who took it much further into proto-psychology. This idea, along with the psychological theories of Pierre Janet on hysterical dissociation in particular, influenced Myers's notion of the subconscious[11] mind which he later reformulated in the early 1890s as the "subliminal self". Myers incorporated and transformed elements of Janet's work with hysterics in the service of both his own parapsychological investigations[12] and his psychological theory of consciousness. The French psychiatrist's experiments with hypnotism, automatic writing and especially his theory of *idées fixes* (the subconscious false beliefs and associations underlying and shaping hysterical symptomology) were folded into Myers's concept of the subliminal self. Janet's *Psychological Automatism* (*L'Automatisme psychologique*, 1889) was the product of his years of research with hysterics as he sought to decipher the causes and meanings of their pathological behaviours. He described and interpreted the dissociated states of these patients as manifestations of active, hidden second personalities that were sequestered in their subconscious. For Janet, these other personalities were the result of traumatic experiences that remained frozen, unprocessed or "unassimilable" islands of unintegrated mentation (Crabtree 1993, 320). The wide variety of automatisms expressed in the patient's trance states that Janet documented, such as spiritism, mediumism, obsessive impulses, fixed ideas, hallucinations and spirit possession demonstrated how individuals could be "controlled" by subconscious forces operating beyond the margins of their ordinary consciousness (Ellenberger 1970, 360).

A Brief Contemporary Clinical Illustration of Janet's Ideas

In Janet's view, the inability of hysterics to process the impact of their traumatic experiences and successfully integrate them into their personality was due to an innate psychological weakness or predisposition. In response to traumatic experiences they are not mentally capable of integrating into their larger personalities, these individuals subconsciously assemble fixed ideas and false associations that generate pathological symptoms. Although Janet's idea of mental degeneration is outdated and no longer accepted, a clinical illustration of the phenomena of hysteria and *idées fixes* from a contemporary psychoanalytic perspective is useful in order to more fully clarify the ways in which trauma is linked to pathological associations. A middle-aged woman *automatically* suffered from debilitating anxiety, guilt and terror of punishment *whenever* she enjoyed herself in ordinary social occasions. She believed that there were "monsters" always waiting to punish her. In her dissociated states she could literally feel them invade her body, first penetrating the soles of her feet, crawling up her legs, clawing through her abdomen and tightening in her throat, where they threatened to choke her. Her body would stiffen as she clutched her throat to stop their progress into her brain. In these moments, she *looked* as if she were possessed by invisible, monstrous demons. After several sessions with a psychoanalytic therapist, the patient was gradually able to remember that during childhood and adolescence her father became violently enraged at any sign she showed of happiness or pleasure in activities not directly approved by him. Her father threatened to smash her fingers for experimenting with nail polish. He beat her severely after she returned from having fun at a high-school dance, tearing her dress off her body while screaming "slut" at her. As she tearfully recounted these episodes, many others, long "forgotten", poured out. She was finally able to retrieve, articulate, and reflect upon previously inaccessible traumas in language accompanied by the affective intensity of her past experiences.

Dissociation or Repression?

Like Myers, whom he influenced, Janet theorized that there are subconscious personalities that surface in dissociated states that can be spontaneously or artificially induced by hypnosis. Myers did not, however, accept Janet's idea that dispositions to pathological dissociation are due to constitutional or innate weakness of the patient. Freud also argued against Janet's view, insisting that the dissociated "splitting of consciousness" (1894, 46) is a psychic, secondary act. He insisted that it is the result of unconscious conflict and repression, not the result of "hereditary taint" or "degenerative atrophy" (47). Whether or not Freud exaggerated Janet's idea that innate, constitutional weakness predisposed individuals to psychopathology (Ellenberger 1970, 539) is beside the point. Contra Janet, Freud's differentiated theory of *"defense"*, *"hypnoid"* and *"retention"* hysterias argued that splitting is "secondary and acquired", and not "primary" (1894, 46–47). Freud also postulated a sexual aetiology of hysteria, where feelings, fantasies and ideas that are "incompatible" with culture and morality become subject to an "intentional forgetting", an unconscious "effort of will" (ibid., 48) that has nothing to do with innate mental degeneracy but everything to do with *repression*. Freud repeatedly sought to distinguish his psychoanalytic theories from Janet's "psychological analysis" (ibid.). His emphasis on *unconscious* conflict, repression and the sexual origins of the pathological symptomology of hysterias, phobias and obsessions help to explain why Myers drew far more heavily on Janet rather than Freud after his collaboration with Breuer on *Studies in Hysteria*.

The theory of dissociation and the existence of *sub*conscious multiple personalities was far more compatible with Myers's psychology of consciousness than Freud's ideas about the sexual origins of repression, conflict and the unconscious. Building on Janet's experimental psychology and experiments with automatic writing for the access it provides to streams of subconscious processes (Taves 2009, 421), Myers maintained that while dissociated states of consciousness may well indicate psychological pathology, and often do, they also reveal the supernormal potentialities of human genius. Myers accepted Janet's finding that hypnotic trance and automatic writing allowed patients to communicate traumatic experiences inaccessible to them in states of ordinary consciousness, but he pushed it further. For Myers, the act of automatic writing in trance states allowed the writer to express knowledge beyond states of ordinary waking consciousness, such as information transmitted through the telepathic communications between the living and the dead. Myers sought to create a "coherent framework for all the data of the multiple strata of human consciousness" (Crabtree 1993, 333) by studying a wide range of "automatisms", the most important of which for him was the somnambulistic trance states of mediums.

In contradistinction to the tripartite Freudian metapsychology of conscious, foreconscious/preconscious and the dynamic unconscious of repression and conflict, Myers ultimately formulated a mental model of a "supraliminal" consciousness, corresponding to the ordinary self, and a "subliminal" consciousness that is manifested in dissociative states and multiple personalities ([1903] 2005, 26, 27). He described the "subliminal" dimension of consciousness as including "all that takes place beneath the ordinary threshold ... outside the ordinary margin of consciousness" (ibid., 21). The subliminal level of the mind also extended far beyond the multiplex self with its many secondary consciousnesses. It represented the "profounder part of man's being" (ibid., 160) whose immense range extends beyond earthly existence. There are two dimensions to Myers's theory of the mind. First there is the level of subliminal consciousness that exits below the supraliminal threshold, a multiplex mind with its multiple consciousnesses. Then there is the Subliminal Self that both underlies and is independent of it. Although Myers is not always clear about the distinction between individual subliminal consciousness and the "Subliminal Self",[13] it seems that the Subliminal Self exists beyond and envelops the subliminal consciousness expressed in the infinite diversity of particular individual selves. His subliminal self resembles Jung's idea of the unconscious far more than Freud's. In a description that discursively rings with key elements of the Myersian subliminal self, Jung describes the "unconscious" as containing "all those psychic components that have fallen below the threshold. ... Moreover we know ... that the unconscious also contains all the material that has *not yet* reached the threshold of consciousness. These are the seeds of future conscious contents" (Jung [1953] 1977, 127–28).

Myers's notion of the Subliminal refers to a transpersonal, cosmic spiritual unity that underlies the multiplex self. This unifying principle of "Individuality" or "Self" flows through the entire universe and connects everything in it. As Hamilton describes it, the "Subliminal Self", or the "Individuality", is a "unifying and organizing power lying beneath the range of personalities" with "enormous potential and a cosmic destiny" (Hamilton 2009, 195). It has a "pre-existence in a Platonic sense"; when released from the body, the soul progresses through "a number of spheres where eventually" it unites with the "ultimate principle while still retaining its individuality" (ibid.). Occasionally, when an individual is in a hypnoid state, an "uprush" (Myers [1903] 2005, 27, 74) from the subliminal region may suddenly occur, an expression of genius or piece of visionary knowledge never displayed before. When this happens, it shows that the borders between the individual subliminal self and the limitless, cosmic Subliminal Self have achieved a heightened permeability. A temporary infusion or influx from the Subliminal Self accounts for instances of supernormal cognition, flashes of brilliance and expressions of talent that do not occur in ordinary supraliminal states. A mystical visionary uprush may also take the form of a psychotic hallucination, a distortion that results from the sheer impact of the experience that floods and overwhelms an individual's confused and terrified mind. Especially important for Myers was how these uprushes could provide visionary glimpses of "the true norm of man". They also reveal traces of the "supernormal" potential of human beings that "transcends existing normality as an advanced stage of evolutionary progress transcends its earlier stage" (ibid., 74). The hidden world of the subliminal self can be a "rubbish-heap" of pathological distortion or a "treasure-house" of superhuman potential yet to be evolved (ibid.). In particular, the trance states of genuine mediums[14] were portals to knowledge of hidden worlds populated by discarnate spirits who "yearn to tell of their bliss" and to "promise their welcome at the destined hour" of bodily death (ibid., 403). In a state of hypnotic trance, subliminal powers are released (ibid., 115) in the form of telepathic communications that flow between the material and transcendent realms.

While Freud accepted, welcomed, and marvelled at both the reality of unconscious communication and its therapeutic value (1912c, 115–116; 1915b, 194), Myers, who coined the term "telepathy", regarded it as crucial evidence of a supernormal capacity achievable by certain people. Telepathic and clairvoyant powers or abilities, especially as manifested in hypnoid trance states, were for Myers indications that a spiritual world existed that was "profounder than those environments of matter which in a sense we know" (Myers [1903] 2005, 160). The spiritual world could reveal itself to human consciousness when the mind temporarily loosened its moorings in waking reality, allowing for intimations of a "cosmic evolution" towards the "ultimate vitalizing Power" of the universe. Telepathy and clairvoyance "indisputably imply this enlarged conception of the universe as intelligible by man" (ibid., 404). Cosmic mind, or consciousness, instantiates itself through a filtering process via the human brain, incarnating itself within a specific biographical life-span Myers identifies with personality, which ends at death. The subliminal self extends beyond the individual personality, maintaining its independent existence before birth and after death. In reality, Myers believes that we are spiritual beings temporarily incarnate or instantiated in finite bodily form (ibid., 405). Under trance conditions, it is possible for the human brain to accommodate the presence of other spirit forms. He writes:

> The human brain is in its last analysis an arrangement of matter expressly adapted to being acted upon by a spirit; but so long as the accustomed spirit acts upon it the working is generally too smooth to allow us a glimpse of the mechanism. Now, however, we can watch an unaccustomed spirit, new to the instrument, installing itself and feeling its way.
>
> (Myers [1903] 2005, 402)

For Myers, telepathy in particular shows that human beings are part of a universal evolutionary process that will bring them closer to actualizing their true spiritual nature, resulting in a "higher level of unitary consciousness" (ibid., 402). Myers concludes his posthumously published *Human Personality and its Survival of Bodily Death* on a prescient note that echoes in a variety of historically updated reformulations within American psychoanalysis to this day. His blending of mystical psychology of human consciousness and psychical research shape his metaphysical theory of evolution. Humanity's evolutionary progress towards higher stages of development shows that what "lies at the root of each of us lies at the root of the Cosmos too. Our struggle is the struggle of the Universe itself; and the very Godhead finds fulfillment through our upward-striving souls" (ibid., 407). This is a remarkable statement of faith, and it undergirded and animated his entire psychology. We will have occasion to recall Myers's words in subsequent chapters.

William James's Mystical Psychology

The breadth of scope and depth of impact of William James's legacy on modern American philosophy, psychoanalytic psychology and the psychology of religion is incalculable (Diakoulakis 2012, 184). James's influence on psychoanalysis, although not often explicitly acknowledged, requires a critical reassessment in order to trace the important ways in which central features of his mystical psychology circulate within the religious, or more accurately, spiritual and mystical unconscious of American psychoanalysis. Part of this reassessment must take into account the enduring influence of Myers on James's thought, which especially in the last decades of James's life, cannot be overemphasized.[15] This means that as distilled through James, the psychological ideas of Myers also reside within contemporary psychoanalysis. The theoretical axis that connects religious or mystical psychoanalysis with the psychology of Myers and James is their shared focus on psychical and paranormal research. This is one of the most important legacies of the psychology of James and Myers for the spiritually oriented psychoanalysts I discuss later. James's interest in psychical research was a crucial part of his efforts to establish a "spiritual basis of reality" with scientific methods and criteria (McDermott 1986, xiv). In this sense, James's incomplete or unsuccessful project (depending on one's point of view) continues on in the work of contemporary American psychoanalysts who, like him, are still searching for a way to reconcile science and what Jeffrey Kripal, the historian of religions, aptly calls a "religion of no religion" (2007a).[16] This ongoing reconciling effort relies largely upon an implicit understanding of the unconscious that tools for a psychological approach that was theoretically suitable to advancing their investigations of mediumistic trance and psychical research agenda (Taves 2003, 313–314).

Myers and James were more optimistically inclined to view the multiplicity of consciousness as evidence of supernormal potential than Janet. The admixture of their own religious sensibilities with their investigations in psychical research produced a spiritualized, mystical psychology of the subconscious that went far beyond Janet. Myers and James developed theoretical frameworks that laid the groundwork for theorizing consciousness and its supernormal capabilities, like telepathy, that both anticipate and are resonant with current psychoanalytic ideas about unconscious communication. Like Myers and James, contemporary psychoanalysis attempts to theorize unconscious communication within current scientific frameworks while preserving a positive role for an all-enveloping transcendent reality in ways Freud rejected. Part of the legacy of Myers and James for contemporary psychoanalysis lies in their implicitly shared *method* of scientifically grounding metaphysically inflected research by providing naturalistic explanations for a diversity of human experiences typically identified as extraordinary, anomalous, mystical, or just plain weird. And behind Myers, James and a contemporary psychoanalysis of unconscious communication stands a wide, loosely organized cultural tradition of American spirituality that threads its way throughout the successive developmental stages of psychoanalysis itself (Fuller 1986, 11). As Merkur more recently observed, "there is indeed a mystical trajectory in psychoanalysis" (2010, 349) that I locate within the intellectual unconscious of American psychoanalysis.

The Varieties of Religious Experience: Religious Psychology

James's *The Varieties of Religious Experience* (1902) is a sustained effort to connect "psychological discourse with a metaphysical horizon" (Fuller 2006, 225). It is *also* true that the *Varieties* is first and foremost a book about the *psychology of* religious feeling and experience than it is about religion. It has very little to do with specific religions understood in any traditional sense. According to one of James's most prolific commentators, the *Varieties* remains the most "influential book" (Taylor 1996b, 84) in the field of the *psychology of* religion. James clearly states that he is interested in exploring the underlying *psychology* of mental states and the ways in which they operate to produce intense, emotional experiences that are interpreted as religious, spiritual, or mystical. As he clarifies in the first lecture, "Religion and Neurology":

> [T]ake the melancholy which, as we shall see, constitutes an essential moment in every complete religious evolution. Take the happiness which achieved religious belief confers. Take the trance-like states of insight into truth which all religious mystics report. These are each and all of them special cases of kinds of human experience of much wider scope. Religious melancholy, whatever peculiarities it may have *quâ* religious, is at any rate melancholy. Religious happiness is happiness. Religious trance is trance. ...
>
> As there thus seems to be no one elementary religious emotion but only a common storehouse of emotions upon which religious objects may draw, so there might conceivably also prove to be no one specific and essential kind of religious object, and no one specific and essential kind of religious act.
>
> (James [1902] 2004, 33, 36)

Two other theoretical distinctions James makes in the *Varieties* are important to note. First, he establishes his unabashed contempt for narrow "medical materialism" ([1902] 2004, 24) that drains religious experience of its power, meaning and knowledge-potential by reducing it entirely to the mechanistic brain functioning of neurological determinism. This perspective is part of a wider, long-standing and frequently repeated objection against what he decries as intolerant, narrow-minded, intellectualistic, logic-obsessed scientific and philosophical attitudes that draw arbitrary distinctions between truth and superstition. In the Hibbert lectures, delivered at Manchester College a few years after publication of *The Varieties*, James reiterates:

> We are so subject to the philosophic tradition which treats *logos* or discursive thought generally as the sole avenue to truth, that to fall back on raw unverbalized life as more of a revealer, and to think of concepts as ... merely practical things ... comes very hard. It is putting off our proud maturity of mind and becoming again as foolish little children in the eyes of reason.
>
> (James 1909a, 755)

This comment is one in a long line of exasperated protests that surface repeatedly in James's writings against the intolerant rationality of narrowly focused scientific investigation that refuses to even acknowledge the existence of metaphysical truths as even potentially manifest in states of consciousness "beyond the margin" (Taylor 1996b) of ordinary awareness.

On this point James is in total agreement with Myers, the main leaders of the SPR, and many other Anglo-American intellectuals of the Victorian-era who lamented the closed-mindedness of "classic-academic" (James [1901] 1986, 193) science. James railed against the narrow focus of laboratory-based psychology that refused to investigate the "absolute metaphysical ground of the universe" (ibid.), which he insisted could be apprehended through careful study of the complexity of human consciousness. Second, it is important to note that James's approach to religion explicitly excludes the "ecclesiastical organization" and "systematic theology" associated with *any* tradition (James [1902] 2004, 37). Religion, for James, has nothing to do with clergy, theology or doctrinal teachings. As far as he is concerned, a theological science of God is a poor attempt to mimic secular science. Neither established religions nor science, due to their political and ideological self-interests, are capable of apprehending the true nature of religious experience. For James, feeling is the "deeper source of religion" (ibid., 372). He adopts a radically subjective experience-based approach to religion described as *"the feelings, acts, and experiences of individual men in their solitude, so far as they apprehend themselves to stand in relation to whatever they may consider the divine"* (ibid., 39). This is by no means a *definition* of religion. Rather, it describes an orientating *perspective* or approach that for James is necessarily more inclusive of the vast diversity of human experiences commonly accepted as "religious" by scholars and lay people. Definitions tend to have hard contours delineating what is both included and excluded within their borders. In contrast, James was interested in the excluded, hard-to-define nature of subjective human experience of unseen, transcendent dimensions of reality that he argued were as worthy of scientific investigation as any orthodox field of inquiry. As far as James is concerned, an adequate interpretation of religion must begin with the "immediate content of the religious *consciousness*" (ibid., 23n, italics added). His *sui generis* approach to religious experience insisted that *all* organized religious belief systems arise out of efforts to articulate, regulate and control universal, emotional and psychological phenomena. His project was to illuminate the nature of the underlying *psychological* core experience that characterized *all* religiosity by differentiating it from cultural and historical particularity and situating it within a thoroughly modern, naturalistic psychology of the *sub*conscious.

His lectures on "Mysticism" (James [1902] 2004, lectures XVI and XVII) in particular offer important insight into both the methodology and the ultimate aim of the entire set. Like the rest of the lectures, James relies on detailed subjective individual reports of mystical experiences while offering little in the way of theoretical reflection. In this sense, the book may be understood as performatively instantiating his method. For James, genuine knowledge comes from close, empathic attention to direct inner experience. Thus, the numerous examples of subjective accounts force his readers to attend closely to the human voices of mystical experience. James insisted that in order to formulate meaningful concepts and theories, the investigator must situate herself "at the point of view of the thing's interior *doing*" (1909a, 750).

Subjective experience takes priority over theory because the *former* gives rise to the *latter*. Theory must not be used to force experience to conform to its own predetermined conceptual demands. It is worth bearing in mind that James came from a liberal, Protestant religious culture whose doctrinal teachings and ecclesiastical authority held little appeal. His father was a Swedenborgian,[18] and Ralph Waldo Emerson, the famous American poet and Transcendentalist, was a close family friend throughout James's childhood. Emerson's philosophy of a cosmic "oversoul" and its harmonizing energies that connect all levels of reality deliberately positioned itself in opposition to traditional Christian theology. While James rejected certain aspects of Emerson's notion of an impersonal Absolute Mind (James 1909a, 666), he too valued religious feeling over church teaching.

These ideas were popular in educated, middle-class sectors of nineteenth-century American society and they lent powerful justification for privileging direct experience as the source of truth and moral insight over the teaching authority of "decaying" religious institutions and their "creaking formality" (Emerson 1838). Whatever James's own critical views of particular aspects of Emersonian philosophy may have been, the legacy of belief in a higher reality accessible to and compatible with internal experience had deep and enduring roots in the cultural context in which he developed his own thought (Taylor 1999b, 182). The religious and philosophical cultural currents of James's time also embraced important elements of spiritualism in its rejection of the category "supernatural". The apprehension or experience of transcendent realities, whether through mediumistic trance, automatic writing or telepathic communication, were understood as operating in accordance with natural laws (Carroll 1997, 66), not in violation of them. James's approach to the complexities of the human mind that blends psychology and spirituality remains an important preoccupation of psychoanalysis and surfaces within some of its most important theorists. In a formulation that remarkably foreshadows Wilfred Bion's and James Grotstein's ideas of "alpha" (formulated) and "beta" (raw) dimensions of mental life and their relationship to the transcendent "O" that I will discuss in greater detail in the next chapter, James describes the subliminal mind as the "B-region" of the personality, which is the "source of our dreams" and "mystical experiences". The "A-region" or supraliminal region of the mind corresponds to the "level of full sunlit consciousness" of the Bionian notion of alpha mentation. James comments further that the B-Region is "obviously the larger part of each of us, for it is the abode of everything that is latent and the reservoir of everything that passes unrecorded or unobserved" ([1902] 2004, 416), the "fountain-head of much that feeds our religion" (ibid., 417). In mystical states of consciousness, "the door into this region seems unusually wide open" (ibid.). For James, mystical experience is the source of *all* religions. As far as he is concerned, it certainly is the source of Christian belief. In fact, the entire *Varieties* appears as both an extended discourse on, and distillation of, the "mystical core of Christianity" (Albanese 2007, 416).

In a letter to Henry W. Rankin written prior to the publication of *The Varieties*, James lends credence to Albanese's assessment of his Gifford lectures in a remarkably clear and concise summation that bears lengthy quotation:

> In these lectures the ground I am taking is this: The mother-sea and fountain-head of all religions lie in the mystical experiences of the individual, taking the word mystical in a very wide sense. All theologies and all ecclesiasticism are secondary growths superimposed, and the experiences make such flexible combinations with the intellectual prepossessions of their subjects, that one may almost say that they have no proper intellectual deliverance of their own, but belong to a region deeper and more vital and practical, than that which the intellect inhabits. For this they are also indestructible by intellectual arguments and criticism. I attach the mystical or religious consciousness to the possession of an extended subliminal self, with a thin partition through which messages make interruption. We are thus made convincingly aware of the presence of a sphere of life larger and more powerful than our usual consciousness with which the latter is nevertheless continuous.
>
> (James in Taylor 1996b, 90–91)

And finally:

> The farther margin of the subliminal field being unknown, it can be treated as by Transcendental Idealism, as an Absolute mind with a part of which we coalesce, or by Christian theology, as a distinct deity acting on us. Something, not our immediate self, does act on our life!
>
> (James in Taylor 1996b, 90–91)

Explorations of the psychology of mystical states of consciousness leads to the source, the *ur*-religion from which all the world's religions and individual beliefs ultimately derive. This view contends that there is a universal religious experience standing behind all manifestations of psychological, historical and cultural diversity that can be detected in the study of pure experience. As a psychologist, James is no different than Freud in assuming that the human mind and its operations share a universal nature that transcends culture and history. As he concludes his letter to Rankin, James demonstrates that he is well aware of the contradictory, circular nature of his theory, which *rejects* Christianity on the one hand while *preserving* its essential core, on the other:

"So I seem doubtless to my audience to be blowing hot and cold, explaining away Christianity, *yet defending the more general basis from which I say it proceeds* (in Taylor 1996b, 91, italics added).

James's understanding of mysticism as a perennial, unitive, and universal expression of unmediated, pure inner experience is strongly contested in religious studies (Hood 2002, 10; Proudfoot 2000, 62; Katz 1978). According to Wayne Proudfoot, who adopts a constructivist notion of mysticism as opposed to a perennial approach:

> [James is] wrong to think that this [unseen moral] order can be located outside of the social products of human history and culture. We do inhabit a pluralistic moral order, but there is nothing in the cosmos that is intimate, social, or morally productive except what we have put there. Language, social practices, institutions, and other cultural products are what make the universe one that can be defined "congruously with our spontaneous powers".
>
> (Proudfoot 2000, 62)

For Proudfoot, there can be no such thing as unmediated consciousness. Freud would agree. When addressing the question of how everything experienced in a life is somewhere preserved in the mind, Freud remarks, in his famous Roman archaeological metaphor, that "all these remains of ancient Rome are found dovetailed into the jumble of a great metropolis" (1930, 70). While the remnants of the most ancient phases in its history are buried somewhere, they cannot be sifted out in their original, pristine form.

Yet the premise of the existence of pure, unmediated or raw experience is crucial to James's views that unitary mystical experiences are potential gateways to transcendent reality. Yet there are traces of ambiguity in his theory, which would seem to imply a monistic view of the universe, which he argues against. He rejects the Transcendentalist notion of a monistic, Absolute mind in favour of a "multiverse" in which "every part, though it may not be in actual or immediate connexion, is nevertheless in some possible or mediated connexion, with every other part however remote, through the fact that each part hangs together with its very next neighbours in inextricable interfusion" (James 1909a, 778). James doesn't clearly address the question of how the "multiverse" relates to his idea of unmediated experience, which is *undifferentiated* experience. James appears to struggle with this question. It is difficult to reconcile his idea of a pluralistic universe/multiverse, the "each-form" (ibid., 649) and the relations between them, with the notion of a cosmic "mother-sea", which is presumably closer to his idea of the "all-form" (ibid., 649). In his lecture, "Concerning Fechner", James ponders the idea of an "earth-soul" that "traces relations between the contents of my mind and the contents of yours", and that everything existing has some form of consciousness (ibid., 705, 706). Just exactly in what ways his multiverse, where everything is connected by a "celestial ocean of ether" (ibid., 704) is ultimately distinguishable from the ideal monism of an Absolute soul is at times difficult to determine. He seems to hold the idea of a cosmic soul, spirit or mind that unites everything in it while preserving traces of particularity and the web of relationships that connect them. For James, in the "immediate moment" of pure experience, "our relation to the object is always one of an intersubjective connection" (Taylor 2010, 416).

As much as James is intent on preserving some traces of particularity beyond their instantiations in concrete "denizens", his idea of a "More" ([1902] 2004, 436) that both contains and flows through the universe and everything in it is certainly at times conceptually close to the notion of an Absolute Mind. For the moment, the tension in James's thought between pure experience and its manifestations in specific consciousnesses whose depths expand into and across transpersonal boundaries, must remain. Be that as it may, James insists that mystical experience must be approached on its *own essential terms*. Mystical states of consciousness are ineffable, noetic, transient and passive. They are dream states (James [1902] 2004, 332), "special" types of consciousness that centre around a common experience of "reconcilability" and feeling of unity (ibid., 335). In mystical states one may experience the presence of God in "flashes of consciousness", similar to Myers's "uprushes", that bring with them a sense of heightened, even ultimate, reality (ibid., 344). The "great mystic achievement", for James, lies in overcoming the barriers between "the individual and the Absolute", expressed in the Christian Pauline formulation that "Christ liveth in me" (ibid., 362). This expression is in line with his idea that careful examination of the mental states of mystics illuminates the existence of multiple personalities, some of whom may show supernormal flashes of brilliance. Altered states reveal not only an expansion of consciousness well beyond the margins of ordinary awareness; they also undermine the pre-eminence of mechanistic, desiccated rationalistic consciousness as they unfold on "orders of truth" beyond the material world to which we may "vitally respond" (ibid., 366).

One of the most interesting cases in the rich assortment of mystical experiences James cites throughout *The Varieties* is the report of J. Trevor, who describes how "impossible" it was for him to accompany his wife and children to church one Sunday morning. To do so, he writes, would have amounted to "an act of spiritual suicide. *And I felt such need for new inspiration and expansion in my life*" (Trevor cited in James [1902] 2004, 343, italics added). Feeling both reluctant and sad in leaving his family to proceed on their own, Trevor instead took a walk with his dog. As he began to enjoy the beauty of the day, his mood lifted. Then:

> [S]uddenly, without warning, I felt that I was in Heaven – an inward state of peace and joy and assurance indescribably intense, accompanied with a sense of being bathed in a warm glow of light ... a feeling of having passed beyond the body, and as if nearer to me than before, by reason of the illumination in the midst of which I seemed to be placed. This deep emotion lasted ... only gradually passing away.
> (J. Trevor cited in James [1902] 2004, 343)

This was not Trevor's only experience of this kind. On other, "rare and brief" occasions, he had "flashes of consciousness" in which he experienced the presence of God. In his writing Trevor appears to be a thoughtful man given to reflectiveness upon the nature and meaning of these experiences. He concludes that "after every questioning and test, they stand out today as the most real experiences of my life":

> [T]heir reality and their far-reaching significance are ever becoming more clear and evident ... *what I was seeking, with resolute determination, was to live more intensely my own life*. ... It was in the most real seasons that the Real Presence came, and I was aware that I was immersed in the infinite ocean of God.
> (J. Trevor cited in James [1902] 2004, 344, italics added)

Trevor's account of his experience of immersion in the "infinite ocean of God" strongly resonates with James's and Myers's views of cosmic consciousness, while at the same time anticipating, with remarkable similarity, Romain Rolland's response to Freud's critique of religion, *The Future of An Illusion* (1927), published decades later. While Rolland agreed with Freud's critique of institutional religions that also corresponds to the views of Myers and James, he disagreed strongly with Freud's thesis that the psychological origins of religious belief lie in the infant's helpless dependency upon the care and protection of its father. Instead, Rolland countered in a passage that could have easily been written by Myers, James or the New England Transcendentalists such as Emerson, that the origins of religious belief have more to do with an "oceanic feeling", which he describes as a *"spontaneous religious sentiment"*, a *"feeling of the 'eternal' ... 'oceanic' sentiment ... a contact ... religious energy* which ... has been collected, canalized and dried up by the Churches, to the extent that one could say that it is inside the Churches (whichever they may be) that true 'religious' sentiment is least available" (in Parsons 1999, 36–37). Another term Rolland used to describe the "religious energy" of the oceanic feeling was that of "a free *vital upsurge*" (ibid.), which is similar to the language of Myers and James. As I pointed out in Chapter 1, while Freud confessed to never having experienced the oceanic feeling described by Rolland (Freud 1930, 65), he did address Rolland's account of the origins of religion in mystical experience with serious, *psychoanalytic* consideration (Hewitt 2014a, 38–44) by linking it to his theory of infantile narcissism. While Freud believed that a sense of oneness with the environment likely characterized infantile experience prior to the differentiation of conscious awareness into self and other, he rejected that it was the source of religion. He conceded that the power of the oceanic feeling may be explained in terms of "the expression of a strong need" in some people to restore a sense of the "limitless narcissism" of early infancy. Freud was able to acknowledge mystical experience only as a psychoanalytic phenomenon, not an ontological one.

What is important about this exchange between Freud and Rolland, and its relevance with regard to Trevor's report of his mystical experience, is how it further highlights important theoretical differences between Freud and James. Like James, Freud also attempts to explain mystical ("oceanic") experience through a psychological approach that takes subjective experience seriously. In contrast to James, however, Freud advances a theoretical explanation that thoroughly separates psychology and mysticism, and that is at odds with Rolland's subjective account. As becomes clear in the concluding chapter of *The Varieties*, James's "radical empiricism" approach to "pure experience" keeps its focus within the bounds of subjective report by accepting its objective truth. Yet, James also states that "no authority emanates from them which should make it a duty for those who stand outside of them to accept their revelations uncritically" ([1902] 2004, 366). Freud would agree with him on this point. However, James significantly tempers his support for the etic perspective of the non-mystical researcher with the comment immediately following, that mystical experiences "open the possibility of other orders of truth, in which, *so far as anything in us vitally responds to them*, we may freely continue to have faith" (ibid., italics added). There is no question for James that the noetic quality of mystical states yields "insight into depths of truth unplumbed by the discursive intellect" (ibid., 329). He also reiterates that "non-mystics are under no obligation to acknowledge in mystical states a superior authority conferred on them by their intrinsic nature" (ibid., 369). Independence of thought in forming explanatory frameworks is essential to any research agenda, and James acknowledges this. But then he seems to reverse his position when he adds, "the existence of mystical states absolutely overthrows the pretension of non-mystical states to be the sole and ultimate dictators of what we may believe" (ibid.). While both these statements generate an interesting, and important tension between the competing claims of science and belief, thereby holding out the possibility for a third way where both can co-exist, James ultimately comes down on the side of belief in his concluding chapter. As Richard Gale has astutely observed, James inevitably fails in his effort to fashion a "have-it-all" science based upon individual experience and faith (in Diakoulakis 2012, 195).

A Non-mystical Psychoanalytic Interpretation of Trevor's Mystical Experience

Although we know very little about J. Trevor, a close psychoanalytic reading of his own words must consider the *possibility* that he was in a depressed emotional state on the morning he opted to take his walk rather than attend church with his family. The restrained, reflective tone of his writing stands in stark emotional contrast to the conviction, flatly stated, that he feared risking "spiritual suicide" by going to church. The reader knows immediately that *something is wrong*. He tells the reader that he needed "new inspiration and expansion" in his life that church could not provide. In the course of his walk he experienced an "indescribably intense" state of "peace and joy", and a "feeling of having passed beyond the body" (Trevor in James [1902] 2004, 343). The luminous "flashes of consciousness" of God's presence he experienced on other occasions, while "rare and brief", were spiritually energizing, the "most real experiences of my life". The "reality" and "far-reaching significance" of these states imparted a sense that he was "living the *fullest, strongest, sanest, deepest* life" (ibid., 344, italics added). From the perspective of non-mystical psychoanalysis, questions arise not only about the reasons for his feelings of diminished vitality in his ordinary, non-mystical states, but also about the real *possibility* that he may have been struggling with anxiety concerning his own mental stability. Psychoanalysis needs to ask why do these experiences count as Trevor's "*sanest*" as well as his "fullest?" From his own account, it appears that the feelings of vitality and strength he experiences in proximity to God are absent in his relationship with his family. If so, why is it that, according to Trevor, only mystical experiences provide him with "the most real experiences of my life" (ibid., 344)? A Jamesian response to this question would interpret Trevor's "flashes of consciousness" as glimpses of an unseen but nonetheless ontologically real "objective presence" (ibid., 61) or "More" (ibid., 439). The emotional and psychological impact on Trevor was transformative, which for James would lend further support to its reality. Regarding Trevor's experience, psychoanalysis would also ask which level of reality is most important to Trevor: the sense of proximity to God, or the heightened vitality and intensity of *feelings* perhaps long absent in his life, from his sense of self, and for which he longs? Is it *God* he experienced, or was he finally able to revivify the emotionally deadened parts of himself through an unconscious creation of a mystical experience?

James would place greater value on the outcome of Trevor's experience, the fact that it produced a positive transformation within him, than on its source. He argued against judging "the worth of a thing ... by its origin" but rather by its consequences, "its fruits for life" (Trevor in James [1902] 2004, 211). Both morally and therapeutically, James has a valid point. The aim of therapy is the alleviation of psychic misery, which as pointed out in the previous chapter, Freud maintained. A psychoanalytic interpretation, such as Freud adopted with his analysis of Rolland's experience of the oceanic feeling, need by no means pathologize mystical experiences, nor should it. In his reply to Rolland, Freud does not attempt to do so. Instead, Freud acknowledges that mystical feeling is "a purely subjective fact" (1930, 64). Freud would agree with James that mystical experience, like any other human experience, is a worthy object of serious scientific exploration by psychology and psychoanalysis. Psychic reality *is* reality, as far as subjective experience is concerned. For psychoanalysis, everything in the human mind, no matter how trivial or outrageous, is worth investigating because it has psychological and emotional meaning for the individual.

A psychoanalytic inquiry into Trevor's mystical experiences must commit itself to exploring its *unconscious* depth dimensions while simultaneously bracketing questions concerning the independent ontological reality of the experience. James's rejection of the unconscious in favour of a limitless, subliminal self allows him to go beyond the margins of the mind in order to pursue the relationship between individual and cosmic consciousness. There is an irony here. Freud delves inward, interpreting mystical experiences in terms of what they reveal about the "dark, inaccessible part of our personality" (1933a, 73), the human unconscious: its phantasies, conflicts, anxieties, desires and repressed pain. His etic psychoanalytic perspective offers explanatory insights that Trevor and James stop short of as they shift their focus outward, away from the psychodynamics of personal experience to consider the "transmundane energies, God, if you will" (James [1902] 2004, 448). As long as the focus remains on the ontological reality of Trevor's mystical experience, a fuller understanding of its personal meaning as to *why* Trevor felt on the brink of emotional or "spiritual suicide" and *why* spiritual experiences are more real for him than his immediate *human* relationships will not be possible. From the perspective of James's mystical psychology, exploration of the mind leads the way to an apprehension of transcendent, spiritual reality, or "God".

"Spirit Redivivus"

In the concluding lecture of *The Varieties*, James returns to Myers's idea of the "subliminal self" a number of times. As far as James is concerned, the concept of "Subliminal Consciousness ... is as true as when it was first written" by Myers in an 1892 essay from which James quotes:

> Each of us is in reality an abiding psychical entity far more extensive than he knows – an individuality which can never express itself completely through any corporeal manifestation. The Self manifests through the organism; but there is always some part of the Self unmanifested; and always, as it seems, some power of organic expression in abeyance or reserve.
> (Myers in James [1902] 2004, 439)

Myers's subliminal self, as it stretches beyond the margins of individual personality, unfolding into the limitless "More" of a transmundane, transpersonal cosmic something that "whatever it may be on its *farther* side", flows into its "*hither* side" as the "subconscious continuation of our conscious life" (ibid., 439). James conceived of the individual mind as a filter; human brains do not *produce* consciousness, they *transmit* it, as he speculates in "Human Immortality" ([1898] 1982). Consciousness pre-exists its incarnation in individual brains. In a brilliant and beautifully evocative, extended metaphor that resonates with the Jewish mystical idea of *"ruah"* (spirit or breath), James writes:

> [The] keys of an organ have only a transmissive function. They open successively the various pipes and let the wind in the air-chest escape in various ways. ... But the air is not engendered in the organ. The organ proper, as distinguished from its air-chest, is only an apparatus for letting portions of it loose upon the world in these peculiarly limited shapes.
> (James [1898] 1982, 87)

Death is not the annihilation of consciousness, but the decay and passing of its vessel:

> And when finally a brain stops acting altogether, or decays, that special stream of consciousness which it subserved will vanish entirely from this natural world. But the sphere of being that supplied the consciousness would still be intact; and in that more real world with which, even whilst here, it was continuous, the consciousness might, in ways unknown to us, continue still.
> (James [1898] 1982, 88)

Here James reformulates the Neoplatonic belief in the immortality of the soul in a way that both preserves and modernizes its most central tenet within a scientific psychological metaphysics. At the same time, James was not able to bring himself to fully endorse the specific features of Myers's belief in "spirit-return" (James [1902] 2004, 448), averring that it was "too early" to judge the truth of his theory (James [1903] 1986: 212).

Despite these hesitations, James cannot bring himself to leave the issue there. His mind vacillated "curiously" ([1909b] 1986, 284) as he struggled mightily to resolve his own internal conflict between his need to believe and the demands of science for empirical evidence. In the "have-it-all" way that characterizes James's attitude to psychical research, he speculates about how immortality might actually work. Towards the end of his "Report on Mrs Piper's Hodgson-Control" (ibid.), James considers immortality as scientifically possible. Friends of his late SPR colleague, Richard Hodgson, reported communications with his spirit as channelled by Mrs Piper during her trance states. In a highly detailed account that draws upon Fechner's ideas on memory, James postulates that if an individual's "memory-processes" are coordinated with "material processes", then for an act "to be consciously remembered", it "must leave traces on the material universe such that when the *traced parts of the said universe systematically enter in activity together* the act is consciously recalled" (ibid., 358). During one's life, these traces abide in one's physical brain. However, with the destruction of the brain in bodily death, these traces somehow continue to exist "in the shape of all the records of [one's] actions which the outer world stores up", so that each and every act that each and every human being makes in some way alters the structure of "the cosmos" (ibid.). We can think of these alterations or marks on the cosmos as analogous to radio frequencies when James refers to "mutually attuned Marconi-stations" that transmit messages carried by "the ether of space" (ibid.).

When Hodgson's friends attempted to contact his discarnate spirit at a séance, the attunements that existed between them and their dead companion in life, along with the "traces of his ancient acts", became activated as the traces of *their* material presence somehow attracted or vibrated with *his*. The traces of his and all earthly existence continue to exist somewhere in the cosmos. While there are many radio frequencies, some can only be accessed with radios *specifically designed* to tune into them. Similarly, the traces of departed individuals may be tuned into by the living bodies of their close associates which "function as receiving stations" (James [1909b] 1986, 358). The bodies of the sitters at the séance can then attract "the right spirits" by "eliciting the right communications from the other side" (ibid.). This mix of empathically vibrating traces of the living and the dead activated in the context of a séance may produce some form of veridical apparition, thus providing evidence for immortality. James sums up this convoluted process by concluding:

> The sitter, with his desire to receive, forms, so to speak, a drainage-opening or sink; the medium, with her desire to personate, yields the nearest lying material to be drained off; while the spirit desiring to communicate is shown the way by the current set up, and swells the latter by its own contributions.
> (James [1909b] 1986, 359)

James, unwilling to commit himself to a conclusive endorsement of the survival of bodily death, nevertheless does so in his painstaking account of what can only be called religious science.

Snakes or Seraphs, Gods or Demons?

In February 1910, six months before he died, James published one of his strangest, most fascinating and deeply touching essays, "A Suggestion about Mysticism". He recapitulates some of the main arguments of his theory as already outlined in *The Varieties* and scattered throughout his writings on psychical research. He reiterates his and Myers's theory that mystical states represent "great extensions" of the ordinary, walking field of consciousness (James 1910, 1272) that allow ingresses of the transmarginal, subliminal dimensions of reality into the subconscious mind of an individual, yielding "mental paroxysms" of insight. In this late essay James concludes decisively that telepathic communication exists (ibid., 1273n1). This statement comes as no surprise given his long involvement with psychic research and his belief in the genuineness of Leonora Piper's spirit-channelling abilities. She was, after all, his "own white crow" (James 1896, 884).[19] As much as he struggled to keep an open mind by considering every possible explanation for the accuracy of her trance communications (James [1898] 1986, 190–191) from the spirit world, they nevertheless had the impact of a "thunderbolt" on him (James 1896, 884). Neither he nor his SPR colleagues could detect in her trance utterances any hint of deception. As far as they were concerned, she did not rely on any of the fraudulent devices employed by many mediums for knowledge that only the deceased and the sitters could have. In reviewing Hodgson's report on Mrs Piper, James postulated the existence of a "floating mind-stuff in the world, infra-human, yet possessed of fragmentary gleams of superhuman cognition, unable to gather itself together except by taking advantage of the trance states of some existing human organism, and there enjoying a parasitic existence which it prolongs by making itself acceptable and plausible under the improvised name of 'spirit control'" (ibid., 191). The hypothesis of a "floating mind-stuff" resonates with his ideas about ether, an "earth-soul" or "flowing sort of reality" in which all "finite beings swim" (James 1909a, 726) and his filter theory of the brain that also helped to explain telepathic communication.

In this final essay on mysticism, James struggles to explain his own experiences as "sudden and incomprehensible enlargements of the conscious field" that carry the weight of "real fact" (1910, 1274). Like Trevor and other numerous reports of mystical experiences presented in *The Varieties*, James reiterates his own experience of the descending movement of the threshold between supraliminal and subliminal consciousness and the enlarged, rapturous and enlivened sense of reality (ibid.) that comes with it. But the experience James reports in this essay was far from blissful. It was terrifying. He recounts the unsettling and disturbing impact of two dreams. One of them "telescoped" into a previous one that was "tragic, elaborate, and with lions". Upon waking, the contents of other dreams flooded his mind, "alternately telescop[ing] into and out of each other". Not surprisingly, this experience both frightened and confused James (ibid., 1276). He could neither differentiate the dreams from each other nor figure out when they occurred. It seemed to him that three different dream systems were operating simultaneously. In his fear and confusion about what was occurring in his mind, he wondered if he was receiving telepathic communications of other people's dreams? Or was he experiencing an invasion of unknown multiple personalities long hidden below the threshold of his own supraliminal self? Even more terrifying for James was the prospect that he was going mad (ibid.).

His uncanny experience was affectively laden with a "sinking, giddying anxiety that one may have when, in the woods, one discovers that one is really 'lost'" (James 1910, 1277). Being lost, unable to find one's way, can easily be accompanied by frightening feelings of helpless vulnerability. These are key features of the uncanny, described by Freud in his own experience of being lost in the streets of Paris and his sense of anxious helplessness when, despite his best efforts and strength of will, he finds himself returning repeatedly to the same place (Freud 1919b, 237). Such experiences are also associated with the anxiety James reports that is intensified by a sense that he was losing his "self", his "foothold" on reality in a dizzying sense of disintegration and "diffusion from his centre" (1910, 1277). As the dreams continued to flood his mind, he desperately wondered "Whose? *whose?* WHOSE?" dreams were they? "Unless I can *attach* them, I am swept out to sea with no horizon and no bond, getting *lost*" (ibid.). He was so frightened that his "teeth chattered" at the dread of where this experience might lead. James's anguished cry for an answer to "WHOSE" dreams were flooding into his mind poses a question about not only the nature of the dreaming mind, but about its agency. James's question lingers as a mystical spectre that surfaces in later psychoanalytic explorations of the question, "who is the dreamer who dreams the dream?"

3

Telepathic "Presencing"[1] in the Analytic Relationship

> The co-participation of the subjectivities of the analysand and the analyst can be likened to the operation of a Ouija board; that is, the actual agent of the movement on the board is never known for sure.
>
> (Grotstein 2000, 30)

James's anxiety and confusion about who is the author of his dreams vividly illustrates manifestations of the "lower mysticisms" that also emerge out of the "subliminal or transmarginal region" of consciousness (James [1902] 2004, 369). For James as well as for Myers, mystical experiences can express either mental pathologies or soaring genius and flashes of supernormal cognition. By far, the majority of mystical experiences reported in *The Varieties* that James considers to be the "most important revelations" are "theological or metaphysical" (ibid., 355) as well as comforting and transformative. Beyond this kind of general description, James offers little in the way of theoretical analysis of the numerous mystical experiences he reports. This is partly due to James's conviction that subjective experience must be accepted on its own terms prior to theorizing it. From a therapeutic perspective, psychoanalysis would agree with James on this point. However, the task of the scholar is to formulate theoretical and conceptual frameworks that assist in explaining experiential phenomena as fully as possible. Mircea Eliade's concept of hierophany is helpful insofar as it contributes to an understanding of the subjective mystical experiences reported by James. It is a concept that is lends deeper insight into the inherent religious nature of contemporary mystical psychoanalysis.

Hierophanies (*hiero*, sacred; *phainein*, to show) occur when dimensions of sacred reality break into ordinary, profane reality, where they can become manifest in *any* form, including altered states of mind and visionary experiences. Influenced by Nicholas of Cusa's doctrine of *coincidentia oppositorum*, or "union of opposites", Eliade explains that the "ultimate nature of the phenomenal world is identical with that of the absolute" (in Kripal 1999, 377). *Every* religious experience is based on a "paradox of opposites". The paradoxical nature of hierophany means it can appear in anything that the subject deems to be sacred, such as an object, a gesture, a creature or any other instance or thing in and through which transcendence may appear. A hierophany is not so much constructed as it is discovered and recognized in extraordinary moments of unsettling, striking encounters with something non-human and entirely other. At the same time, the profane object *remains itself* as it manifests in the sacred. It both "participates in the world and *at the same time* transcends it" (in ibid., 377, italics added). Not only is Eliade's notion of hierophany theoretically compatible with Myers's and James's ideas about the incursions and uprushes from the subliminal regions that reside both within and beyond the boundaries of the human mind, it illuminates them. As mystical experiences of the sacred, these intrusions or irruptions have their origins in a higher, transcendent power that is both internal and external at the same time. They are grasped as structures of the psyche. As will be explored in more detail later, the concept of hierophany is a hermeneutically useful concept that links or bridges the mystical psychologies of Myers and James with mystical psychoanalysis.

Framed in Eliadean terms, hierophanic ingressions of the Jamesian "More" are noetic, ineffable and transformative for those who experience them. As psychoanalysis ponders questions similar to those posed by James about mystical dreaming, such as "whose" dreams are dreamed and what gnostic secrets they hold, it must inevitably confront hierophany. From a spiritually oriented psychological point of view, hierophanic experiences become possible and are facilitated by the permeable and porous nature of consciousness. Psychoanalytic theories of intersubjectivity and mutual recognition agree that there are complex difficulties involved in trying to demarcate fixed psychic boundaries between self and other. The ideal of the inscrutable, blank-screen, non-verbal psychoanalyst is a worn-out caricature that has little basis in reality because silence, body language, and breathing rhythms in themselves can communicate a great deal to the patient about the kind of analyst she is with. Most psychoanalysts would agree with Freud's directive to use their unconscious in the clinical setting, to feel their way into the patient's inner world via the "drift" of each partner's unconscious. The drift of the unconscious in clinical settings is inevitably bidirectional.

Hungarian analyst Sándor Ferenczi (1873–1933), a colleague and friend of Freud, added rhetorical force to the notion of the drift of the unconscious by reformulating it as a "dialogue of unconsciouses" (Ferenczi 1988, 84). The multi-directionality of entwining and intersecting "unconsciouses" is made up of unstable, shifting strands of encoded communications that at times surface in the shared reveries of the clinical moment, or in a later nocturnal dream. Many analysts following Ferenczi have been compelled to accept his observation that "thought-transference" occurs with "remarkable frequency" between the analyst and patient, "often in a way that goes beyond the probability of mere chance". He also thought that the nature of the transference relationship between the patient and analyst may even "promote" telepathic "receptivity" (ibid., 85). As psychoanalysts grapple to explain the inexplicable anomalous events that occur in their consulting rooms, they frequently employ religious language with descriptions such as the "mystery of analytical work" (Sullivan 2010) or the "mysterious dimensions of the psychoanalytic encounter" (Tennes 2007, 505). As will be discussed in the next chapter, some analysts turn to paranormal research as they try to explain their own anomalous experiences in the clinic, which are often perceived as telepathy between the patient and analyst. Still others argue that the inherent, mysterious nature of psychoanalytic work requires the analyst to actively assume the role of a "mystic" (Eigen 1998). The following clinical case illustration represents the kind of strange, anomalous and deeply weird experiences that many analysts have reported.

"Ain't No Mountain High Enough": Telepathy in the Analytic Relationship

One Monday morning Kate, who had been in analysis for several years, recounted her dream of the previous weekend:

> You [the analyst] were in a large house, like a thirties-style mansion or maybe a hotel, and it was on the beach, by an ocean, I think. The house had several large rooms and you were always with large groups of people, talking to them, drinking something, or listening to others. It was a really beautiful place, this huge mansion-type house, on a beach at the edge of a large sea or ocean. I think maybe it had a pool as well, I can't remember. You seemed to be having a good time.[2]

During the weekend in question Kate's therapist had attended a conference on the west coast of the United States. The art deco-styled hotel had a pool overlooking the beach and the ocean beyond. The conference was organized around consecutive plenary sessions attended by large audiences, including the therapist. During the coffee breaks, the therapist, who enjoyed both the intellectual stimulation of exposure to new ideas and the pleasure of reconnecting with old friends, actively participated in group discussions. At no time prior to the conference did the therapist tell Kate that she was going away. Kate did not work in a field with any connection to the mental health profession. Although not impossible, it was highly unlikely that Kate could have had any knowledge about the conference or the therapist's plans to attend it. None of Kate's sessions had been missed or rearranged to accommodate the conference trip. As Kate described her dream, the therapist felt an emotional and physical shock as she silently wondered, *what* is going on here?

A dream like this presents psychoanalysis with a hermeneutical dilemma. Does it focus on the accuracy of detail in the dream, or does it rather try to understand the dream in terms of psychoanalytic theory? In clinical terms, the choice amounts either to moving away from the patient by focusing on the mechanics of telepathy, or moving closer to the patient's experience through psychoanalytic exploration. The latter approach invariably must consider the nature of the psychoanalytic relationship as an integral part of dream interpretation. In the early years of her analysis, Kate was anxious around vacation breaks, especially those that involved unplanned or unforeseen cancellations. Kate feared that she would never see her therapist again. At the time of the conference, there was no sign that Kate had yet developed a robust capacity to "hold" her analyst in mind during times of physical separation. For Kate, "out of sight" *literally* meant "out of mind". On a conscious level she worried that something "bad" would happen to her therapist. Unconsciously, however, Kate feared that her analyst would forget *her*. Kate's internal sense of "continuity of being" (Winnicott [1960] 1990, 47) and "ontological security" (Laing [1959] 1965, 39) depended almost entirely upon her sense of the *therapist's* capacity to hold her in mind. In order to help Kate develop a sense of psychic stability and existential continuity both within herself and with others, the therapist sometimes gave Kate small objects from her office or a written phone number that she could literally "hold onto" during breaks. This in turn helped Kate "hold onto" the therapeutic relationship, which was critical to her "holding onto" her *own* subjective experience. These linking gestures helped Kate contain her anxiety around separations in preparation for later psychic integration that would allow her to develop symbolic, rather than mainly concrete forms of relatedness.

As Kate developed a stronger, more complex sense of ontological continuity and security, she relied less on having simple concrete objects belonging to the therapist during breaks. During one vacation period, Kate borrowed the therapist's pen so she could write her own process notes during the hours where she would normally have been in her analytic session. This mimetic reversal of roles showed a new capacity for play and ability to mentalize another person's mind that in turn allowed Kate to "dream" her analyst into existence and thereby establish an internal connection with her by "playing analyst" to herself. Dreaming is an act of imaginative conjuring where people, places and things are dreamed into existence. What was most significant in this new development was not the *content* of Kate's dreams, but that *she could dream at all*. For much of her traumatized past, Kate inhabited a nightmare world of sustained dread, structured around psychic equivalencies where loss equalled death and separation equalled unbearable isolation. "[A] person unable to dream is trapped in an endless, unchanging world of what is" (Ogden 2007, 577). In her waking dream states of mimetic playfulness, Kate was able to carry on "internal conversations" (Ogden 2001, 8) with her analyst and thereby hold her in mind, which soothed her feelings of anxiety. Her newly acquired ability to dream another into existence by *playing* her analyst meant that Kate could now tolerate, process and verbalize painful feelings of loss during periods of separation.

On the level of conscious awareness, the weekend where Kate's therapist was a half-continent away was no different than any other regularly scheduled weekend break. By that point in the treatment a long period of time had passed since Kate expressed anxiety at routine weekend breaks. There was no reason for the therapist to think that Kate would have any idea about where she was. As it turned out, Kate's dream revealed that she "knew" her therapist's whereabouts and activities with "dumbfounding precision" (Eshel 2006, 1619). Kate's dream was a dramatic demonstration of her ability to remain mentally connected to the therapist during periods of physical separation. Before Kate shared her dream, the therapist was aware that important therapeutic progress had been taking place. In reviewing the weekend, the therapist remembered that she had been thinking about Kate and feeling some pride in her progress as she listened to various speakers discuss their clinical work. She also recalled her own reveries prior to the conference, the happy anticipation of meeting new colleagues, seeing old friends, wondering what it would be like, and how much she was looking forward to it. In hearing Kate's dream she began to wonder if somehow her own reveries and Kate's dream had connected in an intersubjective "construction" of unconscious communication. As Thomas Ogden observes in another context:

> It is disconcerting, to say the least, to recognize that our experiences of dreaming and reverie, which constitute a good deal of what is most personal to and self-defining for us, can no longer be viewed exclusively as our own individual creations.
>
> (Ogden 2001, 12)

Since much of Kate's early life was devoted to crafting survival strategies of self-effacement, it rarely occurred to her to articulate her own needs. Her dream, however, was an eerie and unsettling demonstration that if her *need* was powerful enough, Kate could "find" her therapist wherever she was.

Trauma and Telepathy

Dreams such as Kate's are neither new nor rare in the psychoanalytic literature. While psychoanalysis remains unsure of how to account for them, there are a variety of theoretical speculations about how unconscious communication occurs, and the conditions that facilitate it. Clinical reports of "telepathic" phenomena continue to generate discomfort and confusion within psychoanalysis with the result that it remains inadequately theorized. Unconscious communications ranging from minor synchronicities, where a patient verbalizes the analyst's thought, to seriously weird telepathic dreams such as Kate's all challenge psychoanalysis to reconsider its usual presuppositions about intersubjective knowing, the nature *and* potentialities of human consciousness, and the permeability of psychic boundaries. Whatever theoretical approach is taken, most concur that "telepathic" dreams are commonly associated with trauma-based pathologies (Schore 2012, 177). Myers and James argued that trauma not only produces psychic dissociation, it also ruptures the boundaries of normal consciousness to reveal unseen dimensions of reality. Kripal would describe their approach in terms of a "psychology of mystical trauma" (2007a, 410).

However, a non-mystical psychoanalytic perspective would counter that a life of exposure to sustained trauma, especially from an early age, can create capacities for an exquisite, finely honed sensitivity to the minutest signs of danger that others may not detect. Kate's childhood was characterized by a relentless dread of explosive physical abuse, emotional neglect and abandonment by parents who were threatened by the slightest hint of noncompliance with their image of a "good daughter". Kate shared her parents' bedroom from birth to early adolescence. She suffered frequent and unpredictable beatings by her father at the slightest sign of disobedience. Rather than intervening to protect her child, Kate's mother took refuge in dissociative states that made her "blind" to her daughter's plight. If Kate complained about her father's violence, her mother either denied that the beatings took place or screamed at her not to "disrespect" her father. The only sense of emotional intimacy she had with her parents came from being allowed to sleep in their room. When they abruptly "exiled" her to another room, she was devastated by a sense of rejection and loss that left her feeling confused, isolated and alone. Kate's childhood terror of being "left" was reactivated by her therapist's impending weekend absence as she detected a shift in her analyst's attentiveness.

People who have experienced sustained trauma in their early development are acutely sensitive to the micro-shifts in the feeling states and attentions of others that would be imperceptible to most people. More finely attuned to the feeling states of others than her therapist knew, Kate intuited the subtlest alterations in the therapist's attention towards her. Robert Caper argues that patients with histories of sustained trauma and neglect may be able to intuit the presence of the therapist's "internal objects" such as loving attachment relationships with other people or even one's extra clinical professional life that they have no part in (1997, 270). In other words, the therapist's "passionate relationship" with her own "internal objects" conveys the message that she has a mind of her own (ibid., 271), a private part of herself that is distinct and separate from the patient. Ronald Britton describes the Oedipal dynamics that are relevant to understanding Kate in his discussion of a similar case:

> I came to realize that these efforts of mine to consult my analytic self were detected by [the patient] and experienced as a form of internal intercourse of mine, which corresponded to parental intercourse. *This she felt threatened her existence.*
>
> (Britton 1989, 89, italics added)

Kate's unconscious awareness that her analyst had passions that did not include her reignited the traumatic anxieties of her childhood. As the only sense of belonging she could experience with her parents was shattered by her "expulsion" from their bedroom, Kate's transposed unconscious fantasy of "belonging" to her therapist was suddenly threatened as she felt a slight reduction in her therapist's attention. Memories painstakingly retrieved in the process of forming a coherent narrative of her past temporarily collapsed into a *reliving* of past traumas as her usual sense of safe predictability was disrupted. The finely honed hypervigilance that helped her survive her traumatic childhood flared up as she sensed a subtle "loss" of her therapist. As Kate's unconscious caught the "drift" of the therapist's unconscious west-coast reverie she became frightened at the looming prospect of inchoate loss. The thing she most feared, of course, had already happened in her "loss" of the loving, attentive parents that she never had. This is the most devastating loss of all. With her dream, Kate was able to communicate her experience by setting up a "generative conversation" (Ogden 2004, 1355) that transformed mute trauma into dream images and symbolic representations that she was able to share with her therapist.

"Telepathic" Dreaming?

What is psychoanalysis to make of telepathic dreams? As the unconscious "travels along many pathways" that are not yet understood, it is tempting to describe them "from a mystical point of view [that] may be called telepathic"

(Brown 2011, 7). Freud stated that there is no such thing as a "telepathic" dream. He maintained that unconscious communications transmitted in dreams do not constitute a separate category requiring different interpretive strategies. Dreams are communications between parts of the mind, where daytime experiences unregistered by conscious awareness may become available in dreams. "[D]reams have little to do with telepathy", he insists. "The only reason for discussing the relation between dreams and telepathy is that the state of sleep seems particularly suited for receiving telepathic messages" (Freud 1933b, 37). Freud interprets a man's dream that his wife gave birth to twins on the exact night his daughter actually gave birth to twins in terms of the father's troubled marriage and his relationship with his daughter, who lived far away from him. Freud's interpretation of the dream revealed the man's unconscious wish that he "could put his daughter in the place of his second wife" (ibid., 38). While the dream analysis told Freud "nothing about the objective reality of the telepathic event" (ibid.), it told him a great deal about the unconscious fantasies connected with the dreamer's *relationship* with his daughter. Freud has no doubt that the loving closeness between the father and daughter, intensified by their shared loss of his wife and her mother, would have contributed to the creation of subterranean channels of affectively charged unconscious communication between them. Freud also interprets the dream as bringing the man's dissatisfaction with his present wife, and a wish that his first wife had lived to experience the joy of having grandchildren, closer to the surface of his consciousness. In itself, the question of the *telepathic* nature of the dream is less important to Freud than what it reveals about the relational psychodynamics of this family.

There are a number of psychoanalytic perspectives on "telepathic" dreams. Michael Balint observes that uncanny clinical events like Kate's dream point to a "state of intense positive dependent transference" (Balint 1955, 32) towards the analyst. From Balint's perspective, this kind of "telepathic" dream is a "desperate means of communication" whereby a patient struggles to (re)gain the analyst's "full attention" (ibid.). This observation certainly applies to Kate's dream. Despite (or because of?) the vast geographical distance between Kate and her therapist, she found a way to "join" her therapist by "dreaming her up". For Freud and Balint, psychoanalysis need not try to explain the accuracy of a dream's contents, however astonishing they may be. What is far more important both theoretically and clinically from Freud and Balint's perspective is the developmental growth, signified by the dream, that allowed Kate to regulate her dread of separation by *conjuring* the analyst in her mind. This was a new level of psychological achievement for her. Vitally important psychic changes had been taking place both *within* Kate and within the analytic relationship that neither Kate nor her analyst recognized. Kate found an elegant "telepathic" way to communicate a newly acquired capacity to dream what was taking place in her internal world. Kate was able to break free of the traumatic loop of an "endless, unchanging world of what is" in her newly acquired capacity to dream "formerly undreamable emotional experience" (Ogden 2007, 577). As I discuss in greater detail in Chapter Four, the capacity for dreaming emotional experience is a crucial part of working through trauma.

Whether Kate's dream was a product of clairvoyance and telepathy or any other form of super *natural* or super *normal* power is not only impossible to establish, it is beyond the scope of current psychoanalytic knowledge. What is far more important theoretically and clinically is how psychoanalysis formulates coherent, yet necessarily limited, explanations of putative telepathic dreams. The astounding accuracy of detail in Kate's or any other telepathic dream, while not insignificant, must for the time being be set aside as a mystery which as yet cannot be explained. Freud's view was that, assuming the absence of all possible ordinary explanation, psychoanalysis must admit its ignorance about how this "psychical counterpart to wireless telegraphy" (Freud 1933b, 36) works. For Freud, the imperative to *theorize* such events psychoanalytically takes precedence over explanations of telepathic phenomena as such. Otherwise, both patient and analyst risk opting for a premature conclusion to the analytic process in shifting their attention from their relational dynamics to a focus on the occult quality of those dynamics. Balint appears to have a similar concern in mind with his caution that "in order to study parapsychological phenomena profitably we should not concentrate on either the subject's receptive powers or the healer's or agent's influencing powers, but on the powers *inherent in their mutual relation*" (ibid., 35, italics added). In other words, psychoanalysis needs to think more deeply about the nature of intersubjectivity, self/other relationships and interactions, and the possible multiple unconscious modalities of "knowing" ourselves and others that exceed those of normal verbal communication.

Balint agrees that the putative parapsychological experiences increasingly reported by clinicians (Farrell 1983; Bass 2001; Jacobs 2001; Lazar 2001; Stoller 2001; Eisold 2002; Suchet 2004, 2016; Marcus 1997; Mayer 2008; de Peyer 2016; Farber 2017) are best approached *psychoanalytically* in terms of theory and clinical practice. His view coincides with Freud's approach, which holds that they occur most often in dreams or other hypnoid, altered states and *almost always* in contexts of intense, affectively charged relationships. Considered from Freud's perspective, Kate's unconscious awareness of changes in her analyst remained unformulated until it could be made available to her and her analyst through her dream. This approach again recalls Freud's view that "telepathic messages received in the course of the day may only be dealt with during a dream of the following night. There would then be nothing contradictory in the material that had been telepathically communicated being modified and transformed in the dream like any other material" (1925b, 138). However, for mystical or spiritually inclined analysts this can be a dissatisfying approach that drains psychoanalysis of its mystery and flattens clinical experience, foreclosing explorations of a "More" that beckons from the outer limits of the human mind. These analysts insist that psychoanalysis should be committed to exploring "the mystical path" (Suchet 2016, 747) that promises to reveal transcendent truths within the mind and beyond.

Psychoanalysis and the Occult

Contemporary psychoanalysis has for some time been turning its attention to "telepathic" (*tele*, distance; *pathos*, feeling, suffering) experience as part of its growing interest in the complexities of unconscious communication. As we have seen, the theoretical foundations of these phenomena and their underlying conception of the unconscious are far closer to Frederic Myers and William James than to Freud. Freud's steadfast opposition to supernatural, mystical or spiritual explanations of uncanny human experiences did not prevent him from recognizing and accepting that minds are capable of communicating outside the conventional modalities of verbal and bodily language. As discussed in the previous chapter, Freud counselled cultivating the possibilities for unconscious communication between the patient and analyst. Freud counselled the analyst to catch the "drift" of the patient's unconscious via the latter's free associations by laying himself open to the other (1912b, 116–117) while maintaining his own subjective identity. In this way the minds of both the analyst and patient may meet along interweaving, multivalent and affective communicational avenues that are generated by and envelop them both. Patient and analyst "feel" each other, rather in the way of Aron's description of how "each gets under the other's skin, each reaches into the other's guts, each is breathed in and absorbed by the other" (in Schore 2011, 84). For Freud "thought-transference" (*Gedankenübertragung*) occurs when "an idea emerges from the unconscious" as it "passes over from 'primary process' to the 'secondary process'" mentation (1925b, 138). Most importantly, the relational context of intense affect is the key that opens both parties to a shared "telepathic" communicative experience.

Psychoanalysis, as both a hermeneutic and clinical approach, is committed to understanding the irrational, messy and unpredictable processes whereby minds come to know themselves and the minds of others, sometimes in the strangest and apparently inexplicable ways. Since there is no adequate way to fully explain uncanny forms of unconscious communication, analysts remain at a loss to explain the frequency of uncanny experiences that occur in their consulting rooms. Until analysts find a way to "understand how we intuit what we know" (Eisold 2002, 516), their therapeutic and conceptual focus must confine itself to "what actually occurs *without worrying about how it [can] be explained*" (ibid., 517, italics added). As Helene Deutsch shrewdly commented with regard to her own clinical experiences of unconscious communication, they "confirm that 'occult' powers are to be sought in the depth of psychic life" (1953, 146). However, it should be noted that the definition of "occult" is simply "hidden" or "concealed".[3] Psychoanalysis is inevitably a multidisciplinary enterprise that draws on both the humanities and the sciences. In an effort to uncover the mysteries of unconscious communication, a number of analytic writers have engaged in a dialogue with other disciplines such as religion, quantum physics, paranormal research and occasionally, neuroscience.

However, a necessary caution must be borne in mind. While engagement with other disciplines is important to the vitality and continued relevance of psychoanalysis, it must also be attentive to the defensive aspects of its reliance on these disciplines. Dismissed as passé and irrelevant in university departments of psychology and cognitive science, sidelined by pharmacologically oriented psychiatry and short-term behavioural therapies, or merely by virtue of being relegated to the dustbin of intellectual history, psychoanalysis remains a controversial and divisive subject, clinically and theoretically. A serious consideration of the theoretical importance and clinical implications of uncanny, impossible experience is highly unlikely within strictly medical treatment modalities. James and Myers were right to insist that anomalous experiences are not necessarily pathological. At the same time, it does not mean that they are ontologically veridical. Rather than rushing to explain the inexplicable, Freud advised that psychoanalysis accept the limitations of its capacity to fully explain the mystery of the mind and its complex interactions with other minds. Like William James's radical empiricism that insisted on the importance of subjective experience, Freud argued that psychoanalysis must defend the importance of psychic reality in all its manifestations. Exploring psychic reality brought with it an obligation to hold firmly in mind the difference between the unconscious fantasies underlying internal, psychic reality and the question of transcendent ontological reality. In other words, in a psychologically mature mind, the reality principle is supreme.

In *Moses and Monotheism* (1939), Freud distinguished carefully and at length what he called the "historical truth" of religious imagination and subjective experience from the objective "material truth" of facts. While he did not hesitate to claim that Moses was an Egyptian who was murdered by his own people as a material fact, for example, he also vacillated with respect the *location* of that reality as either psychic (historical) or factual (material). It turns out that for Freud, psychic and factual reality are not only interconnected, they are difficult to separate. Moses may not have been an Egyptian, and the ancient Hebrews may not have murdered him. Moses may never even have existed in in this world. Nonetheless, he is very much alive in religious, cultural memory (Assmann 1997). What the narrative provides Freud with is an interpretive, conceptual framework for attempting to theorize the trans-historical transmission of unconscious trauma whose origins lie in the primordial, inaccessible past. As Freud counselled against mistaking the scaffolding for the building, so the Moses narrative should not be mistaken as providing literal details of the trauma it attempts to represent.

Freud argued that what transpires in the unconscious mind is derived from traces of experience in the external world that become symbolically encoded in myth, religion or art (Hewitt 2008, 2014a). As I will propose in my analysis of Whitley Strieber's stories of his encounters with otherworldly visitors in a later chapter, Freud's distinction between material and historical truth in narratives of trauma allows us to grasp the existential kernel of truth lodged within the strangest rhetorical forms. Traditional scientific methodologies such as replicability, which is a requirement for validating empirical experimental data, cannot as yet explain exactly how unconscious communication works. At the same time, scientific discourses can provide resources for *metaphorical* interpretive strategies that seek to understand how human beings "know" or "read" the minds of others. This question lies at the heart of psychoanalytic inquiry. As Hans Loewald, one of Freud's most creative interpreters, argued decades ago, the locus of therapeutic action takes place *within* the affective intensity of emotional connectedness that occurs *between* the analytic partners. They are not as clearly separate from each other as they perceive (or would prefer) themselves to be. In the clinical space, as Kate's dream amply demonstrated, weird things can happen.

Psychoanalytic Frameworks of Meaning: Freud and Loewald

Hans Loewald's theory of *intersubjective, interpenetrating psyches* and his approach to healthy ego development as a process of differentiation, integration and reconciliation offers a detailed theoretical resource for a psychoanalytic theory of unconscious communication. As he builds upon Freud's ideas of primary and secondary narcissism, Loewald reframes the concept of psychic boundaries. He expands Freud's theory of primary narcissism, which refers to an undifferentiated sense of oneness with the world that originates in the infant/mother psychic matrix. Loewald conceptualizes the emotional interactions between infant and mother as a loosely oscillating movement of an interpenetrating subject/object relation occurring within a shared "love" matrix that envelops them both (2000, 10–12, 553–554). The dream-like psychic fluidity that continuously flows through and around the infant and mother generates interconnected internal mental states that are shaped initially by maternal reveries. Here Loewald extends Freud's ideas about ego and superego differentiation that emerges out of their common source, the id, rather than being sharply separated from each other. In Loewald's view, a reasonably healthy mother is able to mentally receive and reconstitute the developing mind of her infant, which she reflects back. Loewald's description of the dynamic mental processes of the early infant/mother connection can be seen as both operating behind and facilitating unconscious communication within the analytic relationship. The analyst, Freud writes, "is able, from the derivatives of the unconscious which are communicated to him" to reconstruct what the patient is attempting to convey (1912c, 116). In healthy-enough environments, the early, infantile sense of self-in-and-with-other coalesces within an unconscious psychic core that develops into increasingly complex psychological capacities for artistic and intellectual creativity, including mystical or spiritual experiences.

For Loewald, the working through of repressions and other forms of alienated defences allows the conscious and unconscious dimensions of the psyche to establish and strengthen internal linkages between self-states. This capacity also fosters the ability to differentiate between internal fantasies and external realities, which, for both Loewald and Freud, represents an important psychological achievement of human development. The ability to identify and reflect upon one's internal emotional states is a precondition for *thinking* about oneself and relating to others as connected yet distinct. However, internal psychic connections are vulnerable to confusions between unconscious internal fantasy and external reality resulting from a variety of distorting effects due to environmental trauma and/or neglect. The blurring of boundaries between self and others can induce internal states of terror where individuals experience the contents of their minds as "possessed" or colonized to varying degrees by uncanny, terrifying alien "others". In cases of more optimal environmental conditions, psychic linkages between different mental states are established and cultivated. The unconscious can then be a (re)source of vitality and creative energy that enlivens and expands conscious awareness since reflective capacity is no longer impaired. The capacity for linking internal mental states generates thinking about one's feelings, fantasies and experiences of the external world. This in turn facilitates, encourages and supports the healthy and complex relational connections *between* individual minds in both explicit and implicit ways. In other words, human beings communicate with each other through multiple modalities that operate both within and outside of consciousness. Freud insists that the greater part of intra- and inter-psychic mentation occurs unconsciously. As far as he was concerned, unconscious communication between individuals is an "incontestable" fact (Freud 1915b, 194). What Freud could not account for – and what remains unaccounted for to this day – is exactly *how* such unconscious communication occurs.

Psychoanalysis and the Unio Mystica

In his theory of primary narcissism, Freud postulates the existence of an "original libidinal cathexis of the ego" (1914, 75) in earliest infancy that directs itself towards the external world while preserving elements of its original state. He borrows an image from biology that likens this process to the way "the body of an amoeba is related to the pseudopodia which puts it out" (ibid.). According to Freud's speculative arguments, as this outwardly directed movement of libidinal energy draws back into the infant psyche, it carries traces of the loved object that are internalized through fantasy identifications that are part of the process of differentiation of the developing infant's psychological states. Although he never fully articulated a theory of narcissism, he nonetheless characterizes the earliest stages of infancy where the child cannot yet "distinguish his ego from the external world as the source of the sensations flowing in upon him" (1930, 67). The developing child only gradually acquires self-awareness in response to "various promptings" from the external world (ibid.) and the responsiveness of the world in satisfying his desires for food, comfort and contact. However, the neonatal sense of undifferentiated unity with the world remains as an unconscious body-based memory. As Loewald observes, this "primordial type of experience is not unique to the mother–infant matrix. It, or its direct derivatives, are encountered in various forms in adult experience" (Loewald 2000, 554).

As the child gradually accommodates and adjusts to the demands of external reality, s/he incorporates elements of it in a gradual, dialectical process of psychic differentiation, so that the ego, which originally included "everything", achieves the capacity for external *and* internal self-differentiation that is intrinsic to psychological development. However, there is a cost that involves a sense of loss and alienation from the unitary sensibility of early infancy.

It is worth repeating here Freud's view that the "ego-feeling" of mature adulthood is "only a shrunken residue of a much more inclusive – indeed, an all-embracing – feeling which corresponded to a more intimate bond between the ego and the world around it" (1930, 68). In his description of the unitary feeling of inclusiveness that belongs to the infantile and primordial past, Freud acknowledges that it is a real experience that remains preserved in the mind behind and alongside all subsequent forms of development. This means that mystical experience is a psychic amalgam of historical *and* material truth. If the mind at some point regresses "far enough", traces of this originary experience "can once more be brought to light" (ibid., 69) albeit mediated and filtered through later developmental stages. Although by his own admission, Freud could not delve deeper into the infant psyche with his limited theory of primary narcissism, Hans Loewald did. Building and expanding upon Freud, Loewald situates the experience of undifferentiated, "oceanic" oneness as a re-collection of elements of the earliest infant/mother psychic matrix.

Loewald pursues Freud's idea that the developing ego's libidinal energies flow not only towards external objects, but are also internally directed. Thus libidinal forces and processes combine to "establish and maintain the very unity of [one]self" (Loewald 2000, 458). He describes the emergence of the ego as an interplay and intermingling of psychic forces where the love for others and the external world ("object libido") folds back into love of the self ("narcissistic libido"), laden with the traces of internalized object identifications. In this way the libidinal energies informing the child's developing object relations are transformed into intrapsychic interactions with internalized objects. From this perspective, not only are there no strict demarcations between self and other, but self and other are mutually constitutive as the *relational mind* forms through its encounters with the world. Thus, the other exists within oneself, and oneself lies within the other. Finally, in a further reconceptualization and elaboration of Freud's drive theory that is highly relevant to this discussion, Loewald argues that even "*instincts, understood as psychic, motivational, forces, become organized as such through interactions within a psychic field consisting originally of the mother-child (psychic) unit*" (2000, 127–128). This means that what are "naively called objects [play] an essential part in the constitution of the subject ... and what is naively called subject plays an essential part in the organization of objects" so that there is no such thing as a discrete, bounded or separate individual subject *in here* who encounters an equally discrete and bounded individual object *out there*. The idea of Otherness belongs to the self-experience a part of our individual identity, an integral part of who we are.

This internally and externally *relational* subjectivity is always in the process of becoming in its capacity for receptive openness both towards other minds as well as different parts of itself. This concept of mind helps to explain psychoanalytic clinical phenomena such as transference/countertransference and projective identification.[4] As critical theorist Theodor Adorno puts it, human "subjectivity" is "shaped" by the processes of "socialization;" we are "preformed by that being-for-others to the very core of our being" (2006, 71). The psychoanalytic correlate of Adorno's philosophical idea is further elaborated in Loewald's theory of sublimation, a psychic process of inter- and intra-subjectivity that unfolds through complex stages culminating in a *differentiated* unity, or "reconciliation" both within one's self and with the world. The originary "mother–infant matrix of psychic life" (Loewald 2000, 461) unfolds and develops through processes of sublimation, where "narcissism and object libido, identification and object cathexis, are products of differentiation within primary narcissism ... within the mother–infant matrix of psychic life. Sublimation ... involves an internal re-creative return toward that matrix, a reconciliation of the polarized elements produced by individuation and ... by sexual differentiation. Sublimation thus *brings together what had become separate*" (ibid.), resulting in the "reconciliation of the subject-object dichotomy" (ibid., 460).

Loewald's theory of sublimation includes the notion of the transformation of primary into secondary process mentation, through which, as Freud describes in his study on Leonardo da Vinci, passion may be converted into "a thirst for knowledge". According to Freud, Leonardo's "instinct for research" was fuelled by "the divine spark" of affective energy that became transformed into intellectual curiosity.[5] The "driving force" (Freud 1910b, 74) of primary process mobilizes the transformative potential of early narcissistic desire that embraces and identifies with external objects in a self-differentiating and transmuting activity. Loewald describes psychic movement in terms of "contradiction, conflict, spiraling, reconciliation, a dissolving of achieved reconciliations, [and] new resolutions of dissonances" (2000, 448) that culminate in a higher, individuated psychic unity. Loewald goes on to say that if this process of sublimation is disrupted by defensive, alienating repression resulting from trauma-inducing environmental pressures, the connections between the various elements of psychic experience linking primary and secondary process may be distorted and/or broken. This kind of psychic alienation can impair the capacity for symbolization, which is a precondition for reflective thinking.

Loewald's concept of the development of the mind recalls Hegel's idea of "spirit" (*Geist*) as a formless unity that becomes increasingly differentiated and complex in its ongoing interactions with the world. Especially relevant to an exploration of unconscious communication is Loewald's idea that the undifferentiated originary psyche does not "reside in a primordial individual self or individual instinctive core but in a *wider 'subjectivity'* that includes the creative-destructive powers of the parental couple" (516, italics added). On this reading, human beings are predisposed to "reading" and "reaching" each other's minds as part of their innate psychological capacities. Subjectivity is here understood as both created by and independent of human beings interacting with each other. According to Merkur, Loewald went so far as to suggest that "[n]ature itself possesses a subjectivity" (Merkur 2010, 225), and that "the existence of human subjectivity is only possible if subjectivity is an activity on the part of nature" (ibid., 224). This greater subjectivity may be described as a "third" that both envelops and flows through human beings. Ideas such as the "third" and "psychic matrix" of "primordial" experience and their demarcated boundaries may be interpreted in ways that are closely compatible with a secular form of mystical spirituality. Loewald's ideas about the nature of subjectivity that both includes individuals while extending beyond them resonates strongly with Myers's and James's ideas that individual subjectivities swim in a "mother-sea" of consciousness that surrounds and filters through them.

Psychoanalysis as an Expanded Hermenutics of Being

Simply stated, for Loewald psychoanalysis attempts to mobilize new ways of being both with oneself and with others, eventually culminating in the developmental achievement of "a *differentiated unity* (a manifold) that captures separateness in the act of uniting, and unity in the act of separating" (2000, 463). At the same time Loewald, in a close paraphrasing of Freud, acknowledges that the "older, non-discriminating forms of experience persist behind the more advanced ones" (ibid., 553; cf. Freud 1937a, 229). For both Loewald and Freud, psychological development does not proceed in a linear fashion where more advanced, complex phases of mental life absorb and surpass older, less sophisticated forms. Freud could not say with any certainty that "the dragons of primaeval days are really extinct" (1937a, 229). Remnants of early pre-Oedipal, undifferentiated experience may become reactivated "under certain exceptional conditions: in psychosis, in situations of deep intimacy between people, in some drug-related and in *ecstatic states. The intimacy of the infant-mother unity or bond is the prototype*" (Loewald 2000, 553, italics added). What Loewald refers to as the "primordial experience" of infancy and its "direct derivatives" (ibid., 554) can break into consciousness of the adult, in the form of blissful unity with all creation or persecution and possession by monsters and demons.

The parallels with Myers's and James's concept of the "uprushes" or incursions of "seraphs" or "snakes" from the depths of the treasure-house and rubbish-heap of the subliminal self are unmistakable in a passage like this. Although neither Myers nor James is mentioned by Loewald, he is similarly aware of the close association between the heights of mystical experience and the terrifying depths of psychotic breakdown that can occur with the loosening of ego-boundaries. The religious correlates of these psychic states include a range of experiences from oceanic-like feelings at one end to demon possession at the other, depending on the cultural context. "One thing, however, is certain: gods can turn into evil demons when new gods oust them. When one people has been conquered by another, their fallen gods not seldom turn into demons in the eyes of the conquerors" (Freud 1923c, 86). Visions of other worlds or transcendent dimensions of reality may be lauded as saintly or shamanic ecstasy, or pathologized as evidence of mental illness. It may also be a combination of both. In the context of the pathologizing tendencies of the psychiatric world in which he was trained, R. D. Laing comments that "even the same thing, seen from different points of view, gives rise to two entirely different descriptions, and the descriptions give rise to two entirely different theories, and the theories result in two entirely different sets of action" ([1959] 1965, 20). While no definitive theories of unconscious communication are presently available to psychoanalysis, Loewald has provided a compelling basis for a mystical psychoanalysis originating in our earliest human relationships.

"Quantum" Psychoanalysis

Loewald's relational and intersubjective theory of mind is an important contribution to ways in which psychoanalysis can theorize "anomalous" experiences such as Kate's telepathic dream. Although he makes no reference to it, Loewald's ideas about the interconnectedness and fluid subjectivities that characterize the psychic matrix of the mother/infant relation is extremely relevant to the psychoanalytic current interest in quantum physics. Oddly, his theories are rarely invoked by psychoanalysts who use quantum theory to explain their telepathic experiences. Like their nineteenth-century intellectual ancestors, these analysts seek scientific validation to support their theories about the inherent, interconnected and permeable nature of the human mind. They explain clinical events like telepathic dreams (Mayer 1996, 2002, 2008; Bass 2001; Godwin 1991; Lazar 2001; Gargiulo 2010, 2016) as manifestations of quantum interconnectedness that surface in a variety of ways, especially in dreams. Gerald Gargiulo, a former theologian and psychoanalyst, relies heavily on the quantum idea of "nonlocality" or "entanglement" (2016, 8) as providing analogies for analytic understanding of the connected nature of subjectivity (2010, 96). With reference to physicist Werner Heisenberg, Gargiulo argues that it is impossible to rigidly separate the "personal self" from the "objective world" (2016, 24). This leads some analytic writers to interpret instances of unconscious communication as evidence of David Bohm's theory of an "enfolded or implicate order" which envisions "the whole universe [as] in some way enfolded in everything and that each thing is enfolded in the whole" (Bohm 1990, 273).

The idea of an implicate and explicate order informs psychoanalyst James Grotstein's (2000) idea of a "holographic" subjectivity, although he makes no reference to Bohm. Ideas of "non-locality" and Bell's theorem, where "under certain conditions, particles that are at macroscopic orders of distance from each other appear to be able, in some sense, to affect each other, even though there is no known means by which they could be connected" (Bohm 1990, 274) inspire some analysts to speculate about how "the individual boundaried mind and the radically connected mind describe models of the mind that can start to complement each other in new and critically important ways" (Mayer 2002, 94). I will discuss the influence of entanglement on spiritual psychoanalysis in the next chapter. Instead of quantum mechanics, other analytic theorists appeal to neuroscience as well and its theory of "mirror neurons" (Rosenbaum 2011; Grotstein 2009b, 155) or the intuitive powers of right brain function (Schore 2011) for help in explaining unconscious communication.

It is important for psychoanalysis to include insights and perspectives of other disciplines in its effort to enlarge and deepen the scope of its understanding of the human mind. For some interpreters, psychoanalytic theory inevitably raises philosophical questions about the "hermeneutics" of human being (Ricoeur 1970) as it explores the "ground of being, the ground of existence" through a sustained process of "questioning" (Gargiulo 2016, 76). At the same time, psychoanalysts need to proceed with extreme caution as to the manner and extent to which they invoke the astoundingly complicated and counterintuitive theories of quantum physics. Since most analytic thinkers and clinical practitioners are *not* physicists, astronomers or cosmologists, they are not qualified to venture too far into this branch of science with credible epistemological authority. Nor are they are qualified to presume that there is a simple, direct link between the quantum world and the macro world of daily life without solid justification or doing the math.

However, it *is* legitimate for psychoanalysis to describe the interconnected nature of reality with metaphors and analogies carefully drawn from quantum physics. These rhetorical strategies can provide richly suggestive ways for thinking about the permeability of the mind and the phenomenon of unconscious communication (Gargiulo 2010, 95, 96; 2016, 23). Theories of the intersubjective nature of self and other as developed by Loewald, or the philosophical psychology of Adorno on the inherently relational nature of the self, are not necessarily synonymous with "entanglement" as quantum physics understands the term. Rather, psychoanalytic ideas about the "entangled" nature of consciousness are better situated within the tradition of metaphysical psychology initiated by William James, with which they are strikingly compatible. Highly speculative, complex and contested theories ranging from David Bohm's "implicate and explicate" orders of reality to Brian Greene's parallel universes (2005) should be used with caution and care.

These analysts further argue that their use of quantum mechanics aligns with claims that the Newtonian view of reality is misleading since it only applies to the laws of physics that govern the observable world. The laws of time and space that govern Newtonian physics are juxtaposed with the quantum world where these categories don't apply. Quantum theory reveals that light can be measured as either particles or waves, depending on the instrument used. A particle in one location is affected by manipulations made on a particle in another location, irrespective of the distance between them; string theory postulates that all matter in its most infinitesimal form is constituted by combinations of vibrating strings; and most important for psychoanalysis, actions of measurement and observation cannot be separated from their objects. Contrasting "Newtonian" with "quantum" approaches to reality provides psychoanalysis with corresponding metaphorical frameworks that justify their explanations of telepathy against sceptical arguments that dismiss them. The rational, sequential operations of time and space associated with "Newtonian" levels of consciousness is juxtaposed with the hidden, non-rational quantum-like unconscious where the dictates of time, space, and linear, rational thought do not apply. According to Gargiulo, quantum physics provides a model of the world that "mirrors psychoanalytic experience" (2016, 9). The uncertainly principle, which holds that momentum and location cannot be simultaneously established, so that the wave function collapses when either momentum or position is measured, is applied to psychoanalysis. In the act of making a psychoanalytic interpretation, the range of "myriad possibilities" connected with a patient collapses into a "given conclusion" that fixes meaning (ibid., 23). Since "absolute distinctions" between self and other, past and present, here and there, do not exist in the reality of the "micro world" (ibid., 24), then the separate consciousness of a personal self does not exist either. All that can be known is the world as we observe and interpret it, not as it is (ibid., 27). This perspective mirrors James's view that "the world of our present consciousness is only one out of many worlds of consciousness that exist" (James [1902] 2004, 444).

These ideas, updated with respect to current quantum science, are part of a relational ontology of science and spirituality that was already worked out by James and Myers. The singular defining concept that underlies and animates this relational ontology privileges the interconnectedness of all reality against notions of the discrete boundaried mind of the individual self, which is rejected as an illusory fiction borne of the distortions of Newtonian science. There is no demarcated unitary psyche but rather a cosmic spectrum of fluid, interpenetrating psyches originating in a common subliminal realm from which individuals are created or filtered. Consciousness does not belong solely to an individual brain, but exists all around it and flows through it. This effort that combines nineteenth-century science and psychology, reworked and reformulated through psychoanalysis and its use of quantum metaphors, illustrates the unacknowledged, but powerful intellectual legacy of James and Myers. The nineteenth-century notion derived from American mesmerism, that there is a universal magnetic fluid flowing through human bodies that can be tapped into for healing physical and psychological illnesses, is an early modern precursor that roughly anticipates the quantum idea of the interconnected nature of reality. These combined legacies help to shape the cultural contours of a contemporary mystical and scientific psychoanalytic "psychology of anomalous experience" (Blackman 2010, 187).

At the same time, this psychoanalytic psychology of anomalous experience incorporates basic features of Freud's unconscious that disregards time, space and ordinary reality (1915b, 187). The unconscious has "no negation, no doubt, no degrees of certainty" (ibid., 186) and no sense of contradiction. Thus direct knowledge of the unconscious is not available to the analyst, who can only approach and describe it "with analogies" (Freud 1933a, 73). It is important to recall that Freud's term for the unconscious was *Das Unbewusste*, the "unknown", which he later called the "id", *Das Es*, or "it", the "inaccessible part of our personality" (ibid.). The id is composed of repressed contents associated with the individual's life experiences and the non-repressed contents bequeathed through phylogenetic, archaic inheritance. This view of the unconscious does not easily fit with a mystical relational ontology of the subliminal self. For mystical psychoanalysts, the notion of the unconscious is far closer to that of a metaphysical cosmic consciousness, "mother-sea" or Mind at Large that animates the inherently interconnected nature of all reality. Freud's concept of the unconscious is transformed beyond recognition, if not left behind altogether, as psychoanalysis adopts and embraces a

Jamesian belief in a spiritual, cosmic mind as the creator-matrix of the whole universe.

William James Redivivus: James Grotstein's "Mystical Science" of Psychoanalysis

When he was a young medical student, the American Kleinian/Bionian psychoanalyst James Grotstein "witnessed" (2000, 1) a dream in which an angel asks, "Where is James Grotstein?" Another angel replies, "He is aloft, contemplating the dosage of sorrow upon the earth" (ibid., 5). Given that Grotstein later became a psychoanalyst, the dream was prophetic, because psychoanalysts spend their clinical careers "contemplating the dosage of sorrow" suffered by their patients. In *The Interpretation of Dreams*, Freud established dream interpretation as an essential, defining feature of psychoanalytic theory and clinical practice. As the "royal road to a knowledge of the unconscious activities of the mind" (Freud 1900, 608), dreams provide unique access to the dreamer's unconscious. Individuals write, produce, direct and choreograph their own dreams. Dreams "always have a meaning" (Freud 1910a, 38) as they yield knowledge of the *dreamer's* hidden conflicts, desires and fears (ibid., 37). Through the more expansive, reflective self-understanding that emerges through dream interpretation, the patient may be able to transform the distortions of damaged primary process and sublimate them towards more creative, mature and stronger mental life as described by Loewald.

While Grotstein agrees with Freud about the clinical importance of dreams in illuminating unconscious conflicts and fantasies, his approach is radically different than Freud's in a number of key ways. One of his most significant departures from Freud's theory of dreams concerns the question of agency. Grotstein insists that he did not "have" the dream; rather the dream *had* him. The "beautiful and awesome dream" and the "dreamer who dreamed it" were "other than I" (Grotstein 2000, xxvii). As we saw with James at the end of the last chapter, Grotstein also considers the real possibility that dreamers are vehicles or conduits for dreams that are not theirs. He also believes that the dreaming state opens the mind to infusions from transcendent dimensions of reality that lie beyond the material world. Although Grotstein doesn't say who he thinks dreamed the dream he "witnessed", he strongly hints at an answer with his frequent references to the Assyriologist Chaim Tadmor, who "informed me that the ancient Assyrians believed that dreams were the language of the gods, that gods spoke to each other through human dreams, and that humans were forbidden from attending to them or remembering them" (Grotstein 2000, xxvii; 1998, 46). Grotstein, however, was able to remember the heavenly dream that he referred to throughout his life as an "epiphany" and a "mystery" (ibid., xxvii). In his view, the ability to dream is far more than a psychological process that helps the individual understand disturbing emotions. The ability to dream provides evidence of a super normal "preternatural capacity, one possessed by our holographically and numinously functioning ineffable subject of the unconscious" who is neither the one who dreams, nor the one who understands the dream (ibid., xxvii). Although Grotstein returns to these ideas repeatedly throughout his work, it isn't always clear what he is trying to say, which for him is most likely the point. Mysteries must remain mysteries, as far as he is concerned. When and if they reveal dimensions of a mystical, hyper reality, they are to be understood as sacred "witnessings" that bring us closer to ineffable realms that cannot and perhaps should not be deciphered. For Grotstein, it is both erroneous and hubristic to assume that dreams are produced by individuals. Dreams are revelations of an ineffable or ultimate[6] reality that chooses how and when to reveal itself to humans in their dreams (Grotstein 1998, 45).

Freud understood that dreams cannot be fully or completely known. At a certain point in the interpretation of a dream, the analyst and the patient encounter "the dream's navel, the spot where it reaches down into the unknown" (Freud 1900, 525). Freud argued that dreams have manifest and latent content that includes multiple, contradictory and unpredictably shifting story lines that because they are products of the unconscious, have no regard for time and space. Dreams and their interpretations inevitably "branch out in every direction into the intricate network of our world of thought" (ibid.). Freud acknowledges that dreams don't have "definite endings", and are subject to complex mental processes of displacement, condensation, symbolization and endless revision. The fact that there are limits to dream interpretation, however, in no way means for him that dreams have a mystical nature. "I confess", he writes, "that I feel no necessity for making any mystical assumptions in order to fill the gaps in our present knowledge" of dreams (Freud 1910a, 34). In striking contrast to Freud, Grotstein reformulates Freud's understanding of the "dream's navel" in explicit spiritual and mystical language.[7] From this perspective, dreams are the ineffable conduits or "royal roads" that both lead to and interface with the cosmic "Godhead". This "Godhead", a term Grotstein uses frequently but never defines, is an "Ultimate Intelligence", "Ultimate Presence", cosmic "Essence" (Grotstein 2004a; 2004b, 86) or vitalistic energy that flows and filters through the unconscious minds of individuals that it contains and surrounds (Grotstein 1997, 86; 2007, 62; 2009a, 738). The human psyche unfolds to higher orders of Being.

Inevitably, Grotstein's theory of dreams and dreaming requires an equally mystical reconceptualization and retranslation of the unconscious. Freud's view of *Das Unbewusste* ("unknown") is utterly transformed into a "container" or "personified essence" of the cosmic mind, Essence, or Godhead. Grotstein goes on to make the astonishing and puzzling assertion that *Freud's* concept of the unconscious is the "closest to the idea of God that man can possibly contemplate" (Grotstein 2004a, 91). If the unconscious is another way of talking about the divine, it is not an unconscious that Freud would recognize. Freud takes pains to explicitly reject and disavow any possible association of his theory with mystical interpretations or appropriations. None of this seems to trouble Grotstein, who forges on to make the even more outlandish claim that the unconscious is not only divine in nature, it *is* God: "It has been my contention that the unconscious and man's conception of 'God' are congruent" (ibid., 82). Grotstein is unequivocally clear that psychoanalytic exploration of the unconscious in clinical practice can bring both analyst and analysand "as close to 'God' as we are ever likely to arrive" (1997, 83). Dream interpretation in psychoanalysis is the mystical key unlocking the portals to heaven where the discourses of the gods may be overheard. As the sacred interface between heaven and earth and the individual and cosmic mind, dreaming both "exit[s] into" and emerges out of its "numinous origins" (Grotstein 2009a, 746).

At times Grotstein follows his religious reinterpretation of Freud's thought with a sudden reversal in which he accuses Freud of secularizing and demonizing the unconscious (Grotstein 1983, 13; 1998, 41). Perhaps in Grotstein's view, Freud's consistently non-religious treatment of the unconscious is tantamount to demonizing it. For Freud, acknowledging that the human unconscious is the source and dwelling place of spiritual beings both sacred and demonic, is not the same as saying that the unconscious reveals their objective existence. When Freud writes that "certain mystical practices may succeed in upsetting the normal relations between the different regions of the mind" (1933a, 79–80), he is not suggesting that mystical experiences are noetic revelations of gnostic secrets. Rather, he implies that "mystical practices" may lead to dissociative psychological states that temporarily displace ordinary consciousness. Freud does not think there are "ultimate truths" to be found in mystical or any other mental states (ibid., 80). And although he identifies gods and demons as creations of unconscious fantasy, he does not describe the unconscious as "demonic" in nature. We must recall his caution about approaching the unconscious through the use of analogies as he does himself in describing it as "a cauldron full of seething excitations" (ibid., 73). Grotstein does not appear to be interested in such fine distinctions. Instead, he makes the baseless claim that Freud the "atheist" (Grotstein 1998, 46) was prevented from apprehending the cosmic nature of the unconscious because of his intellectual enslavement to positivistic science (Grotstein 2007, 12, 37) that is more suited to the "study of inanimate objects" (ibid., 3) than human beings. He further accuses Freud of losing sight of the "numinous majesty and uniqueness" (Grotstein 1998, 41) of the "ineffable subject of the unconscious" and by taking flight and refuge in "the more acceptable, gentrified ego" (ibid.).

In yet another reversal, Grotstein contradicts his assessment that Freud was a "logical" positivist scientist (Grotstein 2004a, 82) as he also claims that there are mystical elements within *Freud's* concept of the unconscious. Grotstein does not attempt to explain the confusing and contradictory shifts in his treatment of Freud. Instead, he points to the "other Freud" who "speaks with reverence of the elegant organization of dream work" (Grotstein 1998, 49). According to Grotstein, not only does this "other Freud" have a "mystical side" (Grotstein 2007, 105), he goes on to declare that Freud was a "mystic" (Grotstein 2004b, 1096) who was *unaware* that he was a mystic (Grotstein 1998, 56)! This is a clear case of "no" actually meaning "yes". In a stream of dizzying assertions, Grotstein claims that Freud had a misguided belief in the "religion" of "logical positivism" that alienated him from his true mystic self (Grotstein 1998, 46). Following this unsupported claim that Freud was a closet mystic, Grotstein interprets the real meaning of Freud's "ego ideal" or superego as a "way of talking about the 'child God' which Christians have enshrined as 'Christ' but which represents a generic archetype as the 'Messiah'" (Grotstein 1998, 45). While it is by no means clear what Grotstein means by all this, it should in fairness be pointed out that he is not the first or only commentator to read vaguely mystical and "Kabbalistic" themes into Freud's work as he muses that the ego ideal is, "(to use the Kabbalistic nomenclature, 'Sephiroth') the ineffable Subject" (ibid.). In order to justify his reinterpretation of the dream's navel as a mystical portal to the "numinous origins" of "ultimate mystery", "Absolute Truth", or "Ultimate and Infinite Reality" (Grotstein 2009a, 746, 749), Grotstein must do far more than create an "other Freud". But he isn't interested in engaging in an exegesis of Freud's texts. Instead, Grotstein dreams his own dream of Freud the mystic.

Grotstein's Bion: the "Messiah" of Psychoanalysis

This unruly blending of psychoanalysis, religion, spirituality and mysticism that characterizes so much of Grotstein's writing is deeply influenced by the later work of the British psychoanalyst Wilfred Bion (1897–1979). Most of Grotstein's writing is devoted to interpreting and assimilating Bion's notion of "O".[8] Bion explains that he uses the sign O to denote that which is the ultimate reality represented by terms such as ultimate reality, absolute truth, the godhead, the infinite, the thing-in-itself. O ... can "become", but it cannot be "known". It is darkness and formlessness ... its presence can be recognized and felt. ... The religious mystics have probably approximated most closely to expression of experience of it. Its existence is as essential to science as to religion.

(Bion 1970, 26, 30)

In a passage like this, the darkness of Freud's unconscious is transposed to a mystical category. Edna O'Shaughnessy remarks in a comment that equally describes Grotstein's psychoanalytic mysticism, "Bion's thinking becomes less disciplined ... mixing and blurring categories of discourse, embracing contradictions, and sliding between ideas rather than linking them. These features are apparent, *indeed intentional*" (O'Shaughnessy 2005, 1524, italics added). Grotstein is well aware that these kinds of criticisms are often made about Bion's writing style. Nonetheless, his goal is to "scrupulously" present Bion's thought while putting his own "stamp" on it (Grotstein 2004b, 1083). While Grotstein admits that Bion's style leaves readers "inescapably at the mercy of imaginative conjecture" (ibid.), his representation of Bion is often as impenetrable as much of Bion's later work.[9]

After his arrival in Los Angeles from England, Bion became Grotstein's analyst. With Bion, Grotstein "regained the sense of awe and wonder" about who is the "true author" of dreams. In contrast to criticisms that Bion's descriptions of O are "obscure, incoherent" and "highly jargonized" (Blass 2011, 1081), Grotstein evaluates O as signifying "one of the profoundest paradigm changes within psychoanalysis to date. The sweep of its epistemological embrace is so radical that it understandably dismayed many of his analytic cohorts" (Grotstein 1997, 77). Grotstein laments that Bion's later writings on O are dismissed as "mystical", "unscientific", or "psychotic" (ibid.). For Grotstein, Bion is the "wizard", "mystic", "genius", and "messiah" (Grotstein 1983, 1) of psychoanalysis. This idealized representation of Bion and his work elevates him to the status of a prophet whose idea of O may one day be acknowledged as "one of the foremost psychoanalytic discoveries of the century" (Grotstein 1998, 48).

Grotstein is aware (1998, 48) that many writers ignore or marginalize Bion's post-1966 writings on O (Blass 2011, 1081). This does not deter him from writing about the "later Bion" in ways that make it difficult at times to distinguish between his work and Bion's, which can be frustrating for the reader. Grotstein positions himself as a disciple, interpreter and critical commentator, a rhetorical strategy that is quite deliberate. In Grotstein's view, Bion rescues and raises psychoanalysis from a "sensible science" to "its apotheosis in non-sensible intuitionistic science" (Grotstein 1997, 78). Bion, he writes, was explicitly indebted to "the mystics" (ibid., 83). In their shared effort to refashion psychoanalysis as an "intuitionistic science", the act of writing itself becomes for both Bion and Grotstein a mystical act, which helps to explain its deliberately vague and amorphous quality. The "ineffable-subject-of-absolute-ultimate-truth" cannot be delineated or expressed in the intellectual language of psychoanalysis, or any other discipline. Following Kripal's observation that mystical texts are themselves performative acts that create mystical experience through writing, Grotstein's use and incorporation of Bion is better understood when framed in terms of a performative, mystical practice. In other words, Bion and Grotstein are re-engaging the divine through spiritualized psychoanalytic writing. The act of writing itself becomes a "site of the divine's [O's] presence" (Bender 2010, 76) that facilitates a "hierophanic" irruption of the sacred through it.

Grotstein follows Bion's ideas and style of writing so closely that there are times when reading Grotstein, one could also be reading Bion. Through his own mystical psychoanalytic writing, Grotstein interprets and channels Bion's ideas in ways that attempt to produce a hermeneutic merging of their thought. This is understandable given Grotstein's entirely serious declaration that Bion is the "messiah" of psychoanalysis. Grotstein is committed not only to carrying on Bion's work, but also to keeping alive the salvific promise of his visionary mystical psychoanalysis through a kind of literary mimesis that blends them both. For Grotstein, Bion's "cosmic view" of "Man" and the "psyche" (Grotstein 1981, 505, 506) is *both* a psychoanalytic theory *and* a visionary revelation of the "vitalistic" (ibid., 522) sacred Unconscious that links the individual unconscious with the "Godhead", or ultimate absolute truth of infinite reality. In Grotstein's reading of Bion, the therapeutic goal of psychoanalysis has a salvific quality as it aims to help individuals "achieve union" with the "mystical entity" Bion called O (Soffer-Dudek 2015, 938). For Bion, and for Grotstein, O is *not* a metaphor. Rather, it refers to an actual entity (ibid.) or cosmic "ontological reality" (Grotstein 2004b, 1096) that Grotstein sometimes describes in terms of a vitalistic force (2004c, 111; 2009b, 129) that circulates throughout the universe and everything in it. O is a "flowing river of noumena which is paradoxically constant and yet never the same" (Grotstein 1997, 82). With Bion's introduction of O, psychoanalysis enacts a decisive shift, away from Freud's naturalistic approach to the human mind, and towards the realm of "speculative metaphysics" (Soffer-Dudek 2015, 938) and spiritual religiosity. Clinical work is reconceived as a mystical journey towards the revelation of Ultimate Reality, a "sacred analytic passion play" (Grotstein 2000, 237) whereby the analyst-priest (ibid., 244) absorbs the patient's pain (ibid., 233). In this way the analyst helps the patient heal the internal distortions and conflicts that block the path to O, culminating in spiritual, psychic health.

Hierophanic and Gnostic Psychoanalysis

Again, Eliade's notion of hierophany contributes to providing theoretical coherence to Bion's and Grotstein's repetitive, at times rambling descriptions of mystical encounters with the ineffable, absolute truth of O they hope for in the clinical setting. As we saw at the beginning of this chapter, hierophany "refers to any manifestation of the sacred in whatever object throughout history ... [it is] a reality of an entirely different order", a "wholly other" (Eliade and Sullivan 1987, 313). Grotstein's and Bion's idea of the "emotional truth" of a session which ushers in an experience of O becomes somewhat clearer when interpreted in the light of Eliade's description of the paradoxical and dialectic nature of the sacred. The encounter with emotional truth that somehow brings the analyst and patient to the threshold of O is also more accessible when reframed in Eliadean terms. What Grotstein describes as taking place in the encounter with O is a hierophanic encounter.

Like every hierophany, those that occur in clinical contexts express "an incomprehensible paradox arising from the great mystery upon which every hierophany is centred: the very fact that the sacred is made manifest at all" (Eliade and Sullivan 1987, 314). In moments of hierophanic irruption, the consulting room transforms into a sacred space and the session becomes a moment in sacred time. Following this Eliadean line of thought, the encounter with O is a hierophanic experience. Like all such experiences, psychoanalytic hierophanies also "directly affect" the way in which human beings understand themselves and their potential for growth and transformation, or what Eliade describes as "their destiny" (ibid., 315). In applying the concept of hierophany to Grotstein's and Bion's mystical psychoanalytic theorizing, it becomes possible to properly situate it within the Jamesian tradition of psychologized, non-religious spirituality and the "science mysticism" associated with the "religion of no religion" of immediate, subjective experience (Kripal 2007a; James [1902] 2004, 39). This is the tradition to which the work of Bion and Grotstein may be considered as belonging. As well, in Eliadean terms, Grotstein and Bion envision the goal of therapy as facilitating ingressions of the sacred through overcoming the internal pathologies that are barriers against O. Psychoanalytic hierophanies produce transformative experiences that yield deeper levels of authentic self-knowledge for both analyst and patient. They are also gnostic revelations of the sacred as Absolute Truth.

As far as clinical work is concerned, the analyst-mystic sees his role as a spiritual guide who helps his patient receive, absorb and integrate hierophanic moments of sacred revelation. These experiences foster the mental health of both the patient and the analyst who helps the patient tolerate a carefully titrated encounter with O. Grotstein is well aware that mystical experiences can be dangerous if they flood the mind with the overwhelming intensity of primordial, raw emotions that can be unleashed in confronting O. The influx of raw, sensory and unprocessed emotion that Bion calls "beta elements" (James's "B-region") must be carefully managed and titrated in their transformation into "alpha elements" (James's "A-region") of coherent and mentally organized meaning. Both patient and analyst communicate unconsciously in their effort to release "the emotional truths of the analysand's emotions" (Grotstein 2004b, 1085) and transform them through the patient's alpha function. In Grotstein's view, which here recalls Freud, the analyst must open his own unconscious to that of the patient in order to "summon" those emotions that resonate with the patient's (ibid.). The meeting of unconscious minds in the session will hopefully precipitate manifestations the sacred as they create pathways to O.

The analyst helps the patient receive the influx of "Absolute Truth" in ways that can be safely integrated into the patient's own emotional truth. Thus the "beta elements" left over from an original infantile experience of O are projected by the patient into the analyst. The analyst is then able to transform them into spiritual knowledge that can be shared with the patient as "wisdom" of "personal O". Grotstein calls this "last act the achievement of the transcendent position" (Grotstein 2004b, 1087).

Analysts who follow Bion and Grotstein share their view that the goal of therapeutic action is to facilitate manifestations or hierophanies of O, the revelation of what they consider to be the gnostic truth of "the preexisting unity that is ultimate reality" (White 2011, 233). Since these revelatory moments of the sacred occur in space and time in psychoanalytic clinical practice, they share the dialectical nature and structure of hierophany. Mystical psychoanalysis has to confront the "incomprehensible paradox arising from the great mystery upon which every hierophany is centred: the very fact that the sacred is made manifest at all" (Eliade and Sullivan 1987, 314).

Clearly, but without acknowledgement or recognition, the mystical, metaphysical and spiritual psychology of Frederic Myers and William James is a living presence in the psychoanalytic theory of Wilfrid Bion and James Grotstein. In a way, Myers and James, along with strong touches of Jung, reside in the psychanalytic subconscious of them both. Myers and James could have provided theoretical clarification for Bion and Grotstein, as well as resolving much of the confusion in their work, if they had decided to engage their psychological theories. Instead of indulging in occasional condemnations of Freud, Grotstein especially could have drawn upon the Jamesian tradition in American psychology to clarify his own and Bion's thought. By situating his thinking within this intellectual tradition, he could have further clarified his and Bion's theoretical differences with Freud. Unlike James and Myers, Grotstein's mystical approach to psychoanalysis is often mired in needless obfuscations that result from shifting and contradictory uses of the term "unconscious". As we saw in the previous chapter, James clearly rejected the notion of the unconscious in favour of the subconscious or subliminal self. In situating Bion and Grotstein in a Jamesian framework of meaning, it becomes clear that they too are operating with a concept of a subconscious, subliminal self. It may also be pointed out in passing that there is a striking absence of aggression and sexuality in Bion and Grotstein's metaphysical psychology, whereas they are integral psychic forces in the Freudian unconscious. In separating Freud's idea of the unconscious from the spiritual subliminal realms of consciousness, we can see more clearly the ways in which mystical psychoanalysis reformulates and psychologizes the intuitions of religious faith.

4

What Is the "*This*" that Changes Everything?

> A thing becomes sacred in so far as it embodies (that is, reveals) something other than itself.
>
> (Eliade 1958, 13)

While Freud accepted that telepathy occurs in clinical settings, it is clear that he did so rather grudgingly. His ambivalence about thought-transference or unconscious communication, which he regarded as "so close to telepathy" that it could "indeed without much violence be regarded as the same thing" (1933b, 39) is well documented (Jones 1957; Luckhurst 2002; Bass 2004; Rosenthal 2010; Pile 2012; Hewitt 2014a, 2014b; Boyle 2016; Rottenberg 2017). Peter Gay admitted that "what intrigued [Freud] most, inconclusive though he thought the evidence, was telepathy" (1988, 443). However, a nuanced understanding of Freud's "ambivalence" is called for in order to avoid any misunderstanding that Freud struggled with his own internal conflicts around unconscious mystical tendencies such as attributed to him by Grotstein. In line with his consistent methodological commitment to privileging observation over theory (Freud 1915b, 190), Freud remarked with respect to telepathy that he was prepared to believe "what is shown ... to *deserve* belief" (1933b, 31, italics added). As I have argued in greater detail elsewhere (Hewitt 2014a, 85–112), Freud openly acknowledged and marvelled that unconscious communication existed (Freud 1915b, 194). He not only recognized its therapeutic utility, he went so far as to encourage psychoanalysts to use their own unconscious as a "receptive organ" for the patient's unconscious transmissions (Freud 1912c, 115–116).

Decades before his work on the transgenerational transmission of unconscious trauma outlined in *Totem and Taboo* (1913) and *Moses and Monotheism* (1939), Freud accepted that individuals communicate with each other in non-ordinary, unconscious ways that could not be fully understood. He speculated that telepathy may have originated in an "archaic method of communication" which in the "course of phylogenetic evolution" became replaced by the more familiar sensory modalities of verbal language and bodily gestures. If that were the case, Freud mused, it may well be that "the older method" persists "in the background" of psychic life, occasionally reactivated by significant and unexpected changes in specific contexts and conditions of life (1933b, 55). While Freud conceded that unconscious communication can be used as an effective clinical tool, he vacillated for many years about unequivocally acknowledging its existence and his own belief in it (1921, 1922). His ambivalence was related primarily to his fear that unconscious communication, and psychoanalysis by association, would be identified with the widespread spiritualist movements that were prevalent in the late nineteenth and early twentieth centuries (Hewitt 2014a, 85–101). Freud forthrightly admits to his "dread" that psychoanalysis would be tainted by associations with "mysticism" or "spiritualism" if telepathy were "proved true" (1933b, 54). Nonetheless, he finally admitted that telepathy existed as a natural human capacity whose mechanics were still to be explained by science.

Freud was fully aware that in popular culture telepathy was linked with a range of vulgar occult performances associated with table rapping, Ouija boards, automatic writing, levitations, ectoplasmic excretions from the body of the medium during materialization séances, and the channelling of discarnate spirits through mediumistic trance. Nonetheless, he took the view that *beliefs* in such phenomena were as worthy of *psychoanalytic* inquiry as any other form of religious beliefs or subjective mystical experiences. We have seen that as far as Freud was concerned, mediumistic trances were products of the human mind and needed to be understood as psychological phenomena. The human mind was not a receiver or mental conduit for communications from the spirit world. As he commented to Nandor Fodor after reading his study of poltergeists, "The way you deflect your interest from the question of whether the phenomena observed are real or have been falsified and turn it to *the psychological study of the medium*, including the investigation of his previous history, seems to me to be the right steps to take in the planning of research which will lead to some explanation of the occurrences in question" (in Jones 1957, 396, italics added). Freud's studies in diverse areas such as myth, literature, anthropology, religion and culture were all carried out within the framework of psychoanalytic theory.

Both Freud and James emphasized that the importance of approaching subjective experience in its lived immediacy must take precedence to formulating theories about it. Freud's treatment of the psychology of occult experience and beliefs is a part of his critique of religion, and must be considered within that larger framework. For Freud, belief in gods, demons, ghosts or spirit communication should all be subject to critical investigation by psychoanalysis into their origins in unconscious fantasy. This approach aligns with James's view that there is no such thing as *religious* feelings, only feelings and mental states that are *culturally* coded as religious or other "special cases of kinds of human experience of much wider scope" ([1902] 2004, 33). Unlike James, Freud did not concern himself with questions about the ontological independent reality of God or a transcendent "More". As Freud comments quite simply in *The Future of an Illusion*, "To assess the truth-value of religious doctrine does not lie within the scope of the present enquiry" (1927, 33). With respect to the question of subjective belief in gods, Freud's approach implicitly follows Husserl's comment on the intentional object: "It makes no essential difference to an object presented and given to consciousness whether it exists, or is fictitious, or is completely absurd" (in Rennie 2007, 74). From this perspective, "the *concept of consciousness can be seen in a purely phenomenological manner*, i.e., a manner which *cuts out all relation to empirically real existence*" (ibid., 75). This view parallels Freud's psychoanalytic method, which is to analyse the psychology that gives rise to the experience rather than the ontological status of the object of the experience.

"I'm a Forsyth Too"

A fair appreciation of Freud's treatment of unconscious communication must situate it in the larger context of psychoanalytic concepts such as the unconscious, affect, transference, unconscious fantasy and dream interpretation. As Lecia Rosenthal rightly comments, Freud's approach to telepathy is "best understood" within his ongoing metapsychology of the "unconscious in its unverifiability" (Rosenthal 2010, 125). Here it is important to recall that for Freud the unconscious can only be approached through analogies and metaphor, and its existence is inferred. I also agree with Rosenthal's view that, in his explorations of the nature and operations of the unconscious, Freud takes an intersubjective approach by situating the minds of individuals within a "network of exchanges and influences for which no definitive origin or endpoint can easily be determined" (Rosenthal 2010, 133; Hewitt 2014a, 87–88). Here Freud anticipates the contemporary psychoanalytic idea of the intersubjective field, which is similar to Loewald's notion of the "psychic matrix" discussed in the previous chapter. The intersubjective field is a creation of the participants, but it also in turn shapes and influences them and their interactions. As we saw in the discussion of Loewald, the participants interact within the mutually constructed intersubjective field which encompasses them both. They don't stand outside it. This idea of intersubjectivity as a psychic "network" is illustrated in the case of Herr P., who Freud agreed to treat for a limited period of time until he could rebuild his practice following the devastation and chaos of the First World War. A visit in the fall of 1919 from David Forsyth, a British colleague and prospective student of "particular interest" to Freud (1933b, 48), heralded the "promise of better times" and the revival of Freud's professional life (ibid.). Since Forsyth arrived at Freud's office just before the session with Herr P., the meeting with Freud's British visitor had to be postponed. Later, in the session with Herr P. immediately following Forsyth's visit, Herr P. told Freud for the first time that his girlfriend nicknamed him "Herr Von Vorsicht". Understandably "struck by this information" (ibid.) and especially (as Jung would say) its synchronistic quality, Freud carefully reviewed his own associations to this unsettling coincidence as he thought about its psychoanalytic meaning. Herr P., who had spent many years in England and had a "permanent interest in English literature", had previously introduced Freud to Galsworthy's *The Forsyte Saga* (ibid., 49), which he also lent him. Due to what became a shared literary interest between them, the "name 'Forsyte'" became "a part of the secret language which so easily grows up between two people who see a lot of each other" (ibid., 50), as could easily be the case in any analytical therapy.

As Freud pondered the obvious similarities in the pronunciation and linked meanings of *Vorsicht/Forsyth/Forsyte/foresight*, what was happening *between* him and his patient began to dawn on him. As far as Freud was concerned, there was little promise of either professional advancement or "therapeutic success" to be had in working with Herr P. (Freud 1933b, 48). Freud was far more important to Herr P. than Herr P. was to him, and they both knew it. Nevertheless, Herr P. developed a "well-tempered father transference" (ibid.) towards Freud. Understandably, he was opposed to the termination not only of his analysis, but of his *relationship* with Freud. In what must have been an intensely charged, asymmetrical clinical atmosphere of shame, guilt, and fear for a patient who was desperate to remain connected to an analyst who didn't want him, Herr P. found a way to tell Freud he knew what was going on. More than that, Herr P. used his unconscious knowledge of Forsyth's visit to plead with Freud that he was as worthy of professional interest as Freud's more esteemed colleague. "I'm a Forsyth too; that's what the girl calls me" (ibid., 51). Freud was engaged enough with Herr P. to recognize Herr P's iatrogenically induced "melancholy" and "jealousy" (ibid.). He also understood that what Herr P. was *really* telling him: "It's mortifying to me that your thoughts should be so intensely occupied with this new arrival. Do come back to me; after all I'm a Forsyth too" (ibid.). As Freud works through the associations and levels of interpretation of Herr P.'s unconscious knowledge, he wonders, "Could P. have known that Dr Forsyth had just paid me his first visit?" Or was Freud possibly attributing his own knowledge to Herr P? "[W]as it only *my* knowledge about these things that was revealed in his associations?" (ibid., 52) *Whose* knowledge was it? As Freud attempts to think through a multiplicity of possibilities to account for Herr P.'s unconscious knowledge of the Forsyth visit and other private matters related to Freud that he seemed to know about, he admits "I have a feeling that here too the scales weigh in favour of thought-transference" (ibid., 54).

At this point it is important to recall that the word "telepathy" was coined by Frederic Myers. What is most significant about the term "telepathy" is that it refers to the transmission of affect between human beings. Whether or not it can be expanded to include communication between the living and the dead, as Myers believed, is beside the point for this discussion. Certainly Freud would have rejected any such spiritualist application of the concept. For Freud, telepathy is situated within the transference relationship between the patient and the analyst. Since Freud, psychoanalysis has come to view transference as a ubiquitous feature of human interaction inside and beyond the consulting room, a "total situation" that contains all one's emotionally charged object relations, both past and present (Joseph 1985, 447). For Freud, who would agree with this description of transference, it also "always involved the unconscious transfer of affects" (Pile 2012, 55). It is clear that Freud's analytic relationship with Herr P. was compromised by his patient's anxiety at their impending, enforced separation. Herr P.'s iatrogenically induced feelings of humiliation at counting so little for Freud were likely compounded by jealousy of Freud's professional interests that marginalized and excluded him. Resolute as Freud was on the temporary nature of their analytic work, he does express a degree of guilt about his deliberate "disregard" of professional ethics in setting a time limit on the treatment (1933b, 48). As we saw in the discussion of Kate's telepathic dream, trauma is a powerful vehicle of unconscious affect transfer between human beings in intimate relationships as they try to emotionally connect with each other. While clearly aware of all this, Freud does not linger on the nature and meaning of the transfer of affects that was occurring between him and Herr P., nor does he explicitly comment on the traumatic implications of the restriction he imposed on their relationship. Freud's treatment of Herr P. was both ethically and professionally questionable, and he knew it.

Freud and Science

As far as Freud is concerned, theories of unconscious communication must be framed and elaborated within a psychoanalytic "scientific *Weltanschauung*" that is entirely separate from the spiritual and mystical "portions of occultism" (1933b, 54). He rejected all attempts to reduce telepathy to a spiritualist phenomenon (Freud 1922, 220), reasoning that science one day would be able to explain how it worked. From this perspective, he would agree with the view of Myers, James, and the Society for Psychical Research that unconscious communication is a legitimate object of scientific research. Somewhat surprisingly, Freud ultimately maintained that science *itself* stood to benefit from investigating telepathy. It is worth quoting one of Freud's last statements on the topic of science and telepathy at length:

> In my opinion it shows no great confidence in science if one does not think it capable of assimilating and working over whatever may perhaps turn out to be true in the assertions of occultists. And particularly so far as thought-transference is concerned, it seems actually to favour the extension of the scientific – or, as our opponents say, the mechanistic – mode of thought to the mental phenomena which as so hard to lay hold of. The telepathic process is supposed to consist in a mental act in one person instigating the same mental act in another person. What lies between these two mental acts may easily be a physical process into which the mental one is transformed at one end and which is transformed back once more into the same mental one at the other end ... It would seem to me that psycho-analysis, *by inserting the unconscious between what is physical and what was previously called "psychical", has paved the way for the assumption of such processes as telepathy* ... If there is such a thing as telepathy as a real process, we may suspect that, in spite of its being so hard to demonstrate, it is quite a common phenomenon.
> (Freud 1933b, 55, italics added)

Freud could not be clearer that the key to a scientific understanding of telepathy is the unconscious, which is the interface between the physical and mental dimensions of reality. He was also adamant that a genuinely scientific, psychoanalytic investigation into telepathy and the role of the unconscious must occur entirely separately from "revelation, intuition or divination" and the "wishful impulses" (Freud 1933c, 159) associated with spirituality and mysticism. The quest for meaning and the quest for knowledge must not be conflated because for Freud, religious and scientific epistemologies are not "equal in value". Science-based "truth" cannot afford to be "tolerant" or allow for "compromises" with religion if it wishes to protect its "relentlessly critical" attitude (ibid., 160) to knowledge of the world. As far as Freud was concerned, unconscious communication must be subject to the same rigorous standards of scientific methodology applied to any other mental or physical phenomenon. Unlike James and Myers, Freud insisted on the *a priori* epistemically irreconcilability of science with religion in any form. Not only was such a reconciliation impossible in his view, the very attempt to make it was illegitimate. While he could acknowledge the personal and emotional value for people in need of it, he insisted that the epistemological frameworks of religion are completely incompatible with science. Although Freud also recognized that scientific insight is partial, provisional and incomplete in explaining reality (ibid., 174), he nonetheless regarded it as humanity's "best hope for the future" (ibid., 171). In formulating telepathy as a part of the natural, material world that is yet to be explained, Freud is then able to identify it as a legitimate object of scientific inquiry. It is worth restating here that Myers and James, in contrast to Freud, also regarded telepathy as both a natural *and* spiritual phenomenon. Their cosmotheistic and panpsychic view of a divine force or energy that flows through the universe and connects individual minds provided them with an explanation of telepathy that reconciled science and religion.

Parapsychoanalysis

While Freud insisted on separating unconscious communication from spiritualist, religious and mystical explanations, and from occult associations, a number of contemporary psychoanalytic writers have rejected his approach in favour of one that is far closer to James. Although a great deal has been written about the development of psychology and its relationship to psychical research, the relationship between paranormal experience and psychoanalysis remains "relatively unexamined" (Wooffitt 2017, 121). Current psychoanalytic interest in a wide range of paranormal phenomena, especially in the relational literature, can be approached on several levels as a continuation of the research agendas initiated by Myers and James that combined psychical research and psychology. In the implied tradition of this intellectual ancestry, a number of contemporary mystical psychoanalytic writers are fashioning their own brand of science-based spirituality as they grapple with paranormal phenomena, the central focus of which is on telepathic, unconscious communication. They are attempting to blend psychoanalysis and paranormal research into what I call "parapsychoanalysis". The psychoanalytic thinkers covered in this chapter uniformly insist that there are profoundly compelling and clearly demonstrated scientific grounds for accepting the existence of paranormal phenomena. Some of them argue that psychoanalysis is especially well suited to make this case because of its knowledge about the interconnected, permeable nature of the human mind. These psychoanalysts are far more willing to publish their clinical experiences of telepathic communications than analysts of previous generations who felt they lacked "respectable" explanations to account for their experiences (Stoller 2001, 635). Increasingly, contemporary psychoanalysts heavily rely on parapsychological research in their effort to "prove" the objective reality of psi phenomena. Like James and Myers, these writers also complain repeatedly about the "Newtonian-based" biases of "Western scientifically based skepticism" that "resist" what they consider to be highly persuasive, compelling "evidence supporting the existence" of paranormal phenomena (de Peyer 2016, 156, 161). As we have seen, this protest against Newtonian worldviews is an established feature of New Age thought. Some analysts are so confident in their rejection of Western science, and enthusiastic in their embrace of telepathy, that on occasion they succumb to the temptation to psychoanalyze the motivations behind sceptics who reject or seriously question the existence of telepathy and other paranormal claims. One analyst charges that they are either defending themselves against the "intellectual/emotional threat" posed by paranormal research, or that they harbour an "unconscious envy toward those who *do* experience this heightened form of [telepathic] receptivity" (ibid., 161). Older notions of "adepts" who have attained special insight into the mysteries of reality stand behind this kind of speculation, which also resonates with the special role of the psychoanalyst-mystic described in the previous chapter.

The Harp Came Back

The most important advocate for the scientific credibility of paranormal and psi[1] phenomena and their importance for psychoanalysis is Elizabeth Mayer. Her posthumously published book, *Extraordinary Knowing: Science, Skepticism, and the Inexplicable Powers of the Human Mind* (2008), presents findings from a wide range of paranormal research that, as far as she is concerned, provides powerfully persuasive evidence not only for telepathic communication, but also for other psi phenomena that includes clairvoyance, remote viewing, and the efficacy of healing prayer. Mayer's interest in parapsychological research grew out of her own experiences with telepathy that occurred both within and outside her consulting room. She also includes reports from psychoanalytic colleagues about their telepathic experiences. However, one experience stood out for her that was so unsettling that it inspired her to undertake an extensive investigation into paranormal research that preoccupied her for the last fifteen years of her life. Desperate to recover her daughter's stolen, irreplaceable harp, Mayer solicited the services of an Arkansas dowser, Harold McCoy, for help in getting it back. In their first phone conversation, McCoy informed Mayer that the harp was still in Oakland, California, where it was stolen. Assuring her that he would be able to determine its precise location by exercising special mental processes, McCoy asked Mayer to send him a city map and "the light given off by a precious object" (Gilligan, in Mayer

2008, xiii). McCoy not only located the harp, he also later informed Mayer that he ordered the thief, via "thought forms", to be sure to take good care of it (Mayer 2008, 264). Sure enough, the harp was returned, and in "astonishingly good condition". At no point does Mayer question McCoy's claim that he communicated telepathically with the thief, warning him not to damage the harp. Perhaps she found his story plausible because the harp indeed was recovered undamaged, and it was where he said it would be. For Mayer, the success of McCoy's divination technique was enough to convince her that telepathy exists and that minds can impact physical reality over vast distances. Her book is devoted to building a case, mostly upon evidence she painstakingly gathered from her own explorations in paranormal research, for the empirical validation that psi phenomena exists. The experience of the stolen harp and its return is one of the most dramatic among many examples offered in the book that for her prove the reality of "mind-matter anomalies" (ibid.). Even more important for Mayer, the successful outcome she attributed to McCoy's telepathic and divination powers "irrevocably changed [her] familiar world of science and rational thinking" (ibid., 1).

"*This changes everything*", (Mayer 2008, 3) Mayer thought as she brought the harp home. Throughout her book she reiterates how the numerous anomalous experiences she had in her encounters with supernormal reality transformed her life. She describes the stages she went through beginning with initial doubt, her struggles to assimilate her anomalous experiences within her pre-existing worldviews, and the personal transformation that came with accepting that deeper orders of reality lay hidden behind the ordinary. The deeper she delved into the world of paranormal research, the more she felt compelled, at times almost forced, to radically change all her previous beliefs about the nature of reason and reality. As she presents the evidence gathered from a number of scientific and anecdotal sources attesting to the existence of "extraordinary", "anomalous", or paranormal phenomena, she describes how each experience produced an existential shock or "jolt" to everything she thought she knew. In several respects, Mayer's narrative reads like a conversion experience that transformed her previous assumptions about the world in general and psychoanalysis in particular. William James's description of the "candidate for conversion" who is forced to confront the "incompleteness" of previous worldviews and assumptions ([1902] 2004, 187) applies to Mayer's description of confronting her "stunningly inadequate" notions of "space, time, reality and the nature of the human mind" (Mayer 2008, 4). She *converted* (Latin *conversio*, to turn around) from one set of life-organizing assumptions to fully embrace another set that seriously challenged and changed her former view of reality. As she emphatically repeats, the harp episode *"change[d] everything"* for her (ibid.). Again, like the convert James describes as pursuing the "positive ideal which he longs to encompass" ([1902] 2004, 187), Mayer describes the growing need she felt to discover a deeper or "ideal" truth she believed to exist behind the world of personal alienation and intellectual distortion. Her research into the paranormal was not only a search for knowledge, it was even more importantly a spiritual quest for gnostic truth.

Beyond "Daytime" Eyes

Like many contemporary New Age secular mystics, Mayer also believed in the possibility of penetrating the veil of reductionist illusions of ordinary life that block insight into the "wholeness of reality" (Hanegraaff 1998, 371). Mayer began to see that there is a world beyond the one accessible to "sunlit consciousness" (James [1902] 2004, 416). She needed to put aside her "daytime eyes" (Mayer 2008, 215) in order to see the metaphysical "stars" that represented a higher plane of reality:

> Models that explain the feeling of what happens when we see with daytime eyes won't explain seeing with nighttime eyes. If we don't recognize that, we end up like the king's wise men, the ones who proclaimed that stars didn't exist. It was only when the king's fool offered a different model for seeing – that when the sun is shining, you can't see the stars – that the people who'd obediently given up their belief in the stars discovered that the stars once again existed.
>
> (Mayer 2008, 215).

Mayer's prose shimmers with Jamesian sensibility in passages like these, and in her repeated lament that the narrow field of conscious, rational thought is woefully insufficient for apprehending the true nature of transcendent, transpersonal reality. As Mayer attempts to penetrate the gnostic depths of the "this" that changed "everything" for her, she begins to outline a science mysticism of psychoanalysis. The epistemological frameworks associated with traditional scientific and psychoanalytic theories are displaced to make room for a mystical psychology that promises wholeness and balance in aligning the self within the holographic universe that is "mirrored in each of its smallest parts" (Hanegraaff 1998, 368).

Although Mayer describes a number of examples of her encounters with the paranormal and their transformative impact on her, the demonstration by McCoy of his own powers of divination and telepathy are for her the most important. The recovery of the harp that "change[d] everything" for Mayer was a stunning, personal confrontation with the "radical discontinuities" (Doniger 2004, xiii) that suddenly rent the fabric of life as she previously knew it. The narrative account of her long spiritual and psychological journey is punctuated with a wealth of illustrative vignettes and forays into paranormal experiments, discussions with clairvoyants and intuition teachers, her own telepathic experiences and numerous interviews with analysts and other professionals about their anomalous experiences. More than any other psychoanalyst who writes about the paranormal, Mayer immersed herself in studying a wide range of ideas from cognitive science, quantum physics, the history of the Society for Psychical Research, and numerous personal anecdotes about herself and others. She describes the cumulative psychological impact on her of all these experiences that progressively cracked open the familiar "surface of things" (Mayer 2008, 50). Mayer concludes that paranormal research demonstrates the existence of "a world where the barrier between mind and matter might be permeable, where people might be able not only to find a harp from two thousand miles away, but to literally affect its material reality. Investigating that world has stretched my credibility to its limits" (ibid., 264). She ultimately accepts what Myers and James concluded a century earlier: the supernormal potential of the human mind is a reality awaiting evolutionary development.

Mayer's quest for enhanced knowledge about the nature of the mind and its place in the wider fabric of the universe is both scientific and religious. In the last pages of her book, Mayer describes the culmination of her journey as the achievement of enlightened insight into the connectedness of all reality that she intuitively already knew. Ordinary reality, the world as seen with "daytime eyes" is now revealed in its deeper ontological truth as a small part of a vast, cosmic sea of differentiated unity alive with flowing currents of interconnectivity. As it was for James, Mayer views this cosmic interconnectedness as providing the natural conditions of possibility for telepathy. In linking psychoanalysis, mysticism, spirituality, and paranormal science, Mayer can envision a future where human beings will gain access to the supernormal "spectrum of intuitive intelligence" that holds the promise of transcending "the boundaries of time and space" (Mayer 2008, 271) that would deepen our humanity. Along the lines of most New Age religious psychologies, Mayer's work represents a decisive repudiation of a thoroughly irreligious psychoanalysis associated with Freud and Newtonian-based science in favour of a visionary, religious psychology of the human mind within a holistic universe (Hanegraaff 1998, 372). In Grotstein's words, which apply to Mayer, personal subjectivity is "holographically and holistically part of an overall ultimately indivisible subjectivity – the Supraordinate Subject of Being" (Grotstein 2000,

141). From the perspective of the study of religion, the overcoming of pathology is conceived primarily as a spiritual psychological process that culminates in hierophanic encounters with the sacred. Grotstein describes these "epiphanic" (ibid., 138) experiences as "transformation" in an encounter with O that parallels the "spiritual quest" of "the mystics" (ibid., xxi).

It is no wonder that Mayer argues with such firm conviction that mental action *can* alter the physical world (the undamaged harp) and that minds *do* communicate across vast distances. In her view, experiences of "anomalous knowing" challenge all our ordinary notions of space and time, self and other, inside and outside – everything that suggests boundaried separateness not only between individuals but all facets of human and non-human reality. Moments of "anomalous knowing" that irrupt into ordinary experiences as uprushes of super normal insight, as Myers would say, allow us to see *"things as they are* when connectedness, rather than separateness, moves to the foreground of our awareness" (Mayer 2008, 68). Mayer reiterates the variety of ways that paranormal research scientifically validates and explains clinical experiences of telepathic communication for psychoanalysis. In one of the many examples of telepathy she describes throughout her book, Mayer recalls daydreaming about peaches when her patient suddenly tells her that his girlfriend's father called her his "Georgia" peach (1996, 718); another patient knows without being told that Mayer is planning a visit to England (ibid.).

Although there has been a consistent psychoanalytic interest in telepathy since Freud, it has become especially prevalent in American relational psychoanalysis, which seems particularly "receptive" to "anomalous communicative" experiences that occur between patient and analyst (Wooffitt 2017, 119). A number of relational analysts cite Mayer's work as both helping to explain and validate these experiences, many of which do not have quite the same dramatic quality as the story of the stolen harp. Most of the accounts of anomalous experience focus on telepathic communications between the analyst and patient that, again, are at least equally or even more concerned with the nature of telepathy than with psychoanalytic interpretation and meaning. Janine de Peyer describes a clinical moment where the name of her patient's hometown, which she claims not to have known, suddenly occurred to her (de Peyer 2016, 158). On the basis of this and other such experiences where patients appeared to "know" details and events about de Peyer's personal life that she insists they could not have known by ordinary means, she too invokes quantum physics as giving validation to the indisputable reality of telepathy. "If particles in the quantum world communicate instantaneously with one another", she wonders, "jumping from one place to another without seeming to need to travel in between, would it not follow that patients' and therapists' minds would be capable of doing the same thing?" (ibid., 164). This is a common interpretive strategy of the "spiritual twist" (Hanegraaff 2000, 304) often seen in New Age psychological discourses. Drawing upon some of the identical paranormal research as Mayer, de Peyer maintains that telepathic communication is easily explained and scientifically proven by quantum theories of a universal "*resonant interconnectedness* or 'entanglement'" where "minds can affect one another and information is instantaneously accessible by all through *resonant immersion in a ubiquitous, omni-present field*" (de Peyer 2016, 165). For de Peyer, these ideas have the status of established facts.

For analysts like de Peyer and Mayer, psychoanalytic theories that attempt to explain unconscious communication in terms of "empathic attunement" within the therapeutic dyad cannot adequately account for the "actual cognitive and communicative processes that characterize the peculiarly effective transmittal of information" that occurs in telepathic exchanges (Mayer 1996, 719). Heinz Kohut's theory of "cosmic narcissism" that situates the sense of mystical oneness in the infant's "primordial experience of the mother" is similar to Loewald's idea of the psychic matrix that envelops the mother/infant dyad I described at length in the previous chapter. For Kohut, who echoes and extends Freud's idea of primary narcissism also discussed earlier, the originary experience of undifferentiated being and "supraindividual and timeless existence" is "genetically predetermined by the child's primary identity with the mother" (Kohut 1966, 267). For Mayer, theories arguing that an original psychic oneness is the source of empathic relatedness fall short because they fail to explain the accuracy of detail that are a common feature of telepathy.

Other analysts who write on telepathy, like Margaret Arden, point out that psychoanalysis inevitably fails if it tries to explain "subjective experience by means of an objective tool" that include central Freudian ideas. Arden flatly rejects models based on "normal science" because in her view, they are "inappropriate" for theorizing the full extent and potential of intersubjectivity (1988, 75, 84). Mayer also objects that science refuses to treat the findings of paranormal research seriously. Yet in contrast to the emphatic confidence of analysts like Arden and de Peyer, Mayer openly discloses her initial difficulties in reconciling the claims of paranormal research with her own intellectual and rational assumptions. As part of her ongoing efforts to resolve her own doubts, Mayer decided to gain first-hand knowledge of paranormal research by participating in a Ganzfeld experiment. She explains that she needed some "personal experience" in order to fully accept the "ringing conclusions" of "solid, replicable evidence for apparently anomalous information transfer between people". In her view, participating in Ganzfeld experiments promised to provide her with the proof she needed for what it is clear that she already believed: she needed a "compelling hook" on which to hang her need to believe while confronting her own doubts (Mayer 2008, 204). Like William James, she too struggled to create a psychological science of spirituality.

Briefly, the aim of a Ganzfeld experiment is to test the research subject for telepathic reception capacity. The "sender" in the experiment tries to mentally transmit some form of information or visual image to the "receiver", or research subject, who is in another room well out of sight of the sender. Although there is no need here to describe in extensive detail all the specific mechanics of the Ganzfeld experiment (the acoustic chamber to reduce noise, the helmet containing magnetic solenoids, the halved ping-pong balls covering the eyes of the receiver), there are important aspects of Mayer's case that should be noted.[2] At the end of the experiment Mayer, who was the receiver, was given cards displaying various images such as a merry-go-round, scenes of university campuses, and a "bright red sunset", and was asked if any of them matched her own visualizations (Mayer 2008, 205). Unable to recall "a *single memory that remotely resembled any* of the cards", she gave them back to the student researcher (ibid., 206, italics added). He refused to take them. Instead, he "*instructed*" her to review the pictures anyway, and choose one. Reluctant to "screw up his experiment *through lack of compliance*", Mayer chose the red sunset. When the student researcher inquired why she chose that particular image, only then did Mayer feel a "fleeting sensation" as she pondered his question (ibid., italics added).

What that sensation signified only became clear to her after the experiment. When the student came back with the card of the red sunset – the image the sender in another room had been attempting to transmit – Mayer felt her world "turned weird". In an "instant" moment of "overwhelming fear", she felt her "mind split", along with a terrifying sense that her mind was not her own, that she was losing it (Mayer 2008, 207). She felt an uncanny sense of being "walked by the experience" that was similar to a feeling she recalled years earlier when she found a lost watch (ibid., 206–207) her husband had deliberately hidden. She had a sense of "walk[ing] across my mind" as she crossed a barrier into an "inchoate, uncertain mental state", a deeper dimension of "knowing" something that she was "simultaneously certain" she didn't know (ibid., 207). In this moment, the *experimental* nature of the Ganzfeld procedure was subsumed into its *experiential* impact on Mayer. Analysis and discussion of the scientific value of the experiment drops out of the narrative as Mayer dwells rather on how it made her feel. In other words, its truth value seems to have been confirmed by Mayer's affective response to it. As Mayer pondered the intense feelings aroused in her as a result of the

Ganzfeld experiment, she realized what she was searching for all along was the "mystifying feeling behind" the knowing of what she didn't know that she knew (ibid., 210).

For Mayer, the "this" that changed everything, beginning with the recovered harp, was the mystical revelation of the same gnostic secret discovered by William James: the interconnectedness of all reality. Her research in parapsychology ultimately confirmed her own already existing belief in a universal oneness underlying all reality. Mayer states that a powerful "subjective sense of oneness" is "repeatedly" expressed in numerous accounts of "anomalous cognition" as well as in the meditative experiences of religious practitioners (Mayer 2008, 223). Like all seekers on a quest to penetrate the hidden mysteries of nature, Mayer's journey leads inward to the depths of the self, whose "very constitution" is a "microcosm reflecting the macrocosmos in all respects" (Hanegraaff 2003, 362). As her narrative draws to its almost poetic conclusion, Mayer's sense of wonderment and awe increases in the deepening awareness of the true meaning of existence within an interconnected universe. In these last pages, her references to quantum entanglement (2008, 257), the "oceanic feeling" that Freud could not identify in himself (268), her speculations on the holographic universe where the "intangible dynamics" of the quantum world surface in the "microsphere" (ibid., 258), reveal glimpses of a visionary human potential where "mental capacities may defy physical barriers" (ibid.). This is one of several passages that strongly resonates with William James. In fact, Mayer quotes James's own mystical vision of a connected universe, a "mother-sea" containing and grounding "our several minds" through which "fitful influences from beyond leak in", thereby demonstrating the existence of an "otherwise unverifiable connexion" (James [1909b] 1986, 374–375). Since she shares this vision, it is utterly fitting that Mayer turns to James in the last pages of her book (Mayer 2008, 261). For Mayer, her quest to reconcile science with her own mystical intuitions lead her to what she "knew" all along: the sacred connectedness underlying and enveloping all reality that manifests in the "unboundaried capacity of the human psyche" (ibid., 268).

Hierophanic Experience

The long-standing mystical or spiritual dimension that runs through American psychoanalysis does not necessarily include paranormal themes or psychical research. This does not mean that mystical psychoanalysis and parapsychoanalysis require separate methodologies of critical analysis or that they are mutually exclusive. In fact, they go well together, especially since paranormal claims are seen as providing objective validation for the spiritual intuitions that are shared by both mystical psychoanalysis and parapsychoanalysis. Mystical psychoanalysis covers a broad range of religious interests often associated with New Age spirituality as it too identifies "harmony, restoration, and revitalization" (Fuller 1986, 5) as important goals of therapeutic treatment. Spiritually oriented analysts like Gerald Gargiulo explicitly argue that psychoanalysis firmly belongs within "the tradition of Western spirituality in its inquiry into personal meaning and in its efforts to achieve reconciliation" (1997, 1). Like the analysts discussed in both this and the previous chapter, Gargiulo portrays psychoanalysis as a secular, loosely blended admixture of selected elements derived from Christianity, unitive mysticism, and quantum physics. Grotstein declares a kindred affinity with Gargiulo in describing him as a "psychoanalytic mystic" who, like Grotstein, embraces "emptiness, contemplation, infinity, chaos, unpredictability, spirituality, and immanence" (Grotstein 2004d, xi).

For Gargiulo (and, I would add, Grotstein, Mayer, and a number of others), clinical work holds the promise of a psychological "form of salvation" in helping individuals experience their interconnectedness with the "all that is" or "creative life principle" (Gargiulo 1997, 1–2). As we have seen with Mayer, Gargiulo's vision of reality also strongly resonates with James's "mother-sea" of "cosmic consciousness" (James [1909b] 1986, 374) that envelops, animates and connects all existence. The idea of a conscious, cosmic, interconnected universe is a key insight of mystical psychoanalysis. As "midwives of meaning", psychoanalysts are the modern "heirs to Western spiritual traditions" (Gargiulo 1997, 2). Translated into Eliadean terms, Gargiulo is convinced that psychoanalysis can provide the conditions necessary for hierophanic irruptions of the sacred within the analytic space. Psychoanalytic mystics like Grotstein, Gargiulo, and, in her own way, Mayer, believe that clinical work should help their patients encounter inner mysteries that reside in the depths of the unconscious (Spezzano and Gargiulo 1997, xiii).

Whether framed in the directly spiritual language of Bion, Grotstein and Gargiulo, or in the more secularly modified language of paranormal research as embraced by Mayer, the gnostic secret of the psychoanalytic sacred remains the same: the unitary, interconnected nature of all reality, and the potential of psychoanalysis to reveal it. Knowledge and acceptance of this central truth holds the promise of achieving psychological healing and spiritual wholeness. This insight provides the basis of rational plausibility for accepting that telepathic communication occurs between human minds. Again, framed in Eliadean terms, for these analysts the sacred is an "element in the structure of human consciousness" (Rennie 2007, 75). However, this doesn't mean that the sacred is an entity that exists "out there", merely waiting to be revealed "in here". Although not a champion of Freud, Eliade can be invoked to bring clarity and conceptual depth to what mystical psychoanalysts mean by postulating psychoanalysis as a pathway to transcendent dimensions of reality. The psychoanalytic version of the sacred is covered and elaborated through Eliade's description of it as historical, situated, profane, vividly real, authentic and meaningful. In Eliade's view, anything can be a hierophany or manifestation of the sacred, including "*psychological*, economic, spiritual, and social life. There is hardly any object, action, *psychological function*, species of being, or even entertainment that has not become a hierophany [of the sacred] at some time" (Eliade and Sullivan 1987, 313, italics added).

Hierophanies "directly affect the situation of human existence" and alter "the fundamental structures of space and time" (Eliade and Sullivan 1987, 315). The notion of hierophany and the sacred offers a coherent and compatible framework that contributes to a fuller, more delineated and nuanced picture of what Bion and Grotstein are striving for in their descriptions of encounters with O. The idea of hierophany closely corresponds as well to what Mayer struggles to convey with her frequent references to the physical and emotional "jolt" she experienced when confronted with anomalous experiences that continually upended her view of ordinary reality. The profound emotional impact on Mayer of the recovery of the harp and her subsequent study of the paranormal attain fuller clarity, coherence and depth when interpreted as a *hierophanic* experience. Mayer had a mystical experience (or series of them) that brought her to confront the sacred and that also terrified, confused, disoriented, and exhilarated her. It changed "*everything*" because it upended her views of reason and reality that had governed her life. As Eliade writes, "the unknown and the extraordinary are disturbing epiphanies: they indicate the presence of something *other* than the natural" (Eliade 1958, 19). Mystical psychoanalysis might describe them along with Bion and Grotstein as encounters with O, or the "More" posited by James.

"Science Mysticism"

The spiritual unconscious described by Gargiulo and other psychoanalytic writers contains ideas inherited from nineteenth-century traditions such as American mesmerism, Emersonian Transcendentalism, and most importantly, Jamesian metaphysical psychology. All these intellectual traditions saw themselves as naturalistic and scientific. Their mystical, spiritual religious sensibilities firmly rejected traditional theological doctrinal teaching to develop their own forms of a "science mysticism" (Kripal 2010, 123) most suited to exploring the "cosmic enigma" (Caterine 2011, 2) hidden within the natural universe. The mesmerist idea of a magnetic fluid flowing through the universe was psychologized as a cosmic consciousness that became a precursor to transpersonal psychology. Emerson's contention that the spiritual depths of human beings are connected with transcendent realms, and James's idea of the subliminal self as a filtered instantiation originating in a "mother-sea" of cosmic consciousness are all forerunners of mystical psychoanalysis. The psychoanalytic approaches of Grotstein, Gargiulo and Mayer resonate particularly strongly with Emerson's belief that "the currents of Universal Being circulate through me; I am part and parcel of God" (in Fuller 1986, 15). Emerson's description of a Universal Being that flows through him fits well with the later concept of an individual and transpersonal unconscious that became a central theme of mystical psychoanalysis. The idea that a transpersonal unconscious connects and manifests itself in individual minds is crucial for psychoanalytic efforts that attempt to explain the mechanics of telepathic, unconscious communication.

James's effort to reconcile religion and science through psychology is carried forward to the present as spiritually oriented psychoanalysts continue to search for ways to ground psychoanalytic mysticism in the science of contemporary quantum physics.[3] Relational psychoanalyst Melanie Suchet believes that psychoanalysis promises personal transformation "through superconscious states that transcend space and time" (2016, 747). This assertion strongly echoes the views of Myers and James. Her approach advocates that the therapeutic goal must be to encourage patients to pursue personal "transformation of the self through transcendence" (ibid.). In other words, psychoanalysis should foster the production of "superconscious states" because they lead to hierophanic revelations of the sacred. From the perspective of the psychology of Myers and James, superconscious or supercognitive states result when the threshold between ordinary consciousness and the subliminal self is lowered. In Suchet's view, psychoanalytic therapy must tap into and mobilize the individual's inherent "mystical drive" to seek "personal transformation" (ibid.). She follows Bion and Grotstein in arguing that psychoanalysis is a shared, spiritual quest for mystical revelation and spiritual transformation. In the spiritualized clinical field, both the patient and therapist co-create a psychic space, where the illusion of separateness between self and other dissolves, thereby creating pathways for "telepathic interconnectivity" (ibid., 750).

In encounters with O, or moments of hierophanic intrusion, patient and analyst are no longer interacting selves with separate personalities; they no longer have an inviolable, private core of interiority. They transcend the distinctions of ordinary time and space as they become enfolded within a "unified field" that holds them in the "vast sea of quantum potential". The "Divine, the Source, the Absolute" (Suchet 2016, 751) discloses itself as the source of a cosmic, omnipresent "at-oneness". The gnostic secret has been revealed. In this state of mystical unity, both patient and analyst experience a profound *feeling* of "at-oneness" revealing the ontological truth of all existence that lies behind the veil of the illusion of the boundaried mind. Suchet, following Helen Palmer, an intuition teacher who was an important influence on Mayer, advocates the practice of emptying of the mind as a necessary prerequisite for facilitating telepathic communication. Along with Palmer, Suchet believes that once the mind is transformed into a "clear vessel", it can produce the shifts and alterations of consciousness that are necessary for receiving communications from other minds (ibid., 756). As states of ordinary consciousness loosen and dissolve, the "constantly flowing field" (ibid., 751) of "quantum" energies from the cosmic mother-sea irrupt into mystical illumination. In her account of therapeutic action, Suchet vividly describes a thoroughly modern, contemporary psychoanalytic equivalent of a hierophany of the sacred.

The "psychoanalytic mystics" (Merkur 2010) who regard clinical work as a spiritual practice leading to the "all that is" (Gargiulo 1997, 1) rely heavily on quantum theory to give scientific credibility to faith. As previously discussed, they invoke David Bohm's theory of the implicate and explicate orders of reality. For Suchet, Bohm's work lends compelling evidence that reality is a "constantly flowing field" that is "always potentially generative and creative" (Suchet 2016, 751). The quantum idea that what is observed in the physical world is affected by the very act of being observed or measured is another widely cited scientific proof of the interconnected, interpenetrating nature of the universe (Bass 2001, 693). The quantum notion of entanglement, where actions directed to one particle have an identical instantaneous effect on another distant particle, provides another compelling metaphor for what I call a "psychoanalytic physics" of cosmic connectivity. Mystical psychoanalysts assume that quantum physics provides a solid scientific basis for explanations of telepathic communications that occur between patient and analyst. Suchet describes her patient Cleo's dream that Suchet was pregnant before being told about it (Suchet 2004). Anthony Bass presents the case of a patient who "knew" intimate details of his private life, such as his wife's miscarriage, again without being told (Bass 2001, 692). Kate, as discussed in the previous chapter, dreamed her analyst's weekend. It is understandable that anomalous experiences like these will "jolt" the analyst with the shocking suddenness of their unexpected intrusions. While a number of analysts implicitly continue the Jamesian tradition of integrating science and belief as they strive to integrate psychoanalysis, mysticism, and quantum physics, others, no less jolted by their own anomalous experiences, choose not to venture beyond the limits of psychoanalysis in their speculations about telepathic communications in the therapeutic relationship.

Robert Stoller's Telepathic Dreaming

In his posthumously published paper "Telepathic Dreams?" (for which Mayer provided an introduction), psychoanalyst Robert Stoller (2001) recounts a number of telepathic experiences in clinical contexts he had over several years. They began early in his career. His first telepathic dream was about a motorcycle accident involving a young medical student whom he could not identify. A few days after Stoller had the dream, his supervisor, Ralph Greenson, disclosed that his son, a medical student, had been in a motorcycle accident on the same night as Stoller's dream. Greenson's son suffered identical injuries to the man in Stoller's dream (2001, 636). While the dream is understandably shocking because the injuries to the man in the dream corresponded almost identically to those suffered by Greenson's son, Stoller nonetheless approaches the dream in a fairly conservative psychoanalytic way. While accepting that he dreamed about the accident of his supervisor's son on the night it happened, Stoller tries to understand the psychoanalytic meaning of his dream. Using a method similar to the one Freud used in interpreting Herr P.'s telepathic knowledge, Stoller also follows his associations to the dream, first by locating it within the context of his "filial relationship" with Greenson. The maiden name of Stoller's mother was Greene; when she first met Greenson, she remarked that he looked just like her father, who died when Stoller was five. "Was I not then Greenson's grandson?" he wonders (ibid., 638).

Stoller shifts course to describe a series of several dreams that his patients had about *him* in the years following his dream about the motorcycle accident. In one of these dreams, Stoller's patient reported dreaming about "an older man" who crashed through a glass wall. On the night this patient had the dream, Stoller was at a party and indeed did crash through a closed glass door he thought was open (Stoller 2001, 639). In all, Stoller describes thirteen "telepathic" dreams from different patients, all of which contain accurate details about his life he insists they could not have known. The timing of his patients' dreams coincided with the timing of actual events that occurred in his own life. In his effort to account for these telepathic dreams, Stoller looks for the elements they all had in common. His comparative interpretive method shows that in almost every instance "the dream occurred during a *separation* – over a weekend, after an hour was missed or during a time when I was away for an extended period. Second, the patients had few or no associations to the element in the dreams that reproduced the actual events in my life. Third, these details were different from any that had shown up in the patients' dreams before, and they never recurred" (ibid., 650). Separation or anticipation of it, as well as the absence of associations, are common and recurrent themes in psychoanalytic reports of telepathic dreams.

As we have seen with Kate, who dreamed her analyst's weekend with astonishing accuracy, "telepathic" dreams can yield important clinical data about the *relationship* between the patient and analyst that is beyond their conscious awareness. Here we should recall Balint's idea that "telepathic" dreams may represent "desperate" (1955, 32) efforts by the patient to reach a distracted or inattentive analyst. In commenting on Cleo's telepathic dreams of Suchet's pregnancy, Adrienne Harris suggests that a distracted analyst, which as we saw in the case of Kate, can precipitate telepathic knowing in the patient. It is entirely plausible that a pregnant analyst may unwittingly be less focused on her patient than usual (Harris 2004, 294). Suchet had endured painful disappointment in her previous efforts to become pregnant. Perhaps the relief and excitement (Suchet 2004, 269) she felt in becoming pregnant may have been strong enough for Cleo to "pick up". The affective shifts, such as distracted excitement or a slight weakening in the analyst's usual attentive manner, may have enhanced Cleo's usual hypervigilance. This could have made her especially sensitive to the subtle changes occurring in the pregnant body of her analyst, such as "smelling, breathing rates, chemical washes" that are all associated with pregnancy (Harris 2004, 294).

While Stoller provides far less clinical detail about his relationships with the patients whose dreams he reports than Suchet, he does explore some aspects of his "filial relationship" (Stoller 2001, 638) with Greenson. Despite his conscious efforts to maintain a professional and "respectful distance" towards Greenson, he realizes that his father transference to him was "intense" (ibid.). In his efforts to counter the desire for familial intimacy with Greenson by adopting an outwardly distancing behaviour towards him, Stoller greeted him with a perfunctory "hello" at the beginning of their supervisory sessions (ibid., 636). Then, for reasons he could not consciously explain, Stoller departed from his usual greeting on the day following the dream about the motorcycle accident. Instead, he addressed Greenson with a warm "How are you?" that invited a more intimate response. This was the first time Stoller allowed himself to express personal interest in Greenson, which in turn resulted in the disclosure about the near fatal accident of Greenson's son. Stoller's shocked realization that he had dreamed the accident involving Greenson's son on the night it occurred, forced him to confront his own unconscious feelings towards Greenson.

As with Kate's dream, which in hindsight illuminated the changes that were occurring unconsciously between her and her analyst, something similar had probably been occurring between Stoller and his supervisor. On an unconscious level, Stoller desired a deeper, familial intimacy with Greenson that he unwittingly expressed by asking how Greenson was and then telling him about his dream. Stoller's departure from his usual cool formality most certainly startled Greenson into making his personal disclosure. In his readiness to share the story of his son's accident and his emotional reaction to it, Greenson treats Stoller more like a family member than a supervisee. In this way Greenson unconsciously gratifies Stoller's unconscious wish. Something had been going on between them, beyond their conscious awareness, that Stoller finally began to articulate. In line with Freud's idea that dreams are "particularly" well suited to the reception of "telepathic messages" (Freud 1933b, 37), perhaps the really important "message" for Stoller was that he and Greenson were closer than he knew.

Stoller's dream and Greenson's candid response may have provided Stoller with the reassurance he needed that Greenson cared about him more than professionally. Greenson did not hesitate to share with Stoller the details of his son's accident, including his own initial anxiety and the relief he felt when he found out that his son would fully recover. In this sense, the "telepathic" communications that occurred between Stoller and Greenson, Kate and her analyst, Cleo and Suchet, and Freud and Herr P. all point towards the presence of unconscious affective currents within these dyads that eventually surfaced through "telepathic" messages. Stoller is well aware of the complex Oedipal features in his relationship with Greenson. He openly admits the possibility of having unconscious envy towards Greenson's son and feeling guilt about wishing to replace him (Stoller 2001, 636n2). This is as far as he is prepared to go, however. Stoller chooses not to explore his feelings of envy and aggression towards Greenson's son that his dream strongly suggests exist. Although he admits that the dream was disturbing, he ultimately dismisses his "telepathic ability" as a "quirk". Nonetheless, he is forced to acknowledge that his telepathic "quirk" *originated* in his *relationship* with Greenson, and "stopped, also in part because of my relationship with him. In the fall of 1970, I had had enough of it and 'just' turned it off" (ibid., 638). For Stoller, his "telepathic" dreams and those reported by a number of his patients were "outside the psychoanalytic norm" (ibid., 638n7). Although Stoller was forced to admit that telepathic, unconscious communication exists, he refuses to go further in exploring the psychological complexity and implications of it that applied to him. Perhaps it was not the telepathic dimension of his dream that made him so uneasy, but rather what it may have suggested about his youthful feelings towards the older, fatherly Greenson.

Mayer's interest in Stoller's paper centres primarily on the existence and nature of telepathy. This approach is consistent with her later work. Mayer advised her analytic colleagues about the importance of training and cultivating their own telepathic potential (in Martinez 2001, 212). Mayer also encouraged her colleagues in the American Psychoanalytic Association to engage in automatic or "free" writing exercises (ibid., 214). She is reported to have told them that remote viewing research provides "stunning confirmation of the existence of telepathic capacity" (ibid., 212). Mayer's book, finished just before she died after a lengthy and debilitating illness, is a sustained argument supporting the objective ontological reality of paranormal phenomena. In this sense, *Extraordinary Knowing* is more concerned with demonstrating the validity of paranormal claims than with psychoanalysis. In explaining why she wanted to publish Stoller's posthumous paper, Mayer says that it provides additional evidence in support of "significant experimental research [that] has accumulated in recent years to suggest that telepathy – or remote perception, to use its more contemporary designation – may constitute a real and scientifically verifiable phenomenon" (Mayer in Stoller 2001, 633). In Mayer's view, psychoanalysis can make a valuable contribution to "investigating those aspects of remote perception that experimental research has failed to adequately address" (ibid.). Mayer lists a number of authors whose paranormal investigations provide empirical data for explaining the central question for psychoanalysis about "how one mind comes to know another" (ibid., 634). Reversing her earlier view that psychoanalytic concepts like "empathic attunement" cannot adequately explain the "actual cognitive and communicative processes" of telepathic transmission (Mayer 1996, 719), she now suggests that psychoanalysis can contribute to validating paranormal research findings by helping it incorporate a more sophisticated understanding of the "complexity of human relationships" (Mayer in Stoller 2001, 634). As far as Mayer is concerned, psychoanalysis and paranormal research connect through their shared investigations into how minds come to "know" and communicate with other minds (ibid.), both in the consulting room, and across geographical distances. She writes:

> [T]he psychoanalytic situation may be peculiarly suited to investigating those aspects of remote perception that experimental research has failed adequately to address. The science of psychoanalysis allows us to generate hypotheses

about how two people perceive each other and learn to relate in the clinical situation ... the psychoanalytic situation may permit us to look systematically at precisely those variables that objective science, by its nature, cannot adequately capture – things like empathy, affective attunement, and other forms of human connectedness – in terms of their possible relation to anomalous forms of human perception.

(Mayer in Stoller 2001, 634)

Here Mayer delineates the outline of a distinct branch of mystical psychoanalysis that can be called *parapsychoanalysis*.

The Quantum Unconscious

Despite the wide proliferation of books written for a lay readership by leading scientists on the stunningly counter-intuitive and complex theories of quantum physics (Bohm [1980] 2010; Greene 2003, 2005; Kaku 2005, 2014) there appears to be no common agreement in the scientific world that resolves its most important controversy: the nature of reality (Beller 1998, 31). The Nobel laureate and theoretical physicist Richard Feynman famously remarked that "nobody understands quantum mechanics" (in Appelbaum 2012, 119). Moreover, the "interpretive issues in quantum physics" such as "how to understand its relationship to the world" are, according to theoretical physicist and philosopher Karen Barad, "far from settled" (2007, 6). Barad also observes that the "plethora of popular accounts" that surface in a variety of disciplines, within which I include psychoanalysis, attempt to appropriate the "authority of science" in order to support their own ideas (ibid.). In psychoanalysis, simplified readings of concepts such as entanglement, indeterminacy and the question of the relationship between the observer to the observed, are invoked as providing the obvious evidentiary basis for the existence of telepathic communication.

Perhaps the most striking example of the ways in which quantum ideas are assumed to lend empirical validation to clinical experience is illustrated by de Peyer's bold assertion, quoted above, that if particles can jump from one location to another, then surely thoughts can transfer between people. There is a fair degree of disagreement on this point both within science and psychoanalysis. Maria Beller, a historian of science and philosopher, cautions against drawing direct inferences from the quantum realm to the social and political world (1998, 33). Psychoanalyst Joseph Schwartz maintains that Heisenberg's uncertainty principle "says nothing about human agency or objectivity at all" (1995, 49). As far as psychoanalysis is concerned, Schwartz insists that therapeutic insight must be commensurate with what takes place in the therapeutic dyad rather than "making invidious comparisons with the practice of physics" (ibid., 52). Jerome Appelbaum argues that psychoanalysis must be "defined on its own terms rather than those of physics" (2012, 123). At best, psychoanalysis, at least at this point in time, can hope to draw only limited metaphorical inspiration from quantum physics as it envisions new possibilities for understanding the human psyche. Again, we may recall that as far as Freud was concerned, good theory is based on careful clinical observation.

Gargiulo, who engages with quantum ideas throughout most of his work, rightly reminds his readers that he is a "psychoanalyst, not a physicist" (2016, xviii). Despite his modesty, Gargiulo shows little hesitation in drawing freely upon quantum notions such as nonlocality, entanglement and indeterminacy within psychoanalysis on the grounds that quantum theory offers an "alternate model for conceptualizing psychoanalytic clinical experience" (ibid., 22). He does not refer to the complex controversies and different interpretive models that continue to be debated among physicists. In some quarters, controversies relating to theories of the "Copenhagen" school and Einstein on the question of the existence of an objective reality independent of human observation remain unresolved. This is a crucial point to consider for analysts who seek a close theoretical association between quantum ideas, psychoanalysis and clinical practice. Gargiulo uses Heisenberg's idea of indeterminacy, where accurate measurement of either momentum or location of a photon cannot occur simultaneously, so that accuracy in the measurement of one feature is obtained at the expense of the other, to reframe the psychoanalytic notion of interpretation. A clinical intervention in the form of an interpretation about what a patient is communicating is tantamount, for Gargiulo, to the collapse of a wave function when measured (2010, 96; 2016, 12). He regards the quantum idea that reality is a "mist of possibilities" as strongly applicable to the "generic" unconscious (Gargiulo 2016, 7). As he argues is the case with quantum reality, there exists no psychic reality that is in any way "independent" of the analyst's observation, or for that matter, other minds. The psychic reality of the patient comes into being or "collapses" in the moment of interpretation: "just as measurement causes, in quantum mechanics, a wave function to collapse into a particular state, so likewise does a psychoanalytic interpretation create ... out of a myriad of possibilities, a given conclusion" (ibid., 23). In the therapeutic process, analyst and patient encounter each other as instantiated points of created, negotiated meaning within a transcendent "ground of being" (ibid., 7) or "consciousness" that permeates all of nature" (ibid., 54). He further maintains that quantum entanglement accounts for and explains the occurrence of "psychic phenomena" (ibid., 55). From Gargiulo's perspective, quantum mechanics validates his belief that all individual minds are connected in and through an enveloping, transcendent consciousness that animates and flows through all reality.

In order to maintain that quantum mechanics provides obvious validation for a mystical psychoanalysis, Gargiulo neglects to mention the interpretive controversies that continue to be debated both within and beyond the world of theoretical physics. For example, it is worth noting in passing that while Einstein disagreed that there is no such thing as reality independent of observation, he was not so naïve as to accept a "correspondence" approach that posits the world as "presented to us twice – first as it is, and second, as it is theoretically described". According to Beller, for Einstein "the world is given to us only once – through our best scientific theories", grounding his concept of objective reality "in the invariant characteristics of our best scientific theories" (1998, 32). For some commentators, the theory of relativity "is in fact a theory about objective reality" (Lovejoy 1999–2000, 438). With respect to the quantum idea used by de Peyer to support her assertion that thoughts, like "particles", jump from one place to another, physicist John Bell's tongue-in-cheek fable offers a sobering caution for those analysts looking for a quantum equivalent to explain thought transference: "Bertlmann ... always wears one pink and one green sock. If you see a foot with a green sock you know that the other foot has a pink sock. But no signal passes from one foot to the other" (in Lovejoy 1999–2000, 449).

Expanding upon Gargiulo's own caution that he is an analyst and not a physicist, it is equally important to bear in mind that psychoanalysis cannot be considered as a psychological version of quantum physics. However, efforts to establish a scientific basis for spiritual intuitions are certainly not confined to psychoanalysis. Some of the founding figures of quantum mechanics such as Wolfgang Pauli hoped to effect a reconciliation between science and religion (Beller 1998, 29). Niels Bohr believed that the discoveries of quantum mechanics "shook the very foundation of Western epistemology" (Barad 2007, 97). Some scientists, such as Max Born, hoped to expand the implications of the "epistemological lessons" of quantum physics to society and politics (Beller 1998, 29). Whatever the scientific debates may be, the analytic writers discussed here, much as they try, do not and cannot succeed in their efforts to reconcile science with religion. Rather, they are engaged in constructing a "science mysticism" of psychoanalysis. This is evident in Gargiulo's unequivocal declaration that psychoanalysis is a "profound spirituality" (2016, 111). This view, while more simply expressed, resonates with William James as Gargiulo too advocates and embraces a "natural spirituality" that is independent of the "creedal formulations" (ibid., 113) and the doctrinal and ecclesial authority of institutional religions. Defined in this way, Gargiulo dismisses religion as "untenable for an analyzed person" (ibid., 114). Traditional religions may be untenable for psychoanalysis, but mystical spirituality is not. In line with James's notion of the individual mind as a filter and manifestation of cosmic consciousness, Gargiulo writes that human beings are "momentary expressions of what we call intelligence, of what we experience as information and classify as meaning. ... Mind ties us to each other ... [it] is a shared reality" (Gargiulo 2010, 102, 103). We are all connected in a quantum "ground of being, the ground of existence" in our "oneness with everything" (Gargiulo 2016, 7, 75).

Gnostic Psychoanalysis

It should by now be clear that a mystical current promoting a view of the human psyche as connected to "deeper orders of Being" (Fuller 1986, 128) constitutes a significant cultural current within contemporary American psychoanalysis (Boyle 2016). For a mystical, spiritual psychoanalysis, the goal of clinical practice is to "promote spiritual inspiration" that will come from the unconscious (Adams 1995, 473). Belief in the "ineffable" and "transcendent" nature of the human mind (Reiner 2004, 314) as elaborated in the psychoanalytic theories of Bion, Grotstein, Mayer, Suchet, Gargiulo, and others is based on what amounts to updated, contemporary versions of much older ideas that some form of cosmic energy, magnetic fluid, vitalism or ground of being flows throughout all reality. From this perspective, a cosmic Unconscious or Mind takes up temporary residence in the vast diversity of individually instantiated personalities. Exploration of an individual unconscious, if conducted properly, will lead inevitably to the God within, thereby revealing the divine nature of human beings. From this perspective, psychoanalysis promotes the cultivation of "mystical states of awareness" through which the patient can connect with "higher spiritual planes" of reality (Fuller 2001, 25). In this sense American psychoanalysis preserves a number of elements deriving from metaphysical traditions such as represented in Swedenborgian mysticism, Emersonian Transcendentalism, and Jamesian psychology that are also associated with New Age religions. This approach to the inherent divinity of the unconscious stands in striking contrast to Freud's more sobering idea of the unconscious as a dark, chaotic, conflict zone of repressed sexuality and aggressive impulses. It has no connection with the more reassuring and uplifting ideal of a mystical unconscious that shades into the ineffability of "Ultimate Truth".

The clinical implications of mystical psychoanalysis suggest that therapy facilitates engagement with the sacred for both the patient and the analyst.

Thus the consulting room, according to Kerry Gordon, who acknowledges the relevance of Eliade, "becomes a version of what Eliade has called 'sacred space'" (Gordon 2004, 42). Psychoanalysis understood in this way transforms therapeutic action into a gnostic journey of (re)discovery that reveals and reaffirms "our connection to the ineffable" that dwells within the deepest layers of psychic life (ibid., 7). Reconceived in spiritual terms, psychoanalysis becomes both an expression of "the connective imagination" and is the "natural heir to the ancient and primary urge toward gnosis" (Kakar 2009, 155). Clinical practice is a "sacred process" that is "always present" in the therapeutic space (Gordon 2004, 7). It is the sacred duty of the analyst/mystic to lead the "seeker-patient" (Kakar 2009, 106) towards spiritual "enlightenment" (Adams 1995, 473), to experience "the transcendent" (Gordon 2004, 8) and the "irreducibly numinous" (ibid., 11) nature of the self. The goal of self-exploration in the clinical setting envisions mental health as intricately tied to the mystical process of leading the patient to experience her inner divinity. In this way, therapeutic practice facilitates a "psychospiritual regeneration through the repair of our broken capacity for sacred experience" (ibid., 12). Closely following Bion and Grotstein, Gordon too believes that the unconscious is both the location of the "Ineffable Subject", and a "metahuman" (ibid., 21) spiritual force where religion, mysticism, and psychoanalysis converge and release "our sacred potential" (ibid., 41). Or, as relational analyst Lew Aron comments, "psychoanalysis may be envisioned as a religious practice, a form of worship, in which contact is made with the Almighty through immersion in the richness and depth of the inner life and in communion with the Other" (Aron 2004, 450).

The explicitly religious nature of the sacred unconscious, the internal point where the individual psyche intersects with the transcendent could not be farther from Freud's concept of the unconscious. As Robert Fuller (1986) observes about the intrinsic religiosity of American depth psychology, it is indisputably clear that William James's metaphysical psychology provides the interpretive key and theoretical framework of understanding for contemporary mystical psychoanalysis. It does not represent a new trend in American depth psychology, but is rather part of a well-established intellectual and spiritual tradition that remains very much alive in mystical psychoanalysis. It is also important to bear in mind that James's psychological theories, especially as influenced and shaped by Myers, are inextricably enmeshed with his psychic research, particularly with respect to the question of telepathy. The most spiritually or mystically oriented American psychoanalysts are those who continue to confront the question of telepathic or unconscious communication by locating it in parapsychology and current psi research. In this sense psychoanalysis subserves a wider commitment to establishing the independent epistemological truth claims of paranormal phenomena. At the same time, uneasy with traditional religious teachings, doctrines and institutional forms, these analysts represent an important example of the legacy of William James and the cultural currents associated with nineteenth-century spiritualism, mesmerism and transcendentalism (Fuller 1986).

Under the influence of psychoanalysis, spiritualist ideas deriving from the late eighteenth-century and early nineteenth-century American "Great Awakenings" have shifted the location of God away from a remote heaven and encrusted theological, doctrinal authority to dwell in the divine inner world of the individual (Fuller 1986; Carroll 1997; Albanese 2007). I agree with Fuller's view that Jamesian psychology was as much about the "influx of the Divine Mind" (Fuller 1986, 15) into the minds of individual human beings as it was about the multiple nature of hidden levels of consciousness and supernormal potentiality residing within the depths of the subliminal self. This similar blending of psychology and spirituality in mystical psychoanalysis remains as fiercely committed to finding the supernatural within the natural order as was the case with James. In this sense, contemporary mystical psychoanalysis belongs to and is shaped by a religiousness of "no religion" that still thinks of itself as committed to the worldviews of natural science. A major problem that mystical psychoanalysis faces with its insistence on validating its spiritual intuitions through the methodological frameworks of natural science like quantum physics or as emulated by paranormal research is that it inevitably locks itself up within an epistemological narrow-mindedness that it strives to avoid. Efforts to reconcile science and religion are defensive strategies that risk conceptual and theoretical confusion.

To date, there is no fully formulated scientific explanation for unconscious communication or knowledge gained by telepathic means. As far as psychoanalysis is concerned, there doesn't need to be. As I have argued so far, the importance of unconscious communication for psychoanalysis lies in its meaning and significance for the analytic *relationship*. Nothing that occurs in the consulting room is too trivial or unimportant for psychoanalytic inquiry. Everything, including the smallest detail, incomplete remark, facial expression, shift in bodily position, narrative order or silence carries meaning and is worthy of serious investigation. Jung was right to describe synchronicity in terms of *acausal meaning*. It is far less important to establish scientific explanations proving the existence of unconscious communications between the analyst and the patient than to understand what it *means* for them both, for their relationship, and for the therapeutic process. Metaphors drawn from quantum physics about psychoanalytic interpretations "collapsing" dynamic psychic processes into coherent narrative form can be useful. This rhetorical strategy also can provide creatively suggestive ways of thinking about the clinical process. The use of rhetorical or interpretive strategies does not, however, require validation derived from science to "prove" the therapeutic efficacy of psychoanalytic treatment.

Bion and Grotstein, as leading representatives of mystical psychoanalysis, do not concern themselves with establishing scientific warrant for their approach to psychoanalysis. They don't need it. For them, psychological health is achieved through hierophanic encounters with higher planes of spiritual reality. Grotstein in particular is open about his view that psychoanalysis is a deeply "religious" quest leading towards revelations of the gnostic truth of the nature of all reality and the inner depths of the self. The mind, with its capacity to become a conduit for influxes of a cosmic energy or the O of Bionian and Grotsteinian "Ineffable", "Ultimate Truth" contains intimations of humanity's evolution towards the fulfilment of its own supernormal, supernatural potential. Ultimately, the idea of an inherent human supernature of indwelling divinity preserves and reformulates the lasting theological legacy of Jewish and Christian belief that humans are made in the image of God. This, along with the belief in immortality, had to be reconceived in ways that are acceptable to societies increasingly convinced by advances in scientific knowledge. While nineteenth and twentieth century people found it increasingly difficult to believe in an anthropomorphic God sitting in judgment and casting punishment and reward on hapless humans from a remote heaven, it didn't mean that a divine *something* didn't exist. Psychology came to the aid of religious beliefs not only by shifting the locus of divinity to the inner depths of the human mind. It also showed the way to access one's inner divine nature, overcome alienation and achieve mental health. The psychology of Frederic Myers, William James, the Society for Psychical Research and its heir, the paranormal sciences, all represent important and enduring intellectual currents that continue to shape "a modern American mystical religion of no religion" (Kripal 2007a, 11) that covers a vast amount of cultural territory. As one of these cultural currents, contemporary psychoanalysis occupies an important place in this religious landscape.

5

Psychoanalytic Hierophanies: The Sacred in Transit

> This zone, the zone of no-thing, of the silence of silences, is the source. We forget that we are all there all the time.
>
> (Laing 1967, 38)

Jürgen Habermas once remarked that "religion, which has largely been deprived of its world-view functions, is still indispensable in ordinary life for *normalizing intercourse with the extraordinary*" (Habermas 1992, 51, italics added). At least provisionally, and possibly by default, religious language is the necessary, and possibly only, "bearer of a semantic content" capable of articulating "explosive experiences of the extraordinary. Habermas recognizes that even "ordinary life, now fully profane, by no means becomes immune to the shattering and subversive intrusion of extraordinary events" (ibid.). It would not be a misreading of Habermas to assume that what he refers to as "extraordinary" or "explosive" must also include those anomalous experiences (*anōmalos*: uneven, irregular) discussed in the previous chapter. After all, telepathy certainly falls into the category of experiences that exceed the "semantic" competencies of current scientific and philosophical explanatory systems. Habermas is well aware that such experiences cannot be explained on their own terms within the epistemological and conceptual frameworks of philosophy and science. At the same time, Habermas argues there is a legitimate role, mainly relating to the traditional Jewish and Christian monotheisms, for religious intuitions to play in shaping the moral currents of public, political discourses. He makes no reference to mysticism, psi phenomena or paranormal experiences reported by the "rising new demographic of secular people who nevertheless report spiritual experiences" (Kripal 2014, 54).

Although a full critical discussion of Habermas's views on the necessity of including religious discourses in the formulation of public policies and adjudication of social norms is the subject of another study, his observation that philosophy is as yet incapable of translating religious intuitions into "the explanatory force of philosophical language" and "reasoning discourses" (Habermas 1992, 51) is relevant here. The inadequacy of philosophy to articulate religious experience that Habermas points out is a reflection of a deeper failure of his own philosophical approach to seriously consider the *affective power* of subjective extraordinary, anomalous experiences and the impact they have on individuals. While he emphasizes the primacy of extraordinary experience, he does not attempt to theorize it more fully. For Habermas, "extraordinary" experience resists discursive translation because it cannot be fully expressed in terms of philosophical reason. This is a common theme in mystical psychoanalysis emphasizing that telepathic communication cannot be explained by appealing to prevailing forms of intellectual or scientific rationality. This argument is not new. As Wouter Hanegraaff notes with respect to Hermetic writings, "the sources never cease to emphasize the total inadequacy of discursive language. The early twentieth-century Anglican mystic Evelyn Underhill noted that 'only mystics can really write about mysticism'" (in Partridge 2018, 15). William James, writing about his own nitrous oxide-induced mystical experiences concurs with this view: "Depth beyond depth of truth seems revealed ... this truth fades out ... and if any words remain over in which it seemed to clothe itself, they prove to be the veriest nonsense" ([1902] 2004, 335). The externalist, "normalizing" perspective of Habermasian philosophy is inevitably inadequate for apprehending mystical or extraordinary experiences in part because it ignores the nature of *internal, affective, and felt experience.* Psychoanalysis, on the other hand, is dedicated to explorations of subjective experience, *especially* those considered irrational from a philosophical perspective. For psychoanalysis, all subjective experiences are meaningful and potentially intelligible whether they are spiritual, mystical, psi-related, anomalous or paranormal. They all belong to the category of *psychic* reality, a pivotal concept for psychoanalysis because of its connection with unconscious fantasies, desires and, of course, dreams.

Psychoanalytic Spiritualities

There is a significant body of psychoanalytic writing that belongs to a diffuse, sprawling modern spirituality that values the cultivation of "reverence, awe, surrender, and atonement" (Starr 2008, 27) as a clinical goal in the therapeutic setting. A desired sense of connection with a transcendent "More" or divine reality that both resides within the self and sustains it is pursued in order to achieve full mental health. In his discussion of mystically oriented, spiritual psychoanalysts like Bion, Grotstein, and Gargiulo, Gideon Lev points out that they view clinical work as a sacred or "holy" activity (Lev 2017, 226). Psychoanalysis is a "transcendental enterprise" and the analyst is a "practicing mystic" who leads the patient to God (Merkur 2010, 261). The therapeutic session becomes a sustained "form of prayer" in its quest for "the hidden God" (Lev 2017, 232). As we have seen in previous chapters, this "hidden God" does not refer to an entity or divine being as taught by specific theological doctrines and ecclesiastical institutions. Rather, it is imagined as a living, numinous, conscious force, energy or presence that animates and shapes all aspects of the material reality of the natural world. The role of traditional religions, along with their institutional clerical hierarchies, rituals and doctrinal orthodoxies are rejected on the grounds that they attempt to limit, regulate and tame this transcendent power. In other words, to borrow a phrase from Freud used in another context, traditional religions mistake "the scaffolding for the building" (1900, 536). Mistrust of traditional religious institutions and teachings, a stable feature of American spirituality and New Age religions, has deep historical and cultural roots that precede the founding of the Republic.

Jung observes that the effort to harness and contain the overpowering force of direct religious experience through creeds, dogmas and controlled ritual practices helps to protect individuals against the "grave risk" of potential psychological fragmentation that can result from the "onslaught" of "an immediate experience" (Jung [1938] 1973, 55). Jung regards religions as defensive and alienating substitutes for direct spiritual experiences. Feeling and intuitive affect is marginalized and replaced with "suitable symbols invested in a solidly organized dogma and ritual. The Catholic church maintains them by her indisputable authority, the Protestant church … by insistence upon faith and the evangelical message. As long as those two principles work, people are effectively defended and shielded against immediate religious experience" (ibid., 52–53). Although he does not engage with Jung on this point, there are strong traces of Jung's view behind Grotstein's assertion that the unleashed power of numinous experience, or direct, undiluted "O", must be transformed into psychologically digestible elements that the individual can integrate within his own personality structure. This is what Grotstein means when, in drawing upon Bion, he describes this process of psychological metabolization as transforming the inchoate "beta" elements of raw emotional, unconscious experience into the "alpha" elements of conscious, symbolized experience and abstract concepts.

When regarded as a form of transformative spiritual practice, psychoanalysis offers possibilities for "profound healing and change" through revelations of "the divine essence" in a "faith-full state of mind" (Lev 2017, 236). Again, Eliade's idea of hierophany is helpful in providing a deeper understanding of how psychoanalysis implicitly views itself as facilitating experiences of the sacred. In the consulting room, revelations of the dialectical intersections of the individual and cosmic mind become possible. The mystical psychoanalysts discussed so far appear uninterested in developing more robust theoretical and discursive frameworks that would both historically and intellectually situate their loosely formulated intuitions about the spiritual potential of therapeutic work. For Bion and Grotstein, this may be part of an intentional rhetorical strategy to privilege psychoanalysis as a modern and perhaps even unique pathway to revelation of the ineffable sacred. The sacred cannot be expressed in words, but only through the deliberately indefinable cipher and signifier, "O". Merkur states that for Bion, and I would add Grotstein as well, "O" is a theological construct representing God (Merkur 2010, 250) as the originator of all existence. Hence the signifier "O". "O" floats along within an idiosyncratic, highly confusing discursive admixture of attributes that interweave a number of undefined elements loosely picked up from Kabbalistic mysticism, Neoplatonism, Kantian philosophy, perennial mysticism and compatibly suitable scientific theories. At no point do Bion or Grotstein elaborate what they mean by these religious and philosophical themes.

Gargiulo, like many of the analysts discussed here and in previous chapters, relies on a carefully selective understanding of quantum physics as a spiritual, scientific and metaphorical resource for reshaping psychoanalytic theory and clinical practice. Elizabeth Mayer, Janine de Peyer, Melanie Suchet, Gerald Gargiulo and others also fashion their own thematic blendings of quantum physics, parapsychology, and psi theories laced with varying degrees of spirituality into what may also be described as a "religionist"[1] psychoanalysis. They use science as a vehicle to lend credibility to their spiritual intuitions about the nature of reality. The epistemological premises of this form of religionist psychoanalysis are grounded in a persistent and recurrent belief in the existence of a universal, transpersonal and transcendent unitary wholeness. Insight into this gnostic truth and its implications is crucial for overcoming alienation and developing an authentic self capable of apprehending the deeper mysteries of life. Framed in this way, psychoanalysis is both a spiritual *and* therapeutic practice. Religionist psychoanalysts are careful to express their views in secular language that is compatible with contemporary science. Hence, their recurrent appeal to a limited range of quantum theories such as entanglement. In this sense psychoanalysis continues primarily in the tradition of William James and Frederic Myers, with significant but indirect traces of Jung as influenced by them. Yet despite their inestimable importance for mystical psychoanalysis, James and especially Myers are rarely, if ever, cited or even mentioned in passing. In order to unearth the inherent religiosity that infuses mystical psychoanalysis, I will further situate it within the more specific intellectual framework of the study of religions.

Psychoanalysis, the Study of Religion, and Religious Experience

There is no general agreement within the field of the academic study of religion about what constitutes its proper methodological and conceptual frameworks of analysis, or even on the very definition of the term "religion" (Hewitt 2014a, 1–3). While the controversies surrounding these debates yield important insights and perspectives about what constitutes religion and how it should be studied, they are not relevant to the discussion here. My approach to the question of method and theory in the study of mystical psychoanalysis parallels Wouter Hanegraaff's approach to the study of esotericism (1995). I agree with Hanegraaff's recommendation that in the study of religion, the most useful approach is neither "religionist" nor narrowly "reductive". Rather, it navigates a third way that positions emic (believer/insider) and etic (academic/outsider) methodologies within a tensive dialectical relationship. That is to say, I wish neither to dismiss or endorse religionist psychoanalysis, nor its claims to therapeutic healing. While I stress that this approach does not preclude critique, I wish to be perfectly clear that critique is not synonymous with promoting or debunking the theories and worldviews discussed here. My purpose is to contribute to a psychoanalytic, critical understanding of mystical psychoanalysis in a variety of its forms in part by dialogically situating it within the study of religion.

Situating mystical psychoanalysis within this wider theoretical framework draws out some latent implications not only for psychoanalysis itself, but also for a broader reconsideration of the relationship between psychoanalysis and religion. As discussed in Chapter 1, Freud clearly demarcated psychoanalysis from any and all association with religion, on the grounds that religion prohibits critical thought and limits the autonomy of individuals to think for themselves. As I also discussed in earlier chapters, the faith-based epistemologies of religions are for Freud entirely incompatible with methodologies of inquiry based on empirical evidence and rational argument. He would agree with contemporary critical theorists who insist that modern autonomous reason must repudiate faith, which by its nature "depends on a suppressed 'I think' ... [an act of] intellectual suicide" (Bernstein 2013, 165). However, to this day psychoanalysis shows significant traces of uneasiness regarding Freud's uncompromising conclusion that religion and science are irreconcilable. Even Hans Loewald, one of Freud's most sympathetic and brilliant interpreters, disagrees with his views of religion. Freud's attitude to religion most often tends to be either dismissed as part of his personal atheism and commitment to so-called "positivist" or "mechanistic" science (Hewitt 2014a), or merely ignored.

It can be plausibly argued that psychoanalysis, especially in its American form, has always had an undercurrent that, if not directly spiritual, is in many respects strongly compatible with spiritual interpretations partly because of its dedication to exploring the irrational, unseen, and mysterious depths of the human mind. Psychoanalysis does not hesitate to scrutinize all expressions of psychic reality, whether in the form of hallucinations, visions, dreams or neurotic symptoms. It is crucial to bear in mind that for Freud, the most bizarre fantasies and delusions contain kernels of existential truth. The existence of the unconscious, the "dark and inaccessible" part of ourselves (Freud 1933b, 73) which is the key, centrally defining concept of psychoanalysis, is largely inferred through clinical experience. In this sense, it possesses an undeniable element of mystery. As Freud wrote in a letter to Einstein, "There is no greater, richer, more *mysterious* subject, worthy of every effort of the human intellect, than the life of the mind" (in Grubrich-Simitis 1995, 117, italics added). Any adequate attempt to address what some analysts regard as the inherent spiritual nature of psychoanalysis, either against or in spite of Freud, can only benefit from engaging relevant scholars in the field of religious studies.

Jeffrey Kripal: Religion and the "Impossible"

It can be a daunting task to make sense of the complicated, confusing, often muddled and unruly mixture of parapsychology, quantum theories, spirituality, mysticism and esoteric elements that circulate within contemporary psychoanalysis. The formulation of hermeneutical frameworks of meaning that can assist in broadening our critical analysis of contemporary mystical psychoanalysis is greatly helped by utilizing some of the methodological approaches used in the study of religion. A fuller appreciation of mystical psychoanalysis must include identifying it as a religious phenomenon as well as a psychological theory and clinical practice. Just as it is an error to ignore or split off William James's work in psychical research as somehow separate from or irrelevant to his psychology, the same applies to the psychoanalysts discussed in the previous chapters: their insistence on the reality of telepathic communication cannot be divorced from their theories of transference, intersubjectivity or the nature of the human mind. This applies as well to those analysts, like Elizabeth Mayer, who accept the truth claims of paranormal research and the reality of remote viewing, psychokinesis, clairvoyance and telepathy. For them, these phenomena confirm that telepathic communication is a feature of the intersubjective transference relationship between the analyst and the patient. For some psychoanalysts, this goes too far. A well-known analytic colleague expressed a genuine, horrified astonishment at the very idea that

James Grotstein, with whom he was a close friend, was a self-avowed mystic. He seemed to think that describing him in those terms (notwithstanding that Grotstein saw himself that way) was diminishing and insulting. This vignette illustrates an uneasiness with critical analysis that no scholar can afford.

Both psychoanalysis and the study of religion have a shared interest in investigating and understanding the widely diverse and vast array of *human experiences* of unseen, hidden worlds and the figures that populate them. These experiences inevitably involve paranormal phenomena, which must also be included in the study of religion. Most of the psychoanalytic writers I have discussed so far would insist that their mystical inclinations and spiritual insights are thoroughly modern and secular because they are grounded in the nature of reality itself, which they argue is supported by science. I have no interest (or expertise) in adjudicating the incredibly complicated scientific debates regarding the physics of Newton and Einstein, or the mind-bending theories of quantum physics, including the controversies surrounding paranormal research. However, I do contend that the psychoanalytic ideas discussed here are most appropriately, fully and accurately appreciated when examined in the context of religion rather than science. I generally agree with Kripal's assertion that regards "the paranormal [as] another, unexplored, unacknowledged branch of American religious liberalism" (2012a, 248). I think he is also right in asserting that scholars of religion must take the paranormal "seriously" *as a religious phenomenon* that is as worthy of scholarly study as any other. It should go without saying that taking the paranormal seriously in the study of religion in no way requires the scholar to accept its claims to truth.

Throughout his scholarly writings, Kripal advances a brilliantly argued and compelling case for including anomalous human experiences within the study of religion. In his view, the culturally and historically diverse range of anomalous, strange and other-worldly experiences must be treated as inherently religious. While they are often expressed in relation to specific religious and cultural traditions, these experiences have a *sui generis* nature that transcends all forms of symbolic, narrative representation. For Kripal, who explicitly follows William James and, especially, Frederic Myers as enduring influences on his thinking, there are important clues about the nature of human consciousness and its super *normal* potential to be found in these reports. Kripal also understands anomalous experiences as revelatory irruptions of super realities that originate and exist *both* within and beyond individual minds. *Psi* phenomena like telepathy, clairvoyance or premonitory dreams may well be, according to him, instances of our natural capacities and potentialities that remain undeveloped at this stage of human evolution. However, under circumstances that induce altered or hypnoid states of consciousness, intimating visions of our *super* nature and *super* reality may occur. Kripal agrees with the generally held psychoanalytic view that telepathic communication occurs most often with individuals whose life histories include significant trauma. These individuals tend to be more sensitive or prone to communicating unconsciously with others. Kripal thinks they may well possess enhanced capacities for apprehending super realities about whose existence most people are unaware. Cross-cultural religious narratives are replete with examples of insane, traumatized visionaries and shamanic figures who "see" and journey to hidden worlds where they encounter the gods or spiritual beings who inhabit them. In an observation that is highly relevant here, R. D. Laing writes that "the cracked mind of the schizophrenic may *let in* light which does not enter the intact minds of many sane people whose minds are closed. Ezekiel, in Jaspers's opinion, was a schizophrenic" (Laing [1959] 1965, 27). I think Kripal would agree with Laing's sentiment.

Kripal would also acknowledge Habermas's point about the necessary role of religion as providing discursive vehicles and narrative domiciles that are capable of articulating the "explosive experiences of the extraordinary". As far as the analytic writers discussed so far are concerned, unconscious or "telepathic" communications belong to this category of experience. One of the reasons these writers turn to quantum physics and paranormal and parapsychological research is due to what they view as the limitations of Freudian psychoanalysis. Kripal, whose studies in comparative religion are informed throughout by psychoanalytic ideas, correctly observes that religion has become increasingly psychologized in Western societies. Fuller goes even farther in asserting that "[p]sychology has become the secular successor to religion, providing a new vocabulary and new set of theories by which to understand ourselves" and our capacity for becoming "inwardly receptive to the deeper reaches of the universe" (Fuller 2001, 123–124). Spirituality is no longer confined within the bounds of orthodox or traditional theologies and their corresponding teaching authorities, ecclesial institutions and bureaucracies. Mystical psychoanalysis offers a clear example supporting Kripal's insight that modern, Western culture is not becoming "less religious, but *differently* religious" (Kripal 2010, 29). For Kripal an adequate exploration of "extraordinary" or "impossible" experiences requires a methodology forged out of a "dialectic of consciousness and culture" (ibid., 256) that gives serious consideration to the findings of neuroscience, quantum physics, psychoanalysis, philosophy, social sciences *and* the history of religions. These disciplines also provide potentially rich metaphorical, hermeneutical and rhetorical resources that can help to elaborate and clarify the contours of the psychoanalytic mystical imagination.

Kripal would regard the phenomenon of a patient dreaming her analyst's weekend as powerfully suggestive of a "deeper nondual reality that possesses both 'mental' and 'material' qualities that manifest according to the subjective or objective structure of an experience" (Kripal 2010, 257). Instances of "explosive experiences of the extraordinary" such as the "jolt" that Mayer frequently references in describing her own encounters with "extraordinary knowing" become more accessible when subjected to processes of "translation" and "interpretation" (ibid., 257). Interestingly, both translation and interpretation are key features of both religious studies and psychoanalysis. For Kripal, "impossible" experiences belong within the rubric of the "sacred", and thus to the category of religion *and* its academic study. By organizing such experiences within this rubric, they not only acquire theoretical coherence, they also become publicly available for discussion and shared critical examination. It cannot be over-emphasized that for Kripal, the "sacred" is *not* synonymous with supernatural agents commonly associated with the religious rituals and theological beliefs of specific traditions. "The sacred", he writes, "*is* a critical category that can seldom be fit into the categories of faith and piety;" it is a *"third thing"* (ibid., 254).

Kripal embraces Mircea Eliade's idea, which he cites frequently, that "the sacred is an element in the *structure* of consciousness and *not a stage in the history* of consciousness" (Kripal 2010, 255, italics added). The sacred represents a "moment within an always relational dynamic with the natural and social environments, not some easily objective Out There" (Kripal 2007b, 87). What this seems to mean for Kripal is that human beings "are that sense of the sacred", and that the sacred and the human are "two sides of the same coin" (2010, 255). This identification of the human and the sacred implies that interconnected, "fundamentally irreducible" human "trans-subjective" (Kripal 2012b, 231) (un)consciousness and its products belong to the sacred. The sacred dimension that infuses and structures all reality manifests itself in complex, local forms as it moves *"in transit from a traditional religious register"* into modern scientific registers such as the paranormal and psychic research programmes he calls "science mysticism" (Kripal 2010, 9). Psychic phenomena are indicators of hierophanic irruptions of unseen presences, energies or powers that sometimes break through the ordinary bounds of human consciousness. Telepathic experiences in the consulting room as reported by psychoanalysts are easily interpreted as examples of "hierophanic" irruptions within the multiple dialectics of patient/analyst, sacred/profane, and the mystical/natural constitution of being. In upending the organizing elements of ordinary reality like space and time, self and other, these experiences, as Mayer wrote, "change everything".

The Human is Two (or More)

Along with Frederic Myers and William James, Kripal argues that the human personality is "radically multiple" (Kripal 2010, 64). There are some general similarities between this view and psychoanalytic ideas of differentiated agencies of the mind. As we have seen with respect to the ideas of Hans Loewald, Heinz Kohut, and to some extent even Freud, Kripal also speculates that the differentiated dimensions of individual personality emerge out of an originary experience of "psychical unity" that remains "beneath all our phenomenal manifestations" (ibid.). Freud certainly had something like this in mind in connecting Rolland's "oceanic feeling" with his notion of a "limitless narcissism" of pre-Oedipal infancy (Freud 1930, 72). Although he had a far more positive attitude to spirituality than Freud, Loewald also agreed that mystical experiences originate in neonatal experience. From a Loewaldian perspective, in a healthy-enough mind, diverse self-states are experienced as differentiated expressions of a generally *reconciled* sense of individual subjective identity whose origins lie in the unitary oneness of actual infant experience.

Kripal resonates with these ideas as he follows Myers's notion of a "spectrum of consciousness" (Kripal 2010, 65) where submerged aspects or points along the spectrum may surface in consciousness at different times, under different conditions. We may recall that in contrast to Freud's conceptualization of the unconscious, Myers's understanding of the consciousness spectrum of the individual self is neurobiologically and culturally instantiated within a larger psychical unity that both transcends and connects with others. The nature and extent of this kind of psychical unity is elaborated by Loewald, who in strikingly similar fashion to Myers, James, and Kripal, writes, "Individual human mentation, as it develops from the mother–infant matrix, would be but one instance or manifestation of *natura naturans*, of nature's 'subjectivity'. This subjectivity is vaster, 'all-embracing', in comparison to human individual mentation" (Loewald 2000, 516).

For Myers and James, the multiple boundaries separating individuals from each other and the transcendent "mother-sea" of cosmic consciousness running through them are permeable, fluid and unstable. In Kripal's formulation of this idea, "We are thus One *and* Many" (2010, 64). Keeping the psychological theories of James and Myers firmly in mind, Kripal too holds that individual personalities develop awareness by "narrowing the field of consciousness … conceived as operating on a specific band along the spectrum of consciousness within a particular social and historical period" (ibid., 68). Kripal argues that manifestations of individual consciousness are neurobiological embodiments and transmitters of a cosmic conscious energy that ebbs and flows throughout all material reality in a "transitory and constantly shifting" process (ibid., 68) of emergence and retreat. This perspective on the nature of consciousness, which also bears striking similarity to Grotstein's views, leads Kripal to speculate even further that *"what* we see is largely determined by how we see, and *how* we see is in turn largely determined by the restricting structures of society and the brain. So the question becomes: By what methods, by what artifices, can we get around these limiting structures to see more, to reflect and refract a broader band of consciousness?" (ibid., 66).

Visions and Visitors from Other Worlds: the Religious Imagination of Whitley Strieber

Kripal argues that the individually shaped *contents* of human minds along with the experiences generated by human consciousness are socially and culturally negotiated within a variety of domains that include waking and nocturnal dream states, (un)conscious fantasies, and mystical visions. Depending on one's vantage point that judges human visionary and hallucinatory experiences as either psychotic or mystical, they are all mediated and formed by culture. In his co-authored account of the American horror writer Whitley Strieber's visionary experiences of UFOs, interactions with other-worldly visitors and alien abduction, Kripal looks beyond the surface scaffolding of pulp science fiction that characterizes Strieber's narrative. He is far more interested in trying to understand the super reality that seems to be transmitted through Strieber's detailed accounts. In particular, Kripal notices a pattern in Strieber's story that connects it with a number of religious visionary experiences in different historical and cultural contexts. One of the key variables Kripal identifies that is present in virtually all accounts of mystical experience is psychological trauma. Trauma for Kripal is a key that can open the mind to apprehension of other dimensions of reality. In Eliadean terms, trauma facilitates hierophanic irruptions of the sacred.

By Strieber's own account, his personal life history is marked by a series of traumatic experiences that have made him especially sensitive to the kinds of dissociated, altered states of consciousness that are evident in his descriptions of his encounters with aliens or "visitors" from other worlds. In finding a way to represent personal trauma through narrative representation, he gives meaning and coherence to the horrifying, painful abuse and neglect he suffered almost from birth. Equally important, with his publications, he has found a way of communicating with and being heard[2] by a public audience. Tragically, as is the case with so many victims of childhood trauma and abuse, Strieber's caregivers appeared unable to recognize his experiences, and respond to them appropriately. Through narrative, Strieber found a pathway towards potential healing by situating his experiences within widely recognized UFO cultural frameworks that have been present in American folklore since Kenneth Arnold's sighting of flying "shining discs" in 1947. Since then, the expressions "flying saucer" and "UFO" "quickly became household jargon" (Partridge 2005, 170–171).

Arnold's sighting of flying discs inaugurated the "modern waves of sightings and also ushered UFOs into the popular consciousness" (Partridge 2005, 170). Even more important with respect to Strieber, *it provided a consistent vocabulary with which to discuss the phenomenon*" (ibid., 170, italics added). It is also significant that the geographical and historical context of Strieber's alien encounters was the Hudson Valley, a "well-known and well-documented hotspot for UFO activity throughout the twentieth century" (Strieber and Kripal 2017, 86). Between 1982 and 1995, there were more than seven thousand "sightings" of aliens and UFOs in the Hudson Valley (ibid., 89). As Judith Richardson points out in her historical study of the Hudson Valley from the early nineteenth to late twentieth century, "the Hudson River Valley between Manhattan and Albany has developed a reputation as an uncommonly haunted place" populated by the ghosts of Indians, Revolutionary War soldiers, slaves, priests and presidents (Richardson 2003, 2).

As a religious studies scholar, Kripal is well aware that spectral "visitors" from other worlds have "*countless* precedents in the general history of religions", where "strange super beings from the sky ... interact with human beings, provide them with cultural, technological, legal, and ethical knowledge ... demand their submission and obedience, have sex with them ... and generally terrorize, awe, baffle, inspire, and use them" (Strieber and Kripal 2017, 85). Jesus is an example of such a being, represented as the Incarnation of God, who interacts with people, gives them ethical instruction and new religious and cultural norms that challenge established religious, political and familial authorities. Anthropologist and psychoanalyst Melford E. Spiro claims that the "core variable which ought to be designated by any definition of religion" is "the belief in superhuman beings and in their power to assist or to harm man" (1968, 94). This definition of religion easily applies to UFO narratives of interactions with other-worldly beings such as Strieber's, who gave him instruction, had sex with him, terrorized and tortured him, transformed his sense of self, and caused him to look at himself and the world around him "in ways that otherwise would not have been possible" (Strieber and Kripal 2017, 148).

An important part of Kripal's hermeneutical strategy towards Strieber's narrative is to "bracket" the question of the independent ontological reality of specifically who and what he experienced in order to focus on the *meaning* of the experience *for Strieber.* Historical and cultural context, phenomenology, hermeneutics, and comparison, constitute some of the key methodological principles of analysis that Kripal utilizes in his general treatment of mystical, anomalous or spiritual experiences, and he applies these to Strieber. Kripal regards UFO stories of interactions with aliens and abduction as culturally situated religious or mythical narratives that give symbolic expression to "explosive experiences of the extraordinary", (Habermas) "jolts" (Mayer) and epistemological crises precipitated by all anomalous experience. Psychoanalysts take a similar approach as they listen to their patients' stories and struggle along with them to create hermeneutical coherence and meaning to their life histories. Nothing is too trivial, too outlandish, or just plain weird for psychoanalytic inquiry. Analysts know that no matter how weird the narrative scaffolding of any patient account, the patient is telling them that *something* happened, even if the *what* that happened is not always clear. Strieber says that when he wrote about his experiences, he could not "taste the difference between a memory that refers to a concrete event and one that refers to an *intense event* that might not have been so concrete" (Strieber and Kripal 2017, 134, italics added). The "concrete event" may be lost to memory, but the *"intense event"* or affect remains alive and powerful. Detailed recall of an experience matters less than constructing the *meaning* of the experience, which happens by following the affect that infuses psychic reality, which no matter how bizarre or psychotic, *always* contains a kernel of existential truth.

Some psychiatrists are beginning to recognize that there are fine, culturally constructed lines between psychosis and religious or mystical experience (Laing 1967; Jackson and Fulford 1997, 2002). What medical psychiatry tends to define as delusional pathology often includes a wide range of visionary and mystical experiences. As Freud continually reminds us, it is a mistake to disregard these experiences as devoid of truth and meaning. Discourses of delusion may be the only cultural and historically available modes of expression for certain experiences that cannot be assimilated within prevailing normative, political and social frameworks of "sanity". R. D. Laing touchingly illustrates this point with a brief clinical vignette:

> A little girl of seventeen in a mental hospital told me she was terrified because the Atom Bomb was inside her. That is a delusion. The statesmen of the world who boast and threaten that they have Doomsday weapons are far more dangerous, and far more estranged from "reality" than many of the people on whom the label "psychotic" is affixed.
>
> (Laing [1959] 1965, 12)

Like Freud, Laing is able to recognize that the child's psychotic delusion contains a kernel of existential truth that is distorted by the social trauma of sustained anxiety around global threats to human survival that are shaped by specific historical contexts such as the ever-present risk of nuclear war or climate change. Some UFO believers anxiously and unwittingly refashion ancient salvation narratives as expressions of hope that the aliens from outer space will save humanity from itself.

In Search of the Transformed Self

For Kripal the social self is an "adaptive response to the cultural and physical environments" of space and time, much like the Hegelian "autobiography of metaphysical Mind evolving into consciousness" (Kripal 2010, 72). From this Hegelian perspective, it may be further considered that the breakdown of the social ego or false self is indeed a stage on the way to spiritual renewal, as Laing also suggested decades ago (Laing [1959] 1965, 1967). From a Laingian perspective, consciousness alienated from itself in distorted, even delusional temporal and social forms must "die" as a necessary part of a process of self-transformation through the liberation of inner potentialities. Laing illustrates this process of psychological dissolution and renewal in citing Jesse Watkins's account of his own "brief psychotic episode" that followed a period in his life of severe emotional and physical stress. Watkins, who was a sailor and sculptor, did not know Laing at the time of his psychotic episode. At the onset of his psychosis, which occurred over the span of fourteen days (corresponding to the fourteen stations of the Cross, as Watkins notes), Watkins felt that he was "sliding down a chute" (Laing 1967, 121) that propelled him back in time, a "regression" that took him to the brink of existential death (ibid., 123). He had a "particularly acute" sense of the world divided into three levels: an "antechamber level, a central world, and a higher world" (ibid., 127). In his altered state of consciousness, he encountered "gods" who were in charge of this three-tiered cosmos. Laing interprets that Watkins attained a state of "*hyper*-sanity" (ibid., 129) that Watkins himself described as a higher evolutionary stage of being. After several days of immersion in a state of primordial existence where all traces of his former self seemed to have dissolved, Watkins "*decided* to come back" (ibid., 130), reciting the Stations of the Cross as a way of guiding himself back to ordinary reality. Watkins described his experience later as infused with a sense that "everything was so much more real ... than it had been before. The grass was greener, the sun was shining brighter, and people were more alive ... I was much more aware" (ibid., 136). Although Watkins most likely never heard of him, there are strong overtones with Jung's idea that psychotic regression can lead to spiritual realms of primordial reality.

Kripal recounts a similar story, more recently reported by neurosurgeon Eben Alexander, about his experience while in a seven-day coma. Several elements in Alexander's account are strikingly similar to Watkins's narrative. Alexander's coma was an entranceway to a realm of consciousness *"completely free of the limitations of the physical brain"* (in Kripal 2014, 385), composed of visionary images and a sense of moving through a "primordial" state of being he describes as "the Realm of the Earthworm-Eye's View". In a description that bears strikingly similar elements to Watkins's report, Alexander felt that he "regressed back to some state of being from the very beginnings of life" (ibid.). Like Watkins's state of *"hyper-sanity"*, Alexander experienced "hyper" reality through images of the natural and super natural worlds that included not only waterfalls and butterflies, but "shimmering" angelic beings that were "more advanced. *Higher*" (ibid., 386). Both Watkins and Alexander traversed altered states of fluidly shifting consciousness that Laing describes in terms of breakdown and breakthrough, spiritual death and rebirth that both men say profoundly transformed them. Alexander "learned" that "love is the basis of everything" (ibid.). Watkins discovered a heightened sense of aliveness in himself and the world, along with an intensified clarity in his awareness of reality. From Laing's perspective, both Watkins and Alexander went on a soul journey to the depths of inner space and beyond to experience higher, enlightened spiritual truth.

In Laing's view, these kinds of mystical experiences that pass through a state of ego-dissolution leading to the healing of the soul and higher levels of awareness can be *"a natural way of healing our own appalling state of alienation called normality"* (Laing 1967, 136). He further correctly notes that they are common features of shamanic practices of soul flight. Here Laing describes not only a psychological process, but a mystical experience with a long history in Christianity. In the words of thirteenth-century German mystic Meister Eckhart, "No creatures can reach God in their capacity of created things, and what is created must be broken for the good to come out. The shell must be broken for the kernel to come out" (in Strieber and Kripal 2017, 218). Laing, himself a mystically oriented psychoanalyst, clearly has this in mind when he writes that, "The inner world reaches through domains of experience (imagination, reverie, dreams, fantasy, visions …) into realms that we are only beginning to discover. It seems reasonable to me that a man should wish to climb the Mystic Mountain as Mount Everest" (Laing 1964, 592). The parallels with psychoanalysis, whether spiritual or thoroughly secular, are clear: an inward, deeply introspective self-examination, self-questioning, or journey directed towards eventual transformation into a better, more enlivened, enriched and authentic self. On a psycho-spiritual level, this process parallels the Christian idea of death and resurrection, and must be guided by the "true physician priest" (Laing 1967, 133). Freud, who did not regard psychoanalysis as mystical in any sense of the term, expresses the process of psychological transformation in irreligious terms:

> The neurotic who is cured has *really become another man*, though at bottom, of course, he has remained the same; that is to say, *he has become what he might have become at best* under the most favourable conditions. But that is a very great deal.
>
> (Freud 1917b, 435, italics added)

The use of comparison, phenomenology and hermeneutics in theoretically framing and situating anomalous experiences within mysticism and spirituality allows us to see similar features in Kripal's account of his own strange encounter with higher forces or cosmic energies. The experience he returns to frequently throughout his writing is "That Night" in Calcutta, where he was researching the life of the nineteenth-century Hindu mystic and saint, Ramakrishna. For a period of several days, Kripal had been participating in the celebrations of the goddess Kali in the streets and temples of Calcutta. One night while lying in bed, his body asleep but his mind "fully awake", he was seized by or filled with a "powerful electric-like energy [that] flooded [his] body with wave after wave of an unusually deep and uniform arousal" (Kripal 2001, 201). An intensity of "energies" that seemed to have their own consciousness "erupted 'in' in a kind of psychic implosion. As I felt my 'I' being sucked up into an ecstasy that felt entirely too much like death, I watched my legs and torso float uncontrollably towards the ceiling" (ibid.). Psychoanalysis would agree with Kripal that such experiences are "real in the simple sense that *they happen*. What they *mean* is an entirely different issue" (Kripal 2011, 6).

Kripal reflects upon his experience from traditional theoretical perspectives such as historical criticism, philology, textual analysis and psychoanalysis which provide important and necessary tools of interpretation. They also provide him with an enriched and sensitively nuanced appreciation for the "mystic-erotic experiences" of the man he was studying, Ramakrishna (Kripal 2001, 201–202). In considering and addressing these or any other kinds of experiences psychoanalytically, Freud suggests formulating tentative constructions or provisional "conjectures" with the patient that are always in the process of further exploration (Freud 1937b, 265). In this way both analyst and patient can weave together a narrative fabric composed of the diversity of memory traces and repressed material that are embedded in the patient's life history in order to create negotiated meaning. From Freud's perspective, a psychoanalytic interpretation suggesting that Kripal had a mystical dream or hallucination, or suffered an episode of sleep paralysis, in no way negates the value or meaning of the experience, nor does it empty it of its emotional or physical power. Kripal felt as if his brain was "suddenly hooked up to some sort of occult Internet", and that "a portal, had opened" (2011, 6). Freud would insist that experiences such as Kripal's visionary dreaming That Night contain a "kernel of truth", a "fragment of *historical truth*" (Freud 1937b, 268) that encodes the psychic reality of the experience. Freud would unhesitatingly agree with Kripal, as any analyst should, that *something* happened that is deserving of psychoanalytic attention and respectful inquiry. What matters most is the meaning that is negotiated, constructed and shared between not only the analyst and analysand, but also, I would add, by the reader and the text.

Dreaming "Reality" and the "Reality" of Dreams

Psychoanalyst Thomas Ogden writes that we are dreaming all the time, regardless of whether we are asleep or awake, which is important to bear in mind in considering Kripal's insistence that he was awake That Night. Still, he could have been dreaming and awake. Dreaming, Ogden writes, is a "continuous function of the mind that persists even when our dreams are obscured from consciousness by the glare of waking life" (2009, 104). The consulting room is a dream space where analyst and patient dream themselves and each other "into existence" (ibid.) in every session. Dreaming represents the freest, most inclusive and "deeply penetrating form of psychological work" that human beings can accomplish (ibid.). Together in the therapeutic setting, the analyst and patient are engaged in a sustained process of creating "unconscious intersubjective constructions" (Ogden 1997, 567) within a psychic matrix that they create together and that creates them.

Following the logic of the British child psychoanalyst D. W. Winnicott's famous remark that there is no baby without a mother who knows her child as such, Ogden states that there is no such thing as an analyst apart from a patient (2009, 569). He describes the analyst's waking dreams as "reveries" that, if allowed to float freely, facilitate a deep receptivity to the patient's unconscious. The patient's feelings, fantasies, conflicts, fears and desires drift into the analyst's unconscious, stirring up his own corresponding responses, which helps him bring coherence and symbolic form to the patient's unconscious through constructions. From this perspective, psychoanalysis is a "form of human relatedness" that encourages "conversations with oneself that take place at the unconscious-preconscious frontier" where they become "increasingly 'audible' to analyst and analysand" (Ogden 2001, 12). As analyst and patient dream together, they create a joint set of unconscious experiences that produce an "analytic third", which also has a "life of its own" (ibid.). Freud contends that the state of dreaming or reverie becomes accessible in states of consciousness beyond the glare and noise of James's "sunlit consciousness". For Freud, in order to "see" psychoanalytically, the mind must adapt itself "to the dark" (in ibid., 8). As analyst and patient dream together in constructing associations to the patient's dream, it may not always be possible to identify exactly *whose* dream is being dreamed. "Conversations at the frontier of dreaming are not always private", Ogden observes. Our dreams may not always be our own creations (ibid., 12).

In Ogden's view, dreaming and reverie are crucial ways of processing emotional experience. Reveries, or waking dream states, in particular involve an "unconscious internal discourse" that Ogden describes (using Grotstein's formulation) as taking place between the dreamer who dreams, and the dreamer who understands the dream. This unconscious "understanding work" or "unconscious discourse" (Ogden 1997, 587n1) allows us to achieve more profound levels of self-understanding and psychic integration than interpretations that are limited to analysing the fragments of remembered nocturnal dreams. Although Ogden does not say it directly, his ideas on dreaming, reverie, the jointly constructed and constructing analytic third, and the saturating effect of reveries as they "seamlessly melt" into the psychic states of "secondary process" mentation (ibid., 569) strongly suggest that not only are the subjective boundaries of individual minds highly permeable, they may also be considered as part of a larger mind. Dreaming is not simply a product of the mental work involving the differentiated agencies of the unconscious and conscious mind. Rather, dreaming "creates and maintains" the differentiated mind, generates consciousness and is the "principal medium in which we do the psychological work of being and becoming human in the process of attempting to face the reality of, and come to terms with, our emotional problems" (Ogden 2009, 104). In other words, dreaming and reverie are essential for sanity and general healthy mental functioning.

The capacity for dreaming and reverie are linked to the capacity for thinking. The psychological work involved in dreaming generates a "conversation between preconscious aspects of the mind and disturbing thoughts, feelings and fantasies" that struggle towards conscious awareness. For Ogden, this description of the emotional work of dreaming holds for "*every human being who has achieved the differentiation of the conscious and unconscious mind regardless of the epoch in which he is living or the circumstances of his life"* (2004, 1355, italics added). Ogden draws upon Bion's idea that it takes *"two minds to think one's most disturbing thoughts"* (Ogden 2009, 100), such as those of mother/infant, analyst/analysand, different parts of one's personality, individual/society, or reader and text. Every stage of psychological development includes dimensions of experience for which we are "unprepared". Thus, "we are throughout our lives in need of other people with whom to think" (ibid., 100). Kripal's description of "mystical reading and writing" as a "hermeneutical spiral" that advances forward and back on itself in a "continual act of living reflection" (2001, 203) may be considered psychoanalytically in terms of different parts of the self thinking about and through experiences for which it is "unprepared". Like "traditional mystics", Kripal "rereads" and listens to texts in "the lights" (ibid., 203) of his own life and the mystical writers with whom he engages. "In both the mystical and the academic cases, there does not seem to be any identifiable or recoverable experience 'before' language or textuality but a kind of spiraling, infinitely looped textuality" (ibid., 204). Kripal's description of mystical reading and writing resonates in particular with Ogden's idea of dreaming as an unconscious, "continuous function of mind" (Ogden 2009, 104) through which we create "personal, symbolic meaning" by "dream[ing] ourselves into existence" (ibid.).

Nightmares of Absolute Reality

In the opening line of her classic horror novel, *The Haunting of Hill House*, Shirley Jackson writes with striking psychological insight that, "No live organism can continue for long to exist sanely under conditions of absolute reality; even larks and katydids are supposed, by some, to dream" ([1959] 2006, 1). Under the monstrous conditions of "absolute reality", the capacity for dreaming is destroyed; without the ability to dream, thinking is not possible, and without thought, emotional experience remains frozen, unrepresented, unsymbolized, and incommunicable. Psychic space withers into an unending, silent scream that leaves no room for reflective capacity to emerge and develop, or destroys it altogether. Dreaming, writes Ogden, "is our most profound form of thinking". Thus "dream thinking" generates genuine psychological growth", allowing for the creation of psychological meanings, multiple perspectives, and awareness of the distinctions between internal fantasy and external reality (Ogden 2010, 319, 328). It facilitates the capacity for transforming inchoate, raw experience into knowledge not only of self and other, internal and external reality, but of felt subjective experience. As we have seen, Bion and Grotstein would describe this mentation process as the transformation of beta elements into alpha elements that can be used in thinking. Under certain conditions, the capacity for this transformation in mental life becomes impaired, sometimes severely. The brutality inflicted on human beings, especially children, tears apart the fabric of one's emotional and mental universe. The unbearable horror of absolute reality floods and overwhelms the mind. The victim's capacity to think through her or his experience, to forge internal linkages between emotional self-states and external linkages with reality through symbolic representation in language such that one can reflectively organize experience expressed as "*I* feel *this* about *that*" or "*this* happened to *me*" becomes damaged, if not irrevocably ruined.

Adult survivors of sexual and other forms of physical and emotional abuse, no matter how successful they may become in their professional adult lives, are vulnerable to mystifying confusion about the ordinary dynamics of personal, intimate relationships. A successful businesswoman reports childhood memories of nocturnal visits of a vague and frightening dark figure looming in the doorway of her bedroom. "Its" features are blocked by the backlighting of the hallway, so all the little girl sees is a featureless black, quasi-human shape. Such moments become frozen in psychic time, and are deeply embedded in the unconscious. The traumatized child remains sequestered and hidden in the folds of the adult survivor's unconscious. She struggles to remember what "it" did as it climbed into her bed. "Confronted with the horrors" of a repeated, "inescapable shock" such as this, the memory system of an individual "breaks down" (van der Kolk 2015, 178). Gradually she remembers playing with her dolls, then frantically searching for a hiding place the moment she hears "its" heavy footsteps moving somewhere in the house. The safety she experienced in ordinary play turns out to be an illusion as she is gradually crushed by absolute reality. She knows "it" is coming for her, "it" will always be coming for her, even decades later and half a world away.

She does not know who or what "it" is, although over the years she and her therapist have painstakingly gathered clues about "its/his" identity as "it/he" transforms from a monster of personal myth to a sick, entirely human paedophile of all-too-common reality. As an adult, she could never be sure about the reality of minor details in her interactions with others. Frightened and ashamed at her inability to think through her emotional experience and feel the comfortable weight of its reality for her, she cannot sort out "who did what to whom" as she struggles to make sense of minor miscommunications with others that ordinarily may be easily resolved. Trauma undermines the victim's confidence in allowing herself to know what she knows and thus think her own thoughts. The small confusions that sometimes accompany the ordinary flux of daily life leaves her frightened and ashamed. There is nothing ordinary about inhabiting a world where horrors and monsters dwell in the shadows, just below the surface, ready to break through at any moment. A pervasive feeling of dread infuses her reality like a fine psychic mist that prevents her from dreaming her own experience or finding alternative ways of living and being. She is caught in an endless nightmare of absolute reality. This sustained sense of impending catastrophe requires her constant vigilance against the hungry ghosts of unarticulated and unresolved trauma. As Winnicott observes, "clinical fear of breakdown is *the fear of a breakdown that has already been experienced. It is a fear of the original agony*" (1974, 104).

Strieber: Tales of Trauma and Terror

As an adult, Whitley Strieber recounts his numerous encounters with the terrifying "visitors" from worlds beyond who kidnapped and brutally raped him. Strieber's life prior to these encounters was marked from infancy by a series of traumatic experiences, beginning with his mother's inability to produce breast milk and his physiological intolerance for formula substitutes. He describes the first six months of his life as "agony" (Strieber and Kripal 2017, 210). Exhausted from a difficult pregnancy and labour, Strieber's mother spent the second half of his first year in care, separated from her infant son. Strieber suffered an unexplained head injury "at some point", which left him in chronic pain due to a spinal compression (ibid., 211). At the age of six or seven, Strieber recalls that he was part of an experimental programme on a military base where he and other children were "jammed" into a "Skinner" box, a "dark space", and treated as specimens of behaviour experiments. "I remember it as shrill screaming that made us scream, also, as we twisted and struggled", he recalls (ibid.). Strieber describes his frequent dissociated states in which he encountered and interacted with strange beings, or "visitors", who often hurt, terrorized, and occasionally had spectacular sex with him. He describes a feeling of being watched by owls, who he thinks may have been "totem" animals of the "visitors" (ibid., 214) from other dimensions. In one particularly poignant scene, Strieber describes going deep into the woods in search of the owls who were both dangerous predators but also sources of wisdom, which he wanted. "The question was", he writes, "how to take the wisdom without being eaten?"

> Knowing that I was looking at a predator, I nevertheless went out into the woods, went deep, seeking to be helpless in the dark. By this time, I had seen into their eyes and seen the danger there. I knew that I'd been raped, that semen had been *taken* from my body, *and with it the essence of my life and the*

potential for a new child destined to rise up among them, a thought which haunts me to this day.

(Strieber and Kripal 2017, 215, italics added)

These lines vividly capture the monstrous, absolute reality that is the traumatic legacy of the sexually abused child.

Trauma haunts its victims throughout their lives. It depletes vitality, forecloses the future by severely limiting, if not destroying, the potential for a full life. A psychoanalytic reading of Strieber's words just cited will necessarily pose a number of disturbing, unthinkable questions regarding *who* is the predator into whose eyes he looks? Why is he looking into the eyes of the predator? Is he looking desperately for any sign that the predator is not the monster he appears to be, but the loving, protective figure he needs? Is he, like all children, searching to find himself in the gaze of the parent as a loved and cherished child? Is he struggling to protect his mind from splitting by denying the real trauma so that he can create the imaginary protector he should have had? What psychic time zone is he in while looking into the eyes of a predator? Or is Strieber searching for a sign of the "new child" he might become, reflected back to him in the eyes of the "good" part of his tormentor who can give him something of precious value, like wisdom? Perhaps the promise of wisdom offers a pathway to identification with the positive aspects of his abuser/tormentor that will help him form a self capable of both surviving and transcending his experience. Strieber's journey deep into the woods may be understood as the parallel of an inner or spiritual journey in search of meaning, self-knowledge, and perhaps even some shred of love he may have, or certainly *should* have received in early life.

It is important to bear in mind that Strieber's traumas began in infancy, prior to his ability to represent his experiences in language. He was left to *feel* his painful experiences before he could achieve the developmental capacity needed to reflect upon and understand them. From an early age it appears that Strieber had no option but to absorb the raw, cumulative traumas of a difficult birth, milk that poisoned rather than nourished him, and early separation from his mother. Then came physical and emotional abuse he "surely" remembers associated with the Skinner box (Strieber and Kripal 2017, 211). The catastrophic failures of a childhood such as his create for any child a developmental context of threat and deprivation that can "chaotically and malignantly" absorb his emerging "proto-self". The result for the child is that the "surrounding environment cannot be experienced or introjected as a containing, narratable object about which unconscious stories are told, but rather as a chaotic, diffuse mass that is malignantly absorbed into parts of the body, and thus pathologically contained. The younger the foetus or the child is, the more each impingement is registered directly in the unconscious without going through the fragile and not-yet consolidated consciousness. As a result, it can only be experienced as confused bodily sensations, leading to a confused mind" (Durban 2016, 82).

In his writings about his encounters with the "visitors", Strieber attempts to represent, organize and construct meaning around the "malignant" and "chaotically" scattered fragments of his traumatic history. From the vantage point of adulthood, Strieber is able to provide himself with a new life narrative that allows him to transform his traumatic experiences into gnostic revelations that had "the effect of cracking the cosmic egg" (Strieber and Kripal 2017, 212). Kripal, who has written on mysticism in a variety of cultural, religious and historical contexts, agrees that Strieber encountered another plane of reality that was symbolized or manifested in visionary experiences of the alien visitors. He describes Strieber as "easily one of the most psychologically astute mystical writers I have encountered" (Kripal 2015, 166). He creates parallels between Strieber and figures such as Ramakrishna by tracing the connections between sexual trauma and mystical states of consciousness that appear repeatedly in the mystical literature of different cultures. According to Kripal, Ramakrishna suffered sexual abuse early in life. By Ramakrishna's own account, "the House of Mystical Experience can be entered through something as horrible as a Latrine". This does not mean that the house and the latrine are the same; rather the filthy, revolting latrine must be recognized for what it is: the point of access to a "very large and very wonderful House" (ibid., 162).

In the context of his discussion about the connections between mystical experience and trauma, Kripal ventures into dangerous moral territory, and he knows it. While he is aware of the deeply disturbing implications of these juxtapositions, he rightly insists that readers hold in mind the distinction between "the entrance and that which is entered" (Kripal 2015, 162). In his view, trauma can open pathways to higher levels of transcendent experience in religious contexts. Kripal's view of the relationship between trauma and mystical experience should in no way be interpreted as a justification of trauma. Fear and terror are not uncommonly associated with experiences of the *unio mystica* and spiritual power. For example, American Christian serpent handlers risk their lives for what they believe is the higher purpose of obeying Christ's command to take up serpents as stated in the King James Bible (Mark 16:17-18). They describe their ritual use of lethally venomous snakes as intricately connected with the emotional intensity of being filled with the spirit of God (Hood and Williamson 2008). In his cross-cultural studies of mysticism and individual mystics, Kripal finds that suicidal depression may also lead to transformative mystical experience, as was the case with both the French Islamicist and mystic Louis Massignon, and the Hindu saint Ramakrishna (Kripal 2015, 163). Like William James before him, Kripal evaluates mystical experience by its positive and transformative impact on the experiencer rather than on the ways it overlaps "phenomenologically with pathological states" (Wulff 2014, 382). While academics ought to be able to sustain a critical recognition of the distinctions between entrance and entered, these distinctions are easily elided and erased by religious beliefs and their theological justifications.

The well-known biblical story (Genesis 22) of Abraham and Isaac tells of Abraham's intention to sacrifice his son Isaac in unquestioning compliance with God's command. The story of Abraham and Isaac has been interpreted theologically over the centuries as an ultimately positive illustration of Abraham's unwavering faith that is tested by God. According to Jay Bernstein, *this* particular biblical narrative "stands very near the center of Western religious spirituality" (2013, 165) as a testament to the relationship between Abraham and God. From the point of view of Isaac, who had every reason to believe his father would kill him, the situation may well have looked dramatically different. Similarly, the Christian salvation narrative of eternal life is disturbingly unsettled by Jesus's anguished cry from the cross: "My God, why have you forsaken me?" (Matthew 27:46). The father remains silent, abandoning his son to a cruel fate. What are children in any age and any religious tradition to make of stories such as these? In the case of Isaac, how does a child recover when the universe splits apart to reveal that his father is *willing to murder* him? At this point in the narrative of Abraham and Isaac, the religious promise that trauma and betrayal will somehow transmogrify into an uplifting story of transformation and redemption is shattered. At the very moment it was taken, Abraham's internal, psychological decision to sacrifice his son became, for both father and son, the psychic and moral equivalent of the act itself. The heavenly father-god praises the earthly father for his willingness to kill Isaac: "You have not withheld from me your son, your only son" (Genesis 22:13). When the human story is allowed to emerge separately from centuries of theological justification, it becomes apparent that there is no going back, and no going forward in this world for either Isaac or Jesus. These are only two of many religiously idealized and, from a psychoanalytic point of view, deeply troubling narratives that so often portray terror and trauma as necessary experiences along the path to higher levels of spirituality. They continue to influence the Western religious imagination. With respect to the ethical and religious implications of the associations between trauma and mystical experience that Kripal acknowledges, it needs to be more fully understood how and in what ways religious narratives themselves are the transmitters of trauma as they foster these associations, and support them.[3]

The Human Is Two

Kripal explains Strieber's extraordinary experiences with alien visitors in part by appealing to the psychological and psychical researches of William James and Frederic Myers. He invokes their theory that a cosmic consciousness, or "Mind at Large", filters through the human brain, which further explains the psychological nature of anomalous experience generally, and mystical experience in particular. The psychological impact of traumas that fracture the mind also, for Kripal, let in transcendent light. The dissociated trance states that often accompany mystical experiences radically displace ordinary consciousness, emptying it or driving it to the margins of the mind to accommodate a sense of unitary connectedness with all reality. I would argue that the trauma associated with childhood sexual abuse in Strieber's case was an important precondition that facilitated, or even produced, his encounter with the "visitors" from other dimensions. From Ogden's perspective, Strieber may be psychoanalytically understood as finding ways of dreaming his emotional traumas through symbolic narrative representations that in turn allow him to transform and organize the internal malignant chaos caused by childhood abuse. In other words, Strieber has represented and symbolized, in literary form, the internal dialogue between the psychotic and non-psychotic parts of himself as he does the emotional work of creating meaning through his dream narratives.

Kripal expands upon Strieber's narratives by situating them both within psychology, American UFO mythology and the study of mysticism. He notes with reference to psychologist Kenneth Ring that victims of childhood trauma may be acutely prone to experiencing auditory and visual hallucinations as alternate realities, which, psychologically, they are. This is not surprising given that the ways in which trauma haunts the lives of its victims, often emerging in a wide range of dissociated states that conjure visions and voices formed out of personal suffering. Not only childhood trauma, but most forms of emotional crises such as "separation, loss and death are common precipitants of ... spiritual experience" both positive and "malignant" (Ostow 2004, 55). As James reminds us, the "subliminal or transmarginal region" of the mind where both "classical" and "lower" mystical experience originates contains both "seraph and snake" ([1902] 2004, 369).

Kripal considers that most forms of mystical experience recorded in the history of religions are coded narratives that share a gnostic secret about the true nature of reality and human beings. He includes not only mystical experiences associated with the world's religious traditions such as Hinduism, Judaism, Christianity and Islam, but also the visionary experiences that loosely fall within the rather vexed category "paranormal". Like James and Myers, Kripal is interested in the psychology of anomalous experience in terms of what it can reveal about both the nature and potential of human consciousness. It will be clear by now that for Kripal, as well as James and Myers, what is called the "sacred" is *both* thoroughly human *and* transcendent, or transpersonal. Human beings are "two". We each have our own individual biographies and specific personal identities that are structured in terms of our own "neurological, psychological, cultural, linguistic, emotional, political and historical complexities" (Kripal 2015, 164).

For Kripal, this is only part of the human story. He turns to the nineteenth-century German philosopher Ludwig Feuerbach to argue that we are much more than our individual biographies and life experiences. Feuerbach's classic work, *The Essence of Christianity* (1841) is a major text in "the history of Christian mystical literature" (Kripal 2007b, 83) in its unfolding of the gnostic secret that "God is Man and Man is God". Feuerbach's proto-psychoanalytic insight[4] is that God is an unconscious projection of the true nature of human beings, which is "infinite" ([1841] 1957, 2). "Consciousness of God", he writes, "is self-consciousness, knowledge of God is self-knowledge ... God is the manifested inward nature, the expressed self of a man" (ibid., 12–13). Man and God are "identical". The unconscious object of man's worship is man himself, shaped in the form of a supernatural divine being and its attendant theological myths. Religion does not only represent humanity's "childlike condition;" it is also a repository of the "hidden treasures" (ibid., 13) of human developmental potential held in a kind of trust for humanity until it achieves the psychological maturity necessary for reclaiming its true nature. For Feuerbach religions allow man to dream the coded truth of his destiny until he becomes psychologically mature enough to claim his true nature.

A psychoanalytic formulation of Feuerbach's idea of religious dreaming would interpret it as engaging in the emotional work of integrating unconscious knowledge into an expanded and enriched conscious awareness. Both Feuerbach and Kripal maintain that within the vast diversity of the world's religions, human beings are slowly dreaming themselves into fuller existence in their constantly changing awareness of their own true nature. "Religion is a dream, in which our own conceptions and emotions appear to us as separate existences, beings out of ourselves", writes Feuerbach ([1841] 1957, 204). If "dreaming is the key to the mysteries of religion" (ibid., 141), then humanity is dreaming its way to a higher truth that transcends the self-alienation of fractured, traumatized existence marked by isolation and useless suffering ending in pointless death. Kripal interprets Feuerbach's effort to reclaim the divine essence of human nature as an expression of a "mystical humanism" that again sees the "sacred" as a dimension of the human psyche. The relocation of the divine within the human means that humanity is in the process of developing and evolving into its own super normality that is fully natural, historical *and* cosmic. The other-worldly hallucinations or visions reported throughout the world's religions and the varieties of paranormal or psi experiences are thus "ciphers" of other dimensions of mind and reality, intimations of other forms of being human that we are in the process of becoming (Strieber and Kripal 2017, 123).

For Kripal, stories about alien visitations and abduction, psi phenomena or his own mystical experience are not to be taken in the literal form in which they are encountered. The manifest forms of these encounters are intimations of a mystical substance or power whose true nature the human mind cannot grasp. Viewed from an Eliadean perspective, they may be considered as hierophanic irruptions of a sacred, "superconscious energy" that is filtered through the neural systems and "cultural software" of historically situated human beings (Strieber and Kripal 2017, 168). The superconscious cosmos *dreams us* into our individually situated existence. In altered states of consciousness and mystical experiences, we may be able to dream along with it. From the perspective of an historian of religions, Kripal notes that while all mystical and anomalous experiences are culturally and historically formulated and expressed, they bear "striking" resemblances to each other. He draws attention, for example, to the significant "correspondences between Indian Tantric traditions and American abduction literature" (ibid., 170) such as "telepathic communications, channeled revelations … levitation or spiritual flight". Moreover, "central to both are the production of *trance and a broad range of possession states*, both positive and negative. … Sex with discarnate beings is also a central concern of both literatures" (ibid., italics added). These accounts lend themselves to psychoanalytic inquiry not merely because of their common preoccupation with sexuality and desire, although they are relevant. The majority of "close encounter witnesses" include reports of "childhood trauma" (ibid., 208) which is all too often caused by twisted, pathological and degraded forms of sexuality and desire of profoundly sick adults. Psychoanalysis has much to contribute with its hermeneutical frameworks of meaning to a deeper understanding of these experiences.

Sympathy for the Devil

Like the study of religion, psychoanalysis is comparative, and comparison yields insight into the nature of our shared humanity. One of the basic premises of psychoanalysis is that all human beings have minds, feelings, fantasies, desires, and fears, and are vulnerable to the traumatic impact of loss, abandonment and isolation. Psychoanalysis allows us to compare Strieber's experiences with another, very different "close encounter", also with a "visitor" from another world, this time set in seventeenth-century Austria and discussed by Freud (1923c). Psychoanalytic comparison of these contact narratives yields important insights about the interconnections between real trauma, unconscious fantasy and visionary experience that intermingle and circulate within different cultural and historical contexts. In situating these narratives with respect to each other, we are also able to show how individual trauma reflects larger underlying cultural anxieties that danger lurks just beyond the veil of ordinary reality. We also see in comparing these resonant stories of alien contact the ways in which trauma can be linked with possibilities of spiritual transformation.

On the basis of a Latin manuscript that came into his possession, Freud recounts and interprets the tale of a painter, Christoph Haizmann, who sold his soul to the Devil after the death of his father. Freud notes that Haizmann's pact with the Devil was precipitated by the loss of his *father*, which appears to be a mistranslation of the Latin *ex morte parentis* (Heinemann 2000, 49),[5] or death of his parents. Although Freud focuses on the loss of the father, Freud notes that there are significant traces in the story suggesting Haizmann's need for either his mother or some maternal caregiver, as will become evident. According to the priest who knew him, Haizmann was a "wretched man, who was bereft of all help" (Freud 1923c, 75n1) at the time of his meeting with the Devil. A failure as a painter, "trusted by no one", depressed, destitute, unable to work, and fearful for his livelihood (ibid., 103, 102), Haizmann was desperate for security and material support. Isolated and alone in the world, Haizmann belonged to no living being.

In drawing upon psychoanalytic theories, especially his concept of Oedipal conflict and ambivalence, Freud surmises that Haizmann's inability to paint following his father's death may have been an act of "deferred obedience" and acquiescence to his father's objection to his chosen career. From Freud's reading, the fact that Haizmann could not support himself would have made him especially vulnerable to the devil's offer of protection "from the cares of life". Moreover, in "its aspect as deferred obedience, it would also be an expression of remorse and a successful self-punishment" (Freud 1923c, 88) for defying his father's opposition to his wanting to be a painter. Haizmann first turned to the Devil for paternal aid, but eventually he sought refuge with the clergy by entering a Holy Order composed of more socially and religiously acceptable Fathers. With the aid of priests *and*, even more important, the intervention of the Holy Mother of God, Haizmann succeeded in reclaiming his prospects for salvation in exchange for "his freedom and most of the possibilities of enjoyment in life" (ibid., 104). Tormented by the "Evil Spirits" of his own alienated desires, Haizmann had visions of being engulfed in flames as punishment for his sexual fantasies. In such extreme dissociated states, Haizmann felt "surrounded by heat and noisome smells", and heard voices telling him he was being punished for "his vain and idle thoughts" (ibid., 102). He was also prone to frequent seizures and "absences" that were often accompanied by visions.

Haizmann painted the devil's initial appearance to him in the form of an "honest citizen", an ordinary bearded father-figure in a red cloak, leaning on a stick and accompanied by a dog (Freud 1923c, 89, 85). In subsequent visions the devil takes on a terrifying, more explicitly demonic "mythological" appearance, culminating in the image of a "flying dragon" (ibid., 85). In some of Haizmann's paintings the devil has multiple breasts and a huge penis that ends in a snake. The paintings of Haizmann's visionary experiences display a jumble of contradictory symbols of maternal care and nourishment (breasts) and a benign father (beard, cloak and dog) who morphs into a terrifying beast as the literal embodiment of demonic, destructive masculine power (penis/snake). For Freud, this confused riot of fragmented part-objects of male, female, human and monsters that fill Haizmann's visions strongly suggests an ambivalent relationship with his real father, who in all likelihood both supported *and* terrified him. The androgynous devil images may also represent an attempt by Haizmann to heal his own internal splitting of parental fantasy figures as both evil and good, which likely corresponded to his actual childhood experience.

An abusive parent can often appear to a child as two radically different people: the one who loves and protects by day, and the other who inflicts fear and pain by night. It is nearly impossible for a child to psychologically integrate such starkly opposed "parents" into a single figure. Haizmann's initial reliance on the devil for substitute paternal support, protection and a sense of belonging connection eventually shifts in favour of an alliance with Mother church and her male clergy. Although nothing is said in the manuscript about Haizmann's mother, it is doubly significant that the Holy Mother was the one whose intervention ultimately released him from his demonic pact *on the day of her Nativity* (Freud 1923c, 91). On the Holy Mother's birthday, Haizmann is spiritually reborn, and his salvation is assured. It is also worth noting, with reference to Freud's idea of "deferred obedience", that Haizmann gave up not only painting when he took shelter with a new father, the Catholic clergy, but also life's pleasures. As Freud observes in a different context that is relevant here, sons tend to be caught between a culturally directed ethical imperative to emulate the father ideal and be "like" him, while at the same time they are prohibited from possessing what the father *has*: life's pleasures as represented in sexual access to the mother. Some things are "his prerogative" alone (Freud 1923a, 34).

The historical, theological and cultural context of seventeenth-century, Catholic continental Europe provided Haizmann with a rich narrative resource through he could coherently organize the chaos within his body and mind. It also provided him with frameworks of meaning that allowed him to understand and express his emotional traumas. There was nothing incredible or fantastic about Haizmann's visions or pact with the Devil in a cultural and historical context that accepted the corporeal existence of demons. Christian Europe was still torturing and burning women accused of witchcraft, maleficence and sexual intercourse with the Devil. As Europe was inching its way into modernity and grappling with the unsettling impact of Galileo's astronomical discoveries and Newtonian science, the maintenance of belief in the corporeal existence of the Devil would have been an especially important countervailing force against the weakening of faith (Freud 1923c, 87; Clark 1997, 138–140). For Freud, religious beliefs originate in the universal, real experiences of infancy that are inevitably characterized by helplessness, dependency, and the need for protection and safety (1927) during the first several years of life. In Freud's view, the father God of the Jewish and Christian monotheisms is a "father-substitute", and "exalted ... copy" of earthly fathers of individual childhood and human prehistory (1913; 1923c, 85; 1927; 1939).

From a psychoanalytic perspective, Haizmann's visions of the Devil formed a composite picture of unintegrated fragments of the affectively laden real traumas of his early childhood. While an adult may not be able to remember with full accurate clarity the details of early traumas, s/he will have absorbed the affects and feelings of early experience in both the unconscious *and* the body. As Bessel van der Kolk clearly states in the title of his famous study, "the body" *always* "keeps the score" (2015). The traces of unsymbolized and unformulated affects of childhood trauma surface and circulate within narrative frameworks whose details do not necessarily correspond with "material" truth (Freud 1939, 129–130). At the same time, unformulated traumas infuse *psychic* reality (Freud 1913, 159–161) and stain *emotional* truth. Closely following Freud, Ogden maintains that "the psychic registration of a significant experience, whether that registration be conscious or unconscious, is *never* destroyed. It may be suppressed, repressed, displaced, denied, disowned, dissociated, projected, introjected, split off, foreclosed, and so on – but *never* destroyed or demolished. No experience can ever '*unhappen*' psychically" (Ogden 2009, 119, italics added; Freud 1937a, 229). Freud surmises that Haizmann's embrace of the devil as a father-substitute originated in an unconscious but "completely justified memory" (Freud 1939, 130) that morphed into a mythologized distortion of a real father who likely treated the child Haizmann with "devilish" cruelty. While Freud would unhesitatingly view the devil's appearance as a delusion, "in so far as it brings a return of the past, it must be called the *truth*" (ibid.). Anxiety, depression and abject misery were the powerful, irresistible forces that drove Haizmann to the brink of consigning his soul to eternal damnation in return for a sense of belonging ("body and soul") to a replacement father who would take care of him (Freud 1923c, 74) and, I would add, love him.

Finally, as psychologist Lee Kirkpatrick observes, the father-as-God becomes the "exalted" attachment figure (1999, 805) of religious belief as a figure who offers assurance of protection and safety through attachment. The need for attachment to a caregiver who alleviates the infant's unbearable feelings of anxiety about emotional and physical survival is an evolutionary imperative (Hewitt 2008; 2014a, 28). In adulthood, the attachment system is reactivated in times of severe personal crises such as life-threatening illness, physical danger, imposed separation, isolation and the threatened or actual loss of important others. Haizmann's situation following the loss of his father may be understood as comprising all of these elements: seizures, isolation, loss, and fear for his survival because he was unable to support himself. Although Freud died before the development of attachment theory, he anticipates many of its insights in his analysis of Haizmann. Freud generally understood that the unconscious emotional dynamics of infant-parent relationships are operative in religious experiences as well. As attachment research shows (Kirkpatrick 1999, 2005), there are significant correlations between attachment styles and internal models of self, other and environment that are gradually constructed within the complex web of relationships that structure the infant's interpersonal world.

Attachment studies applied to religious beliefs also show important correlations between the attachment styles of relationships with people and with gods, which must also include demons and devils. In commenting on these correlations, Kirkpatrick observes:

> Individuals who possess positive or "secure" generalized mental models of self and of attachment figures may be expected to view God and other deities

in similar terms. Likewise, an "avoidant" orientation towards close relationships may be expected to manifest itself in the religious realm as agnosticism or atheism, or in a view of God as remote and inaccessible.

(Kirkpatrick 1999, 809)

Although there is nothing to suggest that Haizmann was an atheist or agnostic, it is certainly plausible that a kind and loving God was so remote to his own internal sense of himself and his world that he gravitated towards a negative yet recognizable and, for him, more accessible paternal attachment figure in the form of the Devil.

Perhaps something similar happened with Strieber. The alien visitors from distant galaxies expressed far more interest in him than his emotionally remote parental caregivers. As brutal, frightening, painful, seductive and exhilarating as his encounters with the visitors often were, there was intimacy between them, however strange. They paid attention to him, examined and probed him. It may be that the tortures Strieber endured in the protracted physical pain of infancy and the Skinner box of his childhood were imaginatively reconstituted in the rape and painful physical torments he suffered in the alien spaceship (Strieber and Kripal 2017, 36). As Strieber writes, "I am reporting a perception, not making a claim, and there is a world of difference between those two approaches" (ibid., 37). His "perception" may be part of an endlessly repeating feedback loop carrying an ancient trauma that constantly reshapes and reformulates itself in a variety of manifestations corresponding to the various stages of his life, changing life experiences and psychological states. The fragmented shards of emotional shrapnel resulting from childhood trauma tear at the mind in a continual reassembly of past and present experiences. Haizmann's "perception" (using Strieber's term) of the Devil as a substitute paternal attachment figure poignantly illustrates how the "abused child seeks contact with the abusing caregiver because, paradoxically, the predictable, familiar, but adverse experience ... generates a greater sense of safety than an unfamiliar, nonabusive one for which the child has no role-relationship representations" (Fonagy 2001, 80). Freud anticipates this insight with his observation that God the "father-substitute" is a "copy" of the father one experienced in childhood and who aroused ambivalent feelings of affection and hostility. "It is our view", he writes, "that the same ambivalence governs the relations of mankind to its Deity" (Freud 1923c, 85).

Why Not?

The visionary encounters of Strieber and Haizmann with the mythical figures appropriate to their respective historical and cultural locations illustrate some of the ways in which religious and mystical narratives are encoded expressions and re-enactments of psychological trauma. The stories of both Strieber and Haizmann show how they can also offer imaginal possibility and promise not only for surviving trauma's impact, but transforming it. In this respect their visionary narratives give voice to the "soundless apparitions" (van der Kolk 2015, 173) of unformulated, inarticulate frozen pockets of hidden traumatic experiences that haunt the lives of its victims. Autobiographical memories are not precise reflections of reality, not even in the healthiest mind. Rather, they are the stories we tell ourselves and others that "convey our personal take on our own experience", attesting to the "extraordinary capacity of the human mind to rewrite memory" (ibid., 177). In this sense memory is adaptive, social and flexible. It allows for a coherent story of one's life that can be shared with others and when necessary, "modified to fit" changing circumstances (ibid., 182). When confronted with the "horrors" of sudden and "inescapable shock", the memory system breaks down, the "frontal lobe shuts down" and *shuts out* the capacity to symbolize feelings in words, and the "emotional brain" takes over (ibid., 178). Trauma undermines the "adaptive" social function of memory so that memory is forfeited and the individual, unable to remember, is condemned to re-live the past (ibid., 182). The goal of therapeutic treatment is to facilitate the integration of deadened, inchoate fragments of traumatic experience into an "ongoing narrative of life" (ibid.). Unconscious and/or unformulated experiences that lodge in the mind as destructive fragments that can only surface in dissociated states gradually take shape in a coherent story about what happened *in the past* and is now *over* (ibid.). When the therapeutic goal is achieved, the trauma is remembered and left behind, not as a ghost that haunts and terrorizes but as a remembered ancestor returned to its rightful location *in the past.*

Trauma, especially in childhood, produces a lingering "crisis of truth" (Caruth 1995, 6) in which the affect of absolute conviction that *something* happened is dislocated, perhaps irretrievably, from knowledge of *what* happened. In his most boldly speculative, ahistorical history of Jewish identity and survival, Freud "compares the history of the Jews with the structure of trauma" (ibid., 7). He theorizes that the history of the Jews, like the history of all humankind, is structured around an originary trauma of patricide and incestuous desire that is encoded in religious myths (Freud 1913). While the originary trauma is hidden deep within the individual and collective unconscious through repression, the repressed "returns" in a variety of historical and cultural forms. The monsters that haunt and terrorize our nocturnal and waking dreams in dissociated and altered states of consciousness signify the "return of the repressed" (Freud 1919b, 249), experiences both "familiar and old-established in the mind" that return in the form of something feeling new, strange, alien and other (ibid., 241). From his perspective, religions are cultural productions that attempt both to preserve and transform the originary trauma, creating mythic memories through narratives, rituals and moral codes that forbid repetition and also expiate guilt. They are coded testaments establishing connective links between historical and individual trauma that register and shape the "soundless apparitions" that haunt the lives of individuals and societies. As Kripal comments in another context that is relevant here, "*consciousness and culture cannot be collapsed into one another but work together, in incredibly complex ways, to actualize different human potentialities, different forms of reality, different (im)possibilities*" (Kripal 2010, 202).

This is the key to a psychoanalytic understanding of the visionary experiences of Strieber and Haizmann that limits ideas of potentiality, reality and (im)possibility in ways Kripal does not. Rather than proposing that Strieber or Haizmann encountered ontological realities beyond our ordinary world, and rather than dismissing their narratives as pathological delusions without merit, psychoanalysis would do well to follow Freud's advice to look for the existential *kernel of truth* contained in their efforts to articulate, express, shape and give coherent meaning to the traumatic experiences that threatened to overwhelm their minds. From a psychoanalytic perspective, their efforts to name the *what* of the *something* that happened to them may attest to their reasonable strategies for preserving their sanity. Strieber and Haizmann both found meaningful ways to come to terms with lives "structured by trauma". Ogden's attitude to the various defensive strategies devised by his patients to cope with life may be extended to Strieber and Haizmann:

> I find that the idea of "Why not?" has become central to the way I think and speak with patients. ... "Why not feel frightened or sad or jealous?" "Why not keep to yourself the dream you find so embarrassing?" "Why not leave the session early?" These are not rhetorical questions. *"Why not?" is an inquiry into the history of the patient's ways of thinking and feeling which have helped him to stay alive and maintain as much sanity as he could afford under the circumstances.*
>
> (Ogden 2009, 69, italics added)

A critical analysis of mystical visions need not become mired in irresolvable and ultimately useless controversies around the independent, ontological status of the visionary object in either the direction of dismissive debunking or championing endorsement. In the context of a psychoanalytic exploration of mystical phenomena, "why not?" offers richer alternatives for unearthing the deeper meaning of those phenomena and their significance in the mutual quest of analyst and patient for spiritual renewal and transformation. If an otherwise normally functioning patient tells her analyst that she made a pact with the devil, or was abducted by aliens, speaks to Jesus every night before bed, feels comfort when her dead mother visits her in waking dreams, or is terrified of the monsters that penetrate her feet as she falls asleep, the analyst needs to accept that these are real experiences *for the patient*. As Freud comments, "we gradually learn to understand that *in the world of the neuroses it is psychical reality which is the decisive kind*" (1916–1917, 368).

6

Concluding Thoughts on the Psychoanalytic Psychology of Religion

[T]elepathy is a response to a call and can happen only in multiple voices.
(Royle 1995, 78)

"The true psychic reality" is the unconscious, Freud wrote (1900, 613). It belongs to the realm of dreams, fantasies, hallucinations, visions and the entire dimension of the mind associated with the non-rational. As all psychoanalysts know, it can be dangerous territory. Psychic reality can be disturbingly unpredictable and messy, especially when it overtakes external reality. Psychic reality challenges our modern ideas of rationality and autonomy by showing how thin is the veil between the rational and the irrational, fantasy and reality. It is at times both strange and uncanny. It knows neither time nor contradiction, as all dreams attest. Contemporary neuroscientists estimate that consciousness plays a "causal role in less than 5% of cognition" (Solms 2016, 17). Freud declared that the unconscious *"is as much unknown to us as the reality of the external world, and it is as incompletely presented by the data of consciousness as is the external world by the communications of our sense organs"* (Freud 1900, 613). This is a sobering observation, and a blow to narcissistic human pride in the rational mind. As Freud was himself aware, his theory of the unconscious does not tend to attract the "academic respectability granted to scientists engaged in areas of research far removed from the unconscious" (Grubrich-Simitis 2004, 34). Yet it is *the* pivotal concept around which psychoanalysis is constructed. In its effort to illuminate the contradictory, timeless and utterly irrational nature of the unconscious, psychoanalysis does not, and indeed cannot, aspire to the clean theoretical lines associated with experimental research conducted in laboratory contexts.[1]

Freud's attitude to telepathy, which as we have seen he used interchangeably with thought-transference and unconscious communication, was both "unenthusiastic and ambivalent" (1921, 189). Yet it was the only aspect of occult phenomena that he took seriously enough to argue that it should be scientifically investigated. Surprisingly, Freud did express a measure of general sympathy with "occultism". He complained that both psychoanalysis and "occultism" suffer from "contemptuous and arrogant treatment by official science" (ibid., 178). Like William James, Freud also hoped that scientific investigation of telepathic phenomena would lead to the discovery of "more extensive and deeper-reaching natural laws" that would eventually explain it (ibid., 179). Despite his acknowledgement of these points of connection between occultism and psychoanalysis, Freud worried that the latter would suffer from a misplaced identification with the most vulgar aspects of the former – for example, séances, spirit communication and crude mediumistic performances. For this reason, he was ambivalent about telepathy. And yet, he did not deny that telepathy constituted the point of "reciprocal sympathy" (ibid., 178) between psychoanalysis and occultism. Freud also noted that "occultism" and psychoanalysis oppose "everything that is conventionally restricted, well-established and generally accepted" (ibid.). What he strenuously objected to, however, was the mystical and spiritual character of occultism that in his view negated the possibility of obtaining objective knowledge. Believers in the occult were "looking for confirmation and for something that will justify them in openly confessing their faith", he charged (ibid.).

As far as Freud was concerned, psychoanalysis must under no circumstances join forces with the religious, belief-driven occultists. Psychoanalysts are, after all, "incorrigible mechanists and materialists" (Freud 1921, 179) who must refuse the temptation to explain telepathy by any non-scientific means. He thought that most occultists' lack of patience for the slow nature of scientific research, a vital part of the "laborious" psychoanalytic explorations of "unknown mental forces", caused them to accept the easy answers offered by spiritual explanations (ibid., 180). In a curiously ironic twist, Freud basically accused both occultism and official science of sharing similar aims: an obsession with achieving both the "dazzling brilliance" of theory and a "comprehensive view of the universe" (ibid., 179). In contrast to both science and occultism, Freud asserted that psychoanalysis, by its very nature, could only yield "fragmentary pieces of knowledge". Psychoanalysis is inevitably partial, provisional, imprecise and subject to constant revision demanded by the ongoing accumulation of evidence. Freud explained that his acceptance of telepathic phenomena was forced on him by clinical observation (ibid.), as we saw in the case of Herr P., Freud never found a comprehensive theory to explain telepathy. He also he knew that if one ever could be found, it would be a long time in coming (ibid.).

Freud continued to hope that psychoanalysis would be able to forge a way out of the impasse between scientific intolerance on the one hand and occult religious belief on the other. As long as telepathy was regarded as a mental operation of the unconscious, and thus potentially amenable to psychoanalytic explanation, he thought it could be established as a natural, rather than a mystical phenomenon. But Freud knew that the unconscious is a troublesome notion that resisted validation through the methods and standards of scientific inquiry known to him. Freud complained that science and philosophy condemned psychoanalysis as "savouring of mysticism" (Freud 1921, 178). He seemed to understand the inevitability of this association in his own repeated admission that "the mysterious unconscious" (ibid., 180) resists direct empirical observation and description. Nonetheless Freud was committed to what he thought of as a scientific exploration of the mind's mysteries, which possessed its own inherent dangers of importing the very thing he dreaded into psychoanalysis.

It is not hard to see how the very terms that Freud used to describe the unconscious could lend themselves to occult appropriation. Freud feared that public acknowledgement of the objective existence of one occult notion, telepathy, could provoke a wholesale, uncritical acceptance of *every* occult claim, no matter how outlandish. If this happened, the genuine scientific character of psychoanalysis would be swept up by religion and firmly planted within mysticism and the worst popularizations of the occult. Widespread acceptance of pseudo-scientific theories would bring about the "fearful collapse of critical thought [and] the determinist standard of mechanistic science" (Freud 1921, 180). By bringing telepathy into psychoanalysis as a legitimate focus of inquiry, Freud sensed that he was opening the door to the very thing he feared most: the spiritualization of psychoanalysis. Yet he had no choice. As I pointed out previously, Freud accepted not only that telepathy was integral to the dialogical nature of the unconscious, but saw it also as a key part of therapeutic work. But that was as far as he went. Unconscious communication, or telepathy, for him meant that communication between individuals operates through non-verbal pathways of affect transfer that operate outside conscious awareness. It had no mystical significance or meaning. The analyst must find a way to bring these affective forces to consciousness so they can be symbolized and reflected upon by both patient and analyst. Since Freud had experienced instances of telepathic, unconscious communication himself, he had to acknowledge its objective existence. It was not lost on him that by doing this, he put himself and psychoanalysis in a potentially untenable position. This explains his ambivalence and utter lack of enthusiasm for telepathy.

However, despite his clear awareness that he was opening psychoanalysis up to the very thing he repudiated – religion – Freud refused to turn away from confronting telepathy and the task of theorizing it in psychoanalytic terms. This kind of approach is typical of Freud; he often asserted his commitment to stating the truth as he saw it no matter how inconvenient or even harmful the consequences might be to him or anyone else. However one may judge Freud on this point, his intellectual courage is captured rather touchingly by R. D. Laing. When he was still an impressionable young psychiatrist, Laing described Freud as a "hero" who took his theories to the "Underworld" and wielded them like a "Medusa's head" against the terrors within the human mind. Laing seems almost to marvel that Freud "survived" this dangerous journey. Not all mental health professionals do. But the part of this youthfully admiring description of Freud that is relevant to this discussion is Laing's challenge to "see if *we* now can survive *without using a theory that is in some measure an instrument of defence*" (Laing [1959] 1965, 25, italics added). In a way, Laing's challenge has been one of the guiding principles of this book. Throughout my discussion of mystical psychoanalysis and its claims to have discovered gnostic truths about the nature of being and all reality, I have attempted to balance critical analysis with understanding. I have tried to be clear that I have no interest whatsoever in building a case, however scholarly or analytical, that seeks merely to repudiate the spiritual intuitions of the writers discussed here. I do not endorse their claims about the scientific truth of paranormal phenomena; nor do I uncritically examine their accounts of telepathic communications with their patients. I seek to avoid engaging in *defensive* theorizing that closes doors on open-ended and open-minded critical analysis. As scholars of psychoanalysis and the study of religion, it is imperative that we engage the most inconvenient and unsettling challenges to our theoretical premises and critical frameworks with both intellectual rigor and generosity. This approach is not however, to be confused with blind acceptance of any subjective claim to truth about the nature of reality.

I have no cause to doubt any of the clinical reports of telepathic communication examined throughout the book. As a psychoanalyst, I keep the notion of psychic reality firmly in mind as a key hermeneutic tool of analysis. As a scholar of religion, I am committed to taking subjective religious experiences seriously while also situating them within critical explanatory frameworks. Having said this, and given the contested nature of the field of the study of religion and its endless debates and controversies, it cannot be overemphasized that taking these accounts seriously and considering them worthy of scholarly inquiry does not oblige scholars to accept their ontological, independent truth. This is why I bracket claims about the literal reality of telepathy as a "scientific fact" in order to explore them from the perspective of psychoanalysis and the study of religion. But psychoanalysis, as this book clearly demonstrates, is not a homogeneous, monolithic theory. There are a number of opposing and contested views within psychoanalysis concerning the meaning of its most central concept, the unconscious, as I have shown. Although there is a vast literature representing a range of contested views about the unconscious, my approach here has been to explore religious and non-religious interpretations of the unconscious primarily within American psychoanalysis by positioning the latter in a sustained dialectical tension with Freud.

As far as psychoanalysis is concerned, subjective religious experiences belong to the category of psychic reality. This doesn't make them any less real or compelling for the experiencer. A psychoanalytic psychology of religion interprets these kinds of experiences as religious *and* psychological, and attempts to situate them within the life histories and cultural and historical contexts of the experiencer. In this way a psychoanalytic psychology of religion is able to critically explore these kinds of experiences within larger disciplinary frameworks of explanation that include phenomenology, comparison, history and culture. Thus psychoanalytic psychology of religion straddles different worlds as it explores the dream states and fantasy dimensions of specific, subjective human experiences in its effort to formulate explanatory, but always necessarily partial and provisional, frameworks of meaning and knowledge.

The world of psychic reality, of which religious experience is a part, must be accepted and critically investigated in all its so-called irrationality and strange uncanniness because it is a product of the mind. Psychoanalysis, psychic reality, dreams, visions, anomalous experiences, and religion intersect in multiple ways. They represent the bidirectional interactions of mental processes and culture. The products of culture, such as religion, art and science and the capacity for reflective, abstract thought do not exist independently of the "lower reaches of the brain, which generate our basic emotions, feelings, and other instinctual tendencies" (Panksepp 1998, 300). This is a view Freud shared. He was consistent in his view that human beings, with their long evolutionary history, are inextricably enveloped within the natural world. This explains in part why Freud rejected religion. In his view, religion is an expression of humanity's fantasies and aspirations to a grandiose status that is reflected in beliefs in personal immortality and that human beings are created in the image of God. Spiritual or mystical psychoanalysis transforms these beliefs in emphasizing the inherent spiritual nature of human beings. Freud's unconscious originates in animal, bodily impulses, whereas the unconscious of spiritual psychoanalysis is part of a universal, divine cosmic consciousness with which it seeks to unite. Although treated in radically and irreconcilably different ways, religion is a central and defining feature of both forms of psychoanalysis.

Despite this radical difference on the question of religion, both Freud and spiritual psychoanalysis acknowledge the existence of telepathy. In a way, telepathic experience may be considered as almost inevitable in so far as psychoanalysis encourages the expression of fantasies, fears and desires and takes them seriously as sources of psychological knowledge. In the dream space of the consulting room, all kinds of strange and unwelcome thoughts emerge from the minds of the analyst and the patient. In this drift of minds meeting in the unconscious dialogue that is generated between them, unique forms of communication emerge that may reveal deeper levels of interconnectedness between the analyst and patient. As analyst and patient dream together, involuntary images may also emerge within the analyst that resonate with and help to shape the patient's unconscious productions (Balter, Lothane, and Spencer 1980, 491). When minds meet in this way, it may be experienced as a telepathic communication. Whatever it is, telepathy is the axis that connects psychoanalysis and mystical spirituality, science mysticism, parapsychoanalysis, and religion. Since telepathy cannot as yet be reliably reproduced or proven through established scientific methodologies of experimentation, it can only be explained in terms of subjective religious experience. Freud may well have been waging a losing battle from the beginning with his adamant insistence on banning religion from psychoanalysis. His sustained effort to separate psychoanalysis from religion was seriously undermined, if not undone altogether, when he admitted the existence of telepathy. His hope that not only telepathy, but the "mysterious unconscious" could be successfully confined within the limits of psychoanalysis turned out to be as in "vain" (Freud 1921, 180) as he suspected it would.

Notes

Chapter 1

1. In this passage Freud uses the German term *Instinkt,* which means instinct as applied to animals, rather than the far more frequently used border concept *Trieb,* or drive, which combines both somatic and psychological dimensions. The distinction in Freudian drive theory between *Trieb* and *Instinkt* is crucial.
2. For an informative historical and theoretical overview of relational psychoanalysis that briefly but explicitly acknowledges its indebtedness to William James, see Harris (2011).
3. The term "mystical"/"mysticism" has a long history of contested and varied meanings. My use of the term follows William James, who regarded mysticism as a universal religiosity that transcends all particular religious, historical and cultural contexts. His approach is most relevant to the psychoanalytic ideas and theorists studied here.
4. The term "occult" is so broad as to defy strict definition. I have discussed the history of the term and its various meanings in greater detail elsewhere (Hewitt 2017). I use it here to refer to a modern search for spiritual meaning and access to higher planes of hidden realities and deeper dimensions of rationality beyond the ordinary. Alex Owen uses the term "new occultism" to describe this form of modern spirituality (2004, 11ff).
5. For a thorough, scholarly account of their exchange on the topic see Parsons (1999).

Chapter 2

1. Carl Jung contributes to the persistence of this misleading view: "According to [Freudian] theory, the unconscious contains *only* those parts of the personality which could just as well be conscious, and have been suppressed only through the process of education" and repression ([1953] 1977, 127, italics added).
2. The Society for Psychical Research was founded in England in 1882, and its American counterpart in 1885. Freud became an Honorary Member of the SPR in January 1911.
3. Consider, for example, Freud's now famous remark to Hereward Carrington: "If I had my life to live over again I should devote myself to psychical research rather than to psychoanalysis" (in Jones 1957, 392).
4. All italics in quotes are the original author's unless I note otherwise.

5   William James explicitly rejected the notion of an "unconscious" in his *The Principles of Psychology* ([1890] 1950), published more than twenty years before Freud's "Note on the Unconscious". James's notion of the "subconscious" mind was heavily influenced by Myers, and both were influenced by the notion of "divided consciousness" suggested by French psychopathologists (Taylor 1996a, 35; Gauld 1968, 279). Later, the term subconscious would give way to Myers's idea of the "subliminal" realm, which James adopted.

6   Freud's 1915 description of the distinct areas of the mind as unconscious (Ucs.), preconscious (Pcs.), and conscious (Cs.), is often referred to as "the first topography". His later formulation of Ego (*das Ich*), Super-ego (*das Über-Ich*) and unconscious (*das Es*), is known as the "structural model" or "second topography".

7   In *Studies in Hysteria* (1893–1895), co-authored with Josef Breuer, Freud occasionally uses the terms "unconscious" and "subconscious" interchangeably. However, the term "unconscious" as used in the *Studies* seems to anticipate its psychoanalytic meaning as established in the post-*Studies* texts cited above.

8   The term "paranormal" was coined by the German philosopher Max Dessoir in 1889.

9   Any fair history of the SPR must acknowledge that the organization and its investigators were committed to separating the false claims of charlatans from what they considered to be genuine psychic phenomena. By 1885 Richard Hodgson, an SPR investigator, demonstrated that Madame Blavatsky, the founder of Theosophy, was a fraud. The SPR examined each paranormal episode that came to its attention with as much scientific knowledge as was then available to it.

10 According to Richard Noakes, the history of psychical research must be considered as an "episode in late-classical physics" which did not exclude attention to the study of the mind (2008, 326).

11 Janet coined the term "subconscious".

12 According to Henri Ellenberger, Janet had a "lasting suspicion of parapsychological research" (1970, 338)

13 Although Myers is inconsistent in capitalizing the "Subliminal Self", he appears to designate the subliminal self of individuals in lower case while capitalizing the impersonal Subliminal Self.

14 In Myers's view, the famous D. D. Home, Stainton Moses and Leonora Piper were credible mediums whose trance states were capable of simulating an "external intelligence" ([1903] 2005, 120).

15 While I generally agree with Taves's (2009) contention that the "transatlantic network of experimental psychologists and psychical researchers" within which James worked was an indisputable "intellectual inspiration" for the *Varieties*, I hold that the singular influence on James of Myers's theory of the individual subliminal self and the cosmic Subliminal Self as it developed in the context of psychical research was an equally crucial inspiration for his metaphysical psychology, irrespective of whether James agreed with every detail of Myers's views or not.

16 Kripal attributes the phrase to Frederic Spiegelberg, who taught comparative religion at Stanford University (2007a, 8).
17 Although I have emphasized the distinction between the concept "unconscious", which is central to Freudian psychoanalysis and the "subconscious" embraced by Myers and James, most contemporary American psychoanalysts use the term "unconscious", but not always in Freud's sense. I will use the term "unconscious" because that is the term used by psychoanalysis, which has become a taken-for-granted concept that harbours clusters of different meanings, depending upon who is using it.
18 Emmanuel Swedenborg (1688–1772) was a Swedish philosopher and mystic whose visions, spiritual experiences and teachings about the moral and spiritual progress of discarnate beings through various levels of cosmic, spiritual realms became popular in England and the United States in the nineteenth century.
19 The full reference to James's famous thesis on the white crow is, "If you wish to upset the law that all crows are black, you mustn't seek to show that no crows are; it is enough if you prove one single crow to be white. My own white crow is Mrs Piper".

Chapter 3

1 My use of the term is inspired by Ofra Eshel's (2012) idea of "presencing" that evokes the multiple dimensions of potentialities hidden deep within the interstices of analyst/patient interconnectedness that occasionally manifest themselves telepathically in the clinical setting.
2 This is an anonymized account based on one of my own patients.
3 For a fuller discussion of the history of the term "occult" and its role in psychoanalysis, see Hewitt (2017).
4 For example, Herbert Rosenfeld's idea of projective identification as a form of non-verbal *communication* whereby the patient is able to induce the analyst to "feel and understand his experiences" so that the analyst can contain and interpret them to the patient, is relevant here (Rosenfeld 1988, 121).
5 Wilfred Bion later referred to this as an "epistemophilic" or truth drive. See Grotstein (2007, 135–138) and Ogden (2008, 12–18).
6 Grotstein relies heavily on interchanging terms such as "ineffable", "numinous", "Ultimate Reality", and "Absolute Truth" to describe mystical experience, and repeats them with such frequent regularity that they are a key part of his discourse. To cite each and every instance where he uses these terms would be needlessly repetitive and distractingly unwieldly.
7 In Grotstein the terms "spiritual", "religious", and "theological" are not clearly defined or demarcated. At times they overlap. Grotstein also insists that his thinking has nothing to do with religions in their institutional or doctrinal forms.
8 O is an idea, notoriously difficult to define, that Bion introduced in his later work, from about 1965–1966 until his death.

9 Grotstein (in Grotstein and Franey 2008, 94) once remarked that he could not "stand the way [Bion] writes".

Chapter 4

1 "Psi" covers a range of psychic phenomena such as clairvoyance, crisis apparitions, psychokinesis and, most important for the discussion here, telepathy.
2 Psychologist Ray Hyman (1994), who has written extensively on paranormal research, notes that the results of Ganzfeld experiments are often undermined when researchers inadvertently encourage the receiver to rate the targets with "active promptings" at the end of the experiment. By Mayer's own account, it is clear that this is what happened in her case. According to Hyman, "by actively helping the subject to rate the members of the target pool, the experimenter" allows their own biases to "enter the selection procedure" (21).
3 Carl Jung, who had a long friendship with physicist Wolfgang Pauli, also pointed to the relevance of quantum physics for psychology, especially with reference to his notion of synchronicity, an acausal connecting principle ([1955] 2008), well before the analysts discussed here. It should be noted that Pauli, like a number of other late-nineteenth-century and early-twentieth-century physicists, was deeply interested in the metaphysical or mystical implications of quantum mechanics.

Chapter 5

1 Like Wouter Hanegraaff (2008), I use the term "religionist" to designate the insider approach of those analysts who argue that parapsychology and psychoanalysis promise to establish a new paradigm for explaining unconscious communication.
2 Strieber's *Communion: A True Story*, published in 1987, has appeared on bestseller lists and was later made into a movie.
3 For example a number of feminist theologians have long drawn attention to the patriarchal biases of traditional theology that cite the Bible to support the subjugation of women. Some theologians encourage women to remain in family situations even where domestic abuse occurs because of the sanctity of marriage and the family. "Wives, be subject to your husbands as to the Lord ... just as the church is subject to Christ, so must women be to their husbands in everything" (Ephesians 5:22).
4 As I have argued elsewhere, Feuerbach strongly influenced Freud's psychoanalytic critique of religion (Hewitt 2014a, 15–17).
5 At times in his writing Freud uses "father" and "parents" interchangeably. His description of identification and internalization of the "parental agency" or "parental imagos" in the process of super-ego formation includes the mother. Parental/father figures are sometimes composite terms for Freud and emblematic of a number of cultural institutions and authority figures such as educational systems, teachers, and other "ideal models" (1933a, 64).

Chapter 6

1. This situation has begun to change in recent years, however, as scientific journals such as *Neuropsychoanalysis* attempt to integrate psychoanalysis with behavioural and cognitive neuroscientific research and theories. Although a discussion of this field of research lies well beyond the scope of this book, it should be noted that some theorists, clinicians and researchers from both the neurosciences and psychoanalysis are divided about the legitimacy and desirability of efforts to integrate these fields.

References

Adams, Will. 1995. "Revelatory Openness Wedded with the Clarity of Unknowing: Psychoanalytic Evenly Suspended Attention, the Phenomenological Attitude, and Meditative Awareness". *Psychoanalysis and Contemporary Thought* 18: 463–494.

Addison, Ann. 2016. "Jung's Psychoid Concept and Bion's Proto-Mental Concept: A Comparison". *Journal of Analytical Psychology* 61 (5): 567–587. https://doi.org/10.1111/1468-5922.12259

Adorno, Theodor W. 2006. "Lecture 8: Psychology". In *History and Freedom: Lectures 1964-1965*, edited by Rolf Tiedemann and translated by Rodney Livingstone, 69–78. Cambridge: Polity.

Albanese, Catherine. 2007. *A Republic of Mind and Spirit: A Cultural History of American Metaphysical Religion*. New Haven, CT: Yale University Press.

Appelbaum, J. 2012. "Science and Theory in Modern Physics and Psychoanalysis". *International Forum of Psychoanalysis* 21: 117–124. https://doi.org/10.1080/0803706X.2011.592511

Arden, Margaret. 1988. "The Pattern which Connects". *Free Associations* 1: 73–85.

Aron, Lewis. 2004. "God's Influence on my Psychoanalytic Vision and Values". *Psychoanalytic Psychology* 21 (3): 442–451. https://doi.org/10.1037/0736-9735.21.3.442

Asprem, Egil. 2014a. "Psychic Enchantment of the Educated Classes". In *Contemporary Esotericism*, edited by Egil Asprem and Kennet Granholm, 330–350. London: Routledge.

———. 2014b. *The Problem of Disenchantment: Scientific Naturalism and Esoteric Discourse 1900-1939*. Leiden: Brill.

Assmann, Jan. 1997. *Moses the Egyptian: The Memory of Egypt in Western Monotheism*. Cambridge, MA: Harvard University Press.

Balint, M. 1955. "Notes on Parapsychology and Parapsychological Healing". *International Journal of Psychoanalysis* 36: 31–35.

Balter, Leon, Zvi Lothane and James H. Spencer, Jr. 1980. "On the Analyzing Instrument". *Psychoanalytic Quarterly* 49: 474–504. https://doi.org/10.1080/21674086.1980.11926924

Barad, Karen. 2007. *Meeting the Universe Halfway: Quantum Physics and the Entanglement of Matter and Meaning*. Durham, NC: Duke University Press. https://doi.org/10.1215/9780822388128

Barnard, G. William. 2002. "Diving into the Depths: Reflections on Psychology as a Religion". In *Religion and Psychology: Mapping the Terrain*, edited by Diane Jonte-Pace and William B. Parsons, 297–318. London: Routledge.

Bass, A. 2001. "It Takes One to Know One; or, Whose Unconscious Is It Anyway?" *Psychoanalytic Dialogues* 11: 683-702. https://doi.org/10.1080/10481881109348636

———. 2004. "Imagine, I am a Great Soothsayer – The Future is Now". *Studies in Gender and Sexuality* 5 (3): 303-316. https://doi.org/10.1080/15240650509349252

Beller, Mara. 1998. "The Sokal Hoax: At Whom Are We Laughing?" *Physics Today* 51 (9): 29-34. https://doi.org/10.1063/1.882436

Bender, Courtney. 2010. *The New Metaphysicals: Spirituality and the American Religious Imagination*. Chicago, IL: University of Chicago Press. https://doi.org/10.7208/chicago/9780226043173.001.0001

Bernstein, J. M. 2013. "Forgetting Isaac: Faith and the Philosophical Impossibility of a Postsecular Society". In *Habermas and Religion*, edited by Craig Calhoun, Eduardo Mendieta and Jonathan Van Antwerpen, 154-175. Cambridge: Polity.

Bion, W. R. 1970. *Attention and Interpretation*. London: Karnac.

Bishop, Paul. 2010. "The Unconscious from the Storm and Stress to Weimar Classicism: the Dialectic of Time and Pleasure". In *Thinking the Unconscious: Nineteenth-Century German Thought*, edited by Angus Nicholls and Martin Liebscher, 26-56. Cambridge: Cambridge University Press. https://doi.org/10.1017/CBO9780511712272.002

Blackman, L. 2010. "Embodying Affect: Voice-Hearing, Telepathy, Suggestion and Modelling the Non-Conscious". *Body & Society* 16: 163-192. https://doi.org/10.1177/1357034X09354356

Blass, Rachel. 2011. "Introduction to 'On the Value of "late Bion"' to Analytic Theory and Practice". *International Journal of Psychoanalysis* 92: 1081-1088. https://doi.org/10.1111/j.1745-8315.2011.00503.x

Blum, Deborah. 2006. *Ghost Hunters: William James and the Search for Scientific Proof of Life After Death*. New York: Penguin Books.

Bohm, David. [1980] 2010. *Wholeness and Implicate Order*. London: Routledge.

———. 1990. "A New Theory of the Relationship of Mind and Matter". *Philosophical Psychology* 3: 271-286. https://doi.org/10.1080/09515089008573004

Boyle, J. 2016. "Esoteric Traces in Contemporary Psychoanalysis". *American Imago* 73 (1): 95-119. https://doi.org/10.1353/aim.2016.0002

Britton, Ronald. 1989. "The Missing Link: Parental Sexuality in the Oedipus Complex". In *The Oedipus Complex Today: Clinical Implications*, by Ronald Britton, Michael Feldman, and Edna O'Shaughnessy, 83-101. London: Karnac Books. https://doi.org/10.4324/9780429482601-3

Brown, Lawrence J. 2011. *Intersubjective Processes and the Unconscious: An Integration of Freudian, Kleinian and Bionian Perspectives*. London: Routledge.

Burkert, Walter. [1996] 2001. *Creation of the Sacred: Tracks of Biology in Early Religions*. Cambridge, MA: Harvard University Press.

Caper, Robert. 1997. "A Mind of One's Own". *International Journal of Psychoanalysis* 78: 265-278.

Carroll, Bret E. 1997. *Spiritualism in Antebellum America*. Bloomington, IN: Indiana University Press.

Caruth, Cathy. 1995. Introduction to *Trauma: Explorations in Memory*, edited by Cathy Caruth, 3–12. Baltimore, MD: Johns Hopkins University Press.

Castoriadis, Cornelius. 1998. *The Imaginary Institution of Society*. Cambridge, MA: MIT Press.

Caterine, Darryl V. 2011. *Haunted Ground: Journeys through Paranormal America*. Santa Barbara, CA: Praeger.

Clark, Stuart. 1997. *Thinking with Demons: The Idea of Witchcraft in Early Modern Europe*. Oxford: Oxford University Press.

Crabtree, Adam. 1993. *From Mesmer to Freud: Magnetic Sleep and the Roots of Psychological Healing*. New Haven, CT: Yale University Press.

De Peyer, Janine. 2016. "Uncanny Communication and the Porous Mind". *Psychoanalytic Dialogues* 26 (2): 156–174. https://doi.org/10.1080/10481885.2016.1144978

Deutsch, H. 1953. "Occult Processes Occurring During Psychoanalysis". In *Psychoanalysis and the Occult*, edited by George Devereux, 133–146. New York: International Universities Press.

Diakoulakis, Christoforos. 2012. "William James: Belief in Ghosts". In *The Ashgate Research Companion to Nineteenth-Century Spiritualism and the Occult*, edited by Tatiana Kontou and Sarah Willburn, 181–196. Farnham: Ashgate.

Di Censo, James. 1999. *The Other Freud: Religion, Culture and Psychoanalysis*. London: Routledge.

Doniger, Wendy. 2004. Foreword to *Shamanism: Archaic Techniques of Ecstasy*, by Mircea Eliade, translated by Willard R. Trask. Bollingen Series LXXVI. Princeton, NJ: Princeton University Press.

Durban, Joshua. 2016. "Shadows, Ghosts and Chimeras: On Some Early Modes of Handling Psycho-Genetic Heritage". In *Ghosts in the Consulting Room: Echoes of Trauma in Psychoanalysis*, edited by Adrienne Harris, Margery Kalb, and Susan Klebanoff. London: Routledge.

Eigen, Michael. 1998. *The Psychoanalytic Mystic*. London: Free Association Press.

Eisold, K. 2002. "Jung, Jungians, and Psychoanalysis". *Psychoanalytic Psychology* 19: 501–524. https://doi.org/10.1037/0736-9735.19.3.501

Eliade, Mircea. 1958. *Patterns in Comparative Religion*, translated by Rosemary Sheed. New York: New American Library.

Eliade, Mircea and Lawrence E. Sullivan. 1987. "Hierophany". In *The Encyclopedia of Religion*, edited by Mircea Eliade, vol. 6, 313–317. New York: Macmillan.

Ellenberger, H. 1970. *The Discovery of the Unconscious: the History and Evolution of Dynamic Psychiatry*. New York: Basic Books.

Emerson, Ralph Waldo. 1838. "Divinity School Address". Retrieved from http://transcendentalism-legacy.tamu.edu/authors/emerson/essays/dsa.html (accessed 28 January 2019).

Eshel, O. 2006. "Where are You, My Beloved? On Absence, Loss, and the Enigma of Telepathic Dreams". *International Journal of Psychoanalysis* 87: 1603–1627. https://doi.org/10.1516/7GM3-MLDR-1W8K-LVLJ

———. 2012. "A Beam of 'Chimeric' Darkness: Presence, Interconnectedness, and Transformation in the Psychoanalytic Treatment of a Patient Convicted of Sex

Offenses". *Psychoanalytic Review* 99: 149–178. https://doi.org/10.1521/prev.2012.99.2.149

Farber, Sharon K. 2017. "Becoming a Telepathic Tuning Fork: Anomalous Experience and the Relational Mind". *Psychoanalytic Dialogues* 27 (6): 719–734. https://doi.org/10.1080/10481885.2017.1379329

Farrell, D. 1983. "Freud's 'Thought-Transference', Repression, and the Future of Psychoanalysis". *International Journal of Psychoanalysis* 64: 71–81.

Ferenczi, Sándor. 1988. *The Clinical Diary of Sándor Ferenczi*, edited by Judith Dupont and translated by Michael Balint and Nicola Zarday Jackson. Cambridge, MA: Harvard University Press.

Feuerbach, Ludwig. [1841] 1957. *The Essence of Christianity*, translated by George Eliot. New York: Harper & Row.

Fonagy, Peter. 2001. *Attachment Theory and Psychoanalysis*. New York: Other Press.

Freud, E. L. (ed.). 1961. *Letters of Sigmund Freud 1873-1939*, translated by T. & J. Stern. London: Hogarth Press.

Freud, Sigmund. 1954. *The Origins of Psycho-analysis: Letters to William Fliess, Drafts and Notes: 1887-1902*, edited by Marie Bonaparte, Anna Freud, and Ernst Kris. New York: Basic Books. https://doi.org/10.1037/11538-000

———. [1961] 2001. *The Standard Edition of the Complete Psychological Works of Sigmund Freud* (hereafter SE), 24 vols, translated by J. Strachey. London: Vintage/Hogarth.

———. 1894. "The Neuro-psychoses of Defence". SE vol. 3, 45–61.

———. 1900. *The Interpretation of Dreams*. SE vols 4–5.

———. 1908. "'Civilized' Sexual Morality and Modern Nervous Illness". SE vol. 9, 181–204.

———. 1910a. "Five Lectures on Psycho-analysis". SE vol. 11, 9–55.

———. 1910b. "Leonardo da Vinci and a Memory of his Childhood". SE vol. 11, 63–137.

———. 1911. "Formulations on the Two Principles of Mental Functioning". SE vol. 12, 218–226.

———. 1912a. "The Dynamics of Transference". SE vol. 12, 99–108.

———. 1912b. "A Note on the Unconscious in Psychoanalysis". SE vol. 12, 260–266.

———. 1912c. "Recommendations to Physicians Practising Psycho-Analysis". SE vol. 12, 111–120.

———. 1913. "Totem and Taboo". SE, vol. 13, 1–161.

———. 1914. "On Narcissism: An Introduction". SE vol. 14, 73–102.

———. 1915a. "Thoughts for the Times on War and Death". SE vol. 14, 275–300.

———. 1915b. "The Unconscious". SE vol. 14, 166–215.

———. 1916-1917. "The Paths to the Formation of Symptoms". SE 16, 358–377.

———. 1917a. "A Difficulty in the Path of Psycho-Analysis". SE vol.17, 137–144.

———. 1917b. "Transference". SE vol. 16, 431–447.

———. 1919a. "Lines of Advance in Psycho-Analytic Therapy". SE vol. 17, 159–168.

———. 1919b. "The Uncanny". SE vol. 17, 219–252.

———. 1921. "Psycho-analysis and Telepathy". SE vol. 18, 177–193.

———. 1922. "Dreams and Telepathy". SE vol. 18, 197–220. https://doi.org/10.1259/jrs.1922.0064
———. 1923a. "The Ego and the Id". SE vol. 19, 3–66.
———. 1923b. "Two Encyclopedia Articles". SE vol. 18, 235–259.
———. 1923c. "A Seventeenth-Century Demonological Neurosis". SE vol. 19, 72–105.
———. 1925a. "An Autobiographical Study". SE vol. 20, 3–74.
———. 1925b. "Some Additional Notes On Dream Interpretation as a Whole". SE vol. 19, 127–138.
———. 1927. "The Future of An Illusion". SE vol. 21, 5–56.
———. 1930. "Civilization and its Discontents". SE vol. 21, 59–145.
———. 1933a. "The Dissection of the Psychical Personality". SE vol. 22, 57–80.
———. 1933b. "Dreams and Occultism". SE vol. 22, 31–56.
———. 1933c. "The Question of a *Weltanschauung*". SE vol. 23, 158–182.
———. 1937a. "Analysis Terminable and Interminable". SE vol. 23, 211–253.
———. 1937b. "Constructions in Analysis". SE vol. 23, 257–269.
———. 1939. "Moses and Monotheism". SE vol. 23, 7–137.
Freud, Sigmund, and Josef Breuer. 1893–1895. *Studies in Hysteria*. SE vol. 2.
Fuller, Robert C. 1986. *Americans and the Unconscious*. New York: Oxford University Press.
———. 2001. *Spiritual but not Religious: Understanding Unchurched America*. New York: Oxford University Press.
———. 2006. "American Psychology and the Religious Imagination". *Journal of the History of Behavioral Sciences* 42 (3): 221–235. https://doi.org/10.1002/jhbs.20170
Gargiulo, Gerald J. 1997. "Inner Mind/Outer Mind and the Quest for the 'I': Spirituality Revisited". In *Soul on the Couch: Spirituality, Religion, and Morality in Contemporary Psychoanalysis*, edited by Charles Spezzano and Gerald J. Gargiulo, 1–9. Hillsdale, NJ: Analytic Press.
———. 2006. "Ontology and Metaphor: Reflections on the Unconscious and the 'I' in the Therapeutic Setting". *Psychoanalytic Psychology* 23: 461–474. https://doi.org/10.1037/0736-9735.23.3.461
———. 2010. "Mind, Meaning, and Quantum Physics: Models for Understanding the Dynamic Unconscious". *Psychoanalytic Review* 97 (1): 91–106. https://doi.org/10.1521/prev.2010.97.1.91
———. 2016. *Quantum Psychoanalysis: Essays on Physics, Mind, and Analysis Today*. New York: International Psychoanalytic Books.
Gauld, Alan. 1968. *The Founders of Psychical Research*. New York: Schocken Books.
Gay, Peter. 1988. *Freud: A Life for our Time*. New York: W. W. Norton.
Gödde, Günter. 2010. "Freud and Nineteenth Century Philosophical Sources on the Unconscious". In *Thinking the Unconscious: Nineteenth-Century German Thought*, edited by Angus Nicholls and Martin Liebscher, 261–286. Cambridge: Cambridge University Press. https://doi.org/10.1017/CBO9780511712272.011
Godwin, R. W. 1991. "Wilfred Bion and David Bohm: Toward a Quantum Metapsychology". *Psychoanalysis and Contemporary Thought* 14: 625–654.

Goetz, Bruno, Martin Grotjahn and Ernest S. Wolf. 1982. "This is All I Have to Tell About Freud: Reminiscences of Sigmund Freud". *The Annual of Psychoanalysis* 10: 281–291.

Gordon, Kerry. 2004. "The Tiger's Stripe: Some Thoughts on Psychoanalysis, Gnosis, and the Experience of Wonderment". *Contemporary Psychoanalysis* 40: 5–45. https://doi.org/10.1080/00107530.2004.10747234

Greene, Brian. 2003. *The Elegant Universe: Superstrings, Hidden Dimensions, and the Quest for the Ultimate Theory*. New York: W. W. Norton.

———. 2005. *The Fabric of the Cosmos*. New York: Vintage Books.

Grotstein, James. S. 1981. "Wilfred R. Bion: The Man, the Psychoanalyst, the Mystic: A Perspective on his Life and Work". *Contemporary Psychoanalysis*, 17: 501–536. https://doi.org/10.1080/00107530.1981.10746566

———. 1983. "Wilfred R. Bion: The Man, The Psychoanalyst, The Mystic: A Perspective on his Life and Work". In *Do I Dare Disturb the Universe? A Memorial to Wilfred R. Bion*, edited by James S. Grotstein, 1–35. London: Maresfield Reprints.

———. 1997. "Bion, the Pariah of 'O'". *British Journal of Psychotherapy* 14 (1): 77–90. https://doi.org/10.1111/j.1752-0118.1997.tb00354.x

———. 1998. "The Numinous and Immanent Nature of the Psychoanalytic Subject". *Journal of Analytical Psychology* 43: 41–68. https://doi.org/10.1111/1465-5922.00007

———. 2000. *Who is the Dreamer Who Dreams the Dream?: A Study of Psychic Presences*. Hillsdale, NJ: The Analytic Press.

———. 2004a. "Spirituality, Religion, Politics, History, Apocalypse and Transcendence: An Essay on a Psychoanalytically and Religiously Forbidden Subject". *International Journal of Applied Psychoanalytic Studies* 1: 82–95. https://doi.org/10.1002/aps.60

———. 2004b. "The Seventh Servant: The Implications of a Truth Drive in Bion's Theory of 'O'". *International Journal of Psychoanalysis* 85: 1081–1101. https://doi.org/10.1516/JU9M-1TK1-54QJ-LWTP

———. 2004c. "The Light Militia of the Lower Sky: The Deeper Nature of Dreaming and Phantasying". *Psychoanalytic Dialogues* 14 (1): 99–118. https://doi.org/10.1080/10481881409348776

———. 2004d. Foreword to *Psyche, Self and Soul: Rethinking Psychoanalysis, the Self and Spirituality*, by Gerald J. Gargiulo. London: Whurr/Wiley Bros.

———. 2007. *A Beam of Intense Darkness: Wilfred Bion's Legacy to Psychoanalysis*. London: Karnac Books.

———. 2009a. "Dreaming as a 'Curtain of Illusion': Revisiting the 'Royal Road' with Bion as our Guide". *International Journal of Psychoanalysis* 90: 733–752. https://doi.org/10.1111/j.1745-8315.2009.00155.x

———. 2009b. *But at the Same Time, and on Another Level: Psychoanalytic Theory and Technique in the Kleinian/Bionian Mode*. Vol. 1. London: Karnac Books.

———. 2009c. *But at the Same Time and on Another Level: Clinical Applications in the Kleinian/Bionian Mode*. Vol. 2. London: Karnac Books.

Grotstein, James S. and Maureen Franey. 2008. "Conversations with Clinicians: Who is the Writer who Writes the Books?" *fort da* 14: 87–116.

Grubrich-Simitis, Ilse. 1995. "No Greater, Richer, More Mysterious Subject [...] than the Life of the Mind: An Early Exchange of Letters between Freud and Einstein". *International Journal of Psychoanalysis* 76: 115–122.

———. 2004. "How Freud Wrote and Revised his *Interpretation of Dreams*: Conflicts around the Subjective Origins of the Book of the Century", translated by Arnold J. Pomerans. In *Dreams and History: The Interpretation of Dreams from Ancient Greece to Modern Psychoanalysis*, edited by Daniel Pick and Lyndal Roper, 23–36. London: Routledge.

Gyimesi, Júlia. 2009. "The Problem of Demarcation: Psychoanalysis and the Occult". *American Imago*, 66 (4): 457–470. https://doi.org/10.1353/aim.0.0064

Habermas, J. 1992. *Postmetaphysical Thinking: Philosophical Essays*, translated by William Mark Hohengarten. Cambridge, MA: MIT Press.

Hamilton, Trevor. 2009. *Immortal Longings: FWH Myers and the Victorian Search for Life after Death*. Exeter: Imprint Academic.

Hanegraaff, Wouter J. 1995. "Empirical Method in the Study of Esotericism". *Method & Theory in the Study of Religion* 7 (2): 99–129. https://doi.org/10.1163/157006895X00342

———. 1998. "The New Age Movement and the Esoteric Tradition". In *Gnosis and Hermeticism: From Antiquity to Modern Times*, edited by Roelof van den Broek and Wouter Hanegraaff, 359–382. New York: State University of New York Press.

———. 2000. "New Age Religion and Secularization". *Numen* 47 (3): 288–312. https://doi.org/10.1163/156852700511568

———. 2003. "How Magic Survived the Disenchantment of the World". *Religion* 33: 357–380. https://doi.org/10.1016/S0048-721X(03)00053-8

———. 2008. "Leaving the Garden (In Search of Religion): Jeffrey J. Kripal's Vision of a Gnostic Study of Religion". *Religion* 38: 259–276. https://doi.org/10.1016/j.religion.2008.02.001

———. 2012. *Esotericism and the Academy: Rejected Knowledge in Western Culture*. New York: Cambridge University Press.

Harris, Adrienne. 2004. "Haunted Bodies: Commentary on Melanie Suchet's 'Whose Mind is it Anyway?'" *Studies in Gender and Sexuality* 5 (3): 289–302. https://doi.org/10.1080/15240650509349251

———. 2011. "The Relational Tradition: Landscape and Canon". *Journal of the American Psychoanalytic Association* 59 (4): 701–735. https://doi.org/10.1177/0003065111416655

Heinemann, Evelyn. 2000. *Witches: A Psychoanalytic Exploration of the Killing of Women*, translated by Donald Kiraly. London: Free Association Books.

Hewitt, M. A. 2008. "Attachment Theory, Religious Beliefs, and the Limits of Reason". *Pastoral Psychology* 57: 65–75. https://doi.org/10.1007/s11089-008-0136-z

———. 2014a. *Freud on Religion*. Durham: Acumen.

———. 2014b. "Freud and the Psychoanalysis of Telepathy: Commentary on Claudie Massicotte's 'Psychical Transmissions'". *Psychoanalytic Dialogues* 24 (1): 103–108. https://doi.org/10.1080/10481885.2014.870841

———. 2017. "The Psychoanalytic Occult in Freud and Contemporary Theory". In *Religion: Super Religion*, edited by Jeffrey J. Kripal, 43–60. Farmington Mills, MI: MacMillan Reference.

———. 2018a. "Christian Anti-Judaism and Early Object Relations Theory". *Critical Research on Religion* 6 (3): 226–442. https://doi.org/10.1177/2050303218800378

———. 2018b. "Heavenly Republics and Democratic Spiritualities: Grief, Trauma and Social Reform in Nineteenth-Century American Spiritualism". Paper presented at a conference on "Early Christianity, Spirits and Democracy" at the Department for the Study of Religion, University of Toronto, May 5, 2018.

Hill, Peter C., and Ralph W. Hood, Jr. 1999. "Affect, Religion, and Unconscious Processes". *Journal of Personality* 67 (6): 1015–1046. https://doi.org/10.1111/1467-6494.00081

Hood, Ralph W., Jr. 2002. "The Mystical Self: Lost and Found". *International Journal for the Psychology of Religion* 12 (1): 1–14. https://doi.org/10.1207/S15327582IJPR 1201_01

Hood, Ralph W., Jr. and W. Paul Williamson. 2008. *Them that Believe: The Power and Meaning of the Christian Serpent-Handling Tradition*. Berkeley, CA: University of California Press. https://doi.org/10.1525/california/9780520231474.001.0001

Horkheimer, M. and T. W. Adorno. 2002. *Dialectic of Enlightenment: Philosophical Fragments*, translated by E. Jephcott. Stanford, CA: Stanford University Press.

Hyman, Ray. 2010. "Meta-Analysis that Conceals More Than it Reveals: Comment on Storm et al. *Psychological Bulletin* 136 (4): 486–490. https://doi.org/10.1037/a0019676

Jackson, M. and K. W. M. Fulford. 1997. "Spiritual Experience and Psychopathology". *Philosophy, Psychiatry, & Psychology* 4: 41–65. https://doi.org/10.1353/ppp.1997.0002

———. 2002. "Psychosis Good and Bad: Values-Based Practice and the Distinction between Pathological and Nonpathological Forms of Psychotic Experience". *Philosophy, Psychiatry, & Psychology* 9: 387–394. https://doi.org/10.1353/ppp.2003.0059

Jackson, Shirley. [1959] 2006. *The Haunting of Hill House*. New York: Penguin.

Jacobs, T. J. 2001. "On Unconscious Communications and Covert Enactments: Some Reflections on Their Role in the Analytic Situation". *Psychoanalytic Inquiry* 21: 4–23. https://doi.org/10.1080/07351692109348921

James, William. [1890] 1950. *The Principles of Psychology*, two volumes. New York: Dover.

———. 1896. "Address of the President before the Society for Psychical Research". *Science* 3 (77): 881–888. https://doi.org/10.1126/science.3.77.881

———. [1898] 1982. "Human Immortality". In *The Works of William James. Vol. 11: Essays in Religion and Morality*, edited by Frederick H. Burkhardt, Fredson Bowers, and Ignas K. Skrupskelis, 77–101. Cambridge, MA: Harvard University Press.

---. [1898] 1986. "Review of 'A Further Record of Observations of Certain Phenomena of Trance', by Richard Hodgson". In *Essays in Psychical Research*, by William James, 187–191. Cambridge, MA: Harvard University Press.
---. [1901] 1986. "Frederic Myers's Service to Psychology". In *Essays in Psychical Research*, by William James, 192–202. Cambridge, MA: Harvard University Press.
---. [1902] 2004. *The Varieties of Religious Experience: A Study in Human Nature*. New York: Barnes & Noble Classics.
---. [1903] 1986. "Review of *Human Personality and Its Survival of Bodily Death*, by Frederic W. H. Myers". In *Essays in Psychical Research*, by William James, 203–215. Cambridge, MA: Harvard University Press.
---. 1909a. "A Pluralistic Universe". In *William James: Writings 1902-1910*, edited by Bruce Kuklick, 627–819. New York: The Library of America.
---. [1909b] 1986. "Report on Mrs Piper's Hodgson-Control". In *Essays in Psychical Research*, by William James, 253–360. Cambridge, MA: Harvard University Press.
---. 1910. "A Suggestion about Mysticism". In *William James: Writings 1902-1910*, edited by Bruce Kuklick, 1272–1280. New York: The Library of America.
Jones, Earnest. 1957. *The Life and Work of Sigmund Freud: The Last Phase*, vol. 3. New York: Basic Books.
Joseph, Betty. 1985. "Transference: the Total Situation". *International Journal of Psychoanalysis* 66: 447–454.
Jung, C. G. [1938] 1973. *Psychology & Religion*. Clinton, MA: Yale University Press.
---. [1953] 1977. *Two Essays on Analytical Psychology*, translated by R. F. C. Hull. Bollingen Series XX. Princeton, NJ: Princeton University Press.
---. [1955] 2008. *Synchronicity: An Acausal Connecting Principle*. London: Routledge.
---. [1956] 1990. "Two Kinds of Thinking. In *Symbols of Transformation*, translated by R. F. C. Hull. Bollingen Series XX. Princeton, NJ: Princeton University Press.
---. 1963. *Memories, Dreams, Reflections*, edited by Aniela Jaffé and translated by Richard and Clara Winston. New York: Vintage.
Kakar, Sudhir. 2009. *Mad and Divine: Spirit and Psyche in the Modern World*. Chicago, IL: University of Chicago Press. https://doi.org/10.7208/chicago/9780226422893.001.0001
Kaku, Michio. 2005. *Parallel Worlds: A Journey Through Creation, Higher Dimensions, and the Future of the Cosmos*. New York: Anchor Books.
---. 2014. *The Future of the Mind*. New York: Doubleday.
Katz, Stephen. 1978. *Mysticism and Philosophical Analysis*. New York: Oxford University Press.
Keeley, J. P. 2001. "Subliminal Promptings: Psychoanalytic Theory and the Society for Psychical Research". *American Imago* 58: 767–791. https://doi.org/10.1353/aim.2001.0021
Kelly, Emily Williams. 2007. "F. W. H. Myers and the Empirical Study of the Mind-Body Problem". Chap. 2 in *Irreducible Mind: Toward a Psychology for the 21st Century*,

by Edward F. Kelly, Emily Williams Kelly, Adam Crabtree, Alan Gauld, Michael Grosso, and Bruce Greyson. Lanham, MD: Rowman & Littlefield.

Kirkpatrick, Lee. 1999. "Attachment and Religious Representations and Behaviour". In *Handbook of Attachment*, edited by J. Cassidy and P. R. Shaver, 803–822. New York: Guilford.

———. 2005. *Attachment, Evolution, and the Psychology of Religion*. New York: Guilford.

Kohut, Heinz. 1966. "Forms and Transformations of Narcissism". *Journal of the American Psychoanalytic Association* 14: 243–272. https://doi.org/10.1177/000306516601400201

Kripal, Jeffrey J. 1999. "'The Visitation of the Stranger': On Some Mystical Dimensions of the History of Religions". *Cross Currents* 49 (3): 367–386.

———. 2001. *Roads of Excess, Palaces of Wisdom: Eroticism and Reflexivity in the Study of Mysticism*. Chicago, IL: University of Chicago Press.

———. 2007a. *Esalen: America and the Religion of No Religion*. Chicago, IL: University of Chicago Press.

———. 2007b. *The Serpent's Gift: Gnostic Reflections on the Study of Religion*. Chicago, IL: University of Chicago Press.

———. 2010. *Authors of the Impossible: The Paranormal and the Sacred*. Chicago, IL: University of Chicago Press.

———. 2011. *Mutants and Mystics: Science Fiction, Superhero Comics, and the Paranormal*. Chicago, IL: University of Chicago Press.

———. 2012a. "The Dominant, the Damned, and the Discs: On the Metaphysical Liberalism of Charles Fort and its Afterlives", in *American Religious Liberalism*, edited by Leigh E. Schmidt & Sally M. Promey, 227–251. Bloomington, IN: Indiana University Press.

———. 2012b. "Mind Matters: Esalen's Sursem Group and the Ethnography of Consciousness". In *What Matters? Ethnographies of Value in a (Not So) Secular Age*, edited by Ann Taves and Courtney Bender, 215–247. New York: Columbia University Press. https://doi.org/10.7312/columbia/9780231156851.003.0008

———. 2014. *Comparing Religions: Coming to Terms*. Chichester: Wiley Blackwell.

———. 2015. "The Traumatic Secret: Bataille and the Comparative Erotics of Mystical Literature". In *Negative Ecstasies: Georges Bataille and the Study of Religion*, edited by Jeremy Biles and Kent L. Brintnall, 153–270. New York: Fordham University Press.

La Barre, Weston. [1970] 2010. *The Ghost Dance: The Origins of Religion*. Maidstone: Crescent Moon Publishing.

Laing, R. D. [1959] 1965. *The Divided Self: An Existential Study in Sanity and Madness*. London: Penguin Books.

———. 1964. "Review of the book *General Psychology* by Karl Jaspers". *International Journal of Psychoanalysis* 45: 590–593.

———. 1967. *The Politics of Experience and The Bird of Paradise*. London: Penguin Books.

Laplanche, J. and J-B Pontalis. 1973. *The Language of Psychoanalysis*, translated by Donald Nicholson-Smith. New York: W.W. Norton.

Lazar, S. G. 2001. "Knowing, Influencing, and Healing: Paranormal Phenomena and Implications of Psychoanalysis and Psychotherapy". *Psychoanalytic Inquiry* 21: 113-131. https://doi.org/10.1080/07351692109348926

Lev, Gideon. 2017. "Getting to the Heart of Life: Psychoanalysis as a Spiritual Practice". *Contemporary Psychoanalysis* 53 (2): 222-246. https://doi.org/10.1080/00107530.2017.1295773

Loewald, H. 2000. *The Essential Loewald: Collected Papers and Monographs*. Hagerstown, MD: University Publishing Group.

Lovejoy, Derek. 1999-2000. "Objectivity, Causality and Ideology in Modern Physics". *Science & Society* 63 (4): 433-458.

Luckhurst, Roger. 2002. *The Invention of Telepathy: 1870-1901*. Oxford: Oxford University Press.

Mack, Michael. 2003. "Testing the Compatibility of Psychoanalysis and Contemporary Neuroscience: Freud between Spinoza and Kant". *Avello Journal: The Unconscious* 2 (1): 3-27.

Marcus, D. M. 1997. "On Knowing What One Knows". *Psychoanalytic Quarterly* 66: 219-241. https://doi.org/10.1080/21674086.1997.11927532

Marcuse, Herbert. [1955] 1962. *Eros and Civilization: A Philosophical Inquiry into Freud*. New York: Vintage Books.

Martinez, Diane Lawson. 2001. "Intuition, Unconscious Communication and Thought 'Transference'". *Journal of Applied Psychoanalytic Studies* 3 (2): 211-219. https://doi.org/10.1023/A:1010169813039

Mayer, E. L. 1996. "Changes in Science and Changing Ideas about Knowledge and Authority in Psychoanalysis". *Psychoanalytic Quarterly* 65: 158-200. https://doi.org/10.1080/21674086.1996.11927487

———. 2002. "Freud and Jung: The Boundaried Mind and the Radically Connected Mind". *Journal of Analytical Psychology* 47: 91-99. https://doi.org/10.1111/1465-5922.00291

———. 2008. *Extraordinary Knowing: Science, Skepticism, and the Inexplicable Powers of the Human Mind*. New York: Bantam Books.

McDermott, Robert A. 1986. "Introduction". In *Essays in Psychical Research: William James*, by William James, xiii-xxxvi. Cambridge, MA: Harvard University Press.

Merkur, Dan. 2010. *Explorations of the Psychoanalytic Mystics*. Amsterdam: Rodopi. https://doi.org/10.1163/9789042028609

Myers, F. W. H. [1903] 2005. *Human Personality and Its Survival of Bodily Death*, edited by Susy Smith (abbreviated from the original). Mineola, NY: Dover.

Nicholls, Angus, and Martin Liebscher, eds. 2010. Introduction to *Thinking the Unconscious: Nineteenth-Century German Thought*, 1-25. Cambridge: Cambridge University Press. https://doi.org/10.1017/CBO9780511712272.001

Noakes, Richard J. 1999. "Telegraphy is an Occult Art: Cromwell Fleetwood Varley and the Diffusion of Electricity to the Other World". *British Journal for the History of Science* 32 (4): 421-459. https://doi.org/10.1017/S0007087499003763

———. 2008. "The 'World of the Infinitely Little': Connecting Physical and Psychical Realities". *Studies in the History and Philosophy of Science* 39: 323–334. https://doi.org/10.1016/j.shpsa.2008.06.004

Ogden, T. 1997. "Reverie and Interpretation". *Psychoanalytic Quarterly* LXVI: 567–595. https://doi.org/10.1080/21674086.1997.11927546

———. 2001. "Conversations at the Frontier of Dreaming". *fort da* 78: 7–14.

———. 2004. "On Holding and Containing, Being and Dreaming". *International Journal of Psychoanalysis* 85: 1349–1364. https://doi.org/10.1516/T41H-DGUX-9JY4-GQC7

———. 2007. "On Talking-as-Dreaming". *International Journal of Psychoanalysis* 88: 575–589. https://doi.org/10.1516/PU23-5627-04K0-7502

———. 2008. "Bion's Four Principles of Mental Functioning". *fort da* 14B: 11–35.

———. 2009. *Rediscovering Psychoanalysis: Thinking and Dreaming, Learning and Forgetting*. London: Routledge.

———. 2010. "On Three forms of Thinking: Magical Thinking, Dream Thinking, and Transformative Thinking". *Psychoanalytic Quarterly* 79: 317–347. https://doi.org/10.1002/j.2167-4086.2010.tb00450.x

O'Shaughnessy, Edna. 2005. "Whose Bion?" *International Journal of Psychoanalysis* 86 (6): 1523–1528. https://doi.org/10.1516/DDJD-MC5U-Y13N-YPUA

Ostow, Mortimer. 2004. "Psychodynamics of Spirituality". *International Journal of Applied Psychoanalytic Studies* 1: 47–60. https://doi.org/10.1002/aps.57

Owen, Alex. 2004. *The Place of Enchantment: British Occultism and the Culture of the Modern*. Chicago, IL: University of Chicago Press. https://doi.org/10.7208/chicago/9780226642031.001.0001

Panksepp, Jaak. 1998. *Affective Neuroscience: The Foundations of Human and Animal Emotions*. New York: Oxford University Press.

Parsons, William B. 1999. *The Enigma of the Oceanic Feeling: Revisioning the Psychoanalytic Theory of Mysticism*. New York: Oxford University Press.

Partridge, Christopher. 2005. *The Re-Enchantment of the West: Alternative Spiritualities, Sacralization, Popular Culture, and Occulture*, vol. 2. London: T. & T. Clark International.

———. 2018. *High Culture: Drugs, Mysticism, and the Pursuit of Transcendence in the Modern World*. New York: Oxford University Press.

Paul, Robert. 1991. "Freud's Anthropology: A Reading of the 'Cultural Books'". In *The Cambridge Companion to Freud*, edited by Jerome Neu, 267–286. Cambridge UK: Cambridge University Press. https://doi.org/10.1017/CCOL0521374243.012

———. 2010. "Yes, the Primal Crime Did Take Place: A Further Defense of Freud's *Totem and Taboo*". *Ethos: Journal of the Society for Psychological Anthropology* 38 (2): 230–249. https://doi.org/10.1111/j.1548-1352.2010.01137.x

———. 2015. *Mixed Messages: Cultural and Genetic Inheritance in the Constitution of Human Society*. Chicago, IL: University of Chicago Press.

Pile, Steve. 2012. "Distant Feelings: Telepathy and the Problem of Affect Transfer Over Distance". *Transactions of the Institute of British Geographers* 37 (1): 44–59. https://doi.org/10.1111/j.1475-5661.2011.00458.x

Proudfoot, Wayne. 2000. "William James on an Unseen Order". *Harvard Theological Review* 93 (1): 51–66. https://doi.org/10.1017/S0017816000016667
Reiner, Annie. 2004. "Psychic Phenomena and Early Emotional States". *Journal of Psychoanalytic Psychology*. 49: 313–336. https://doi.org/10.1111/j.1465-5922.2004.00464.x
Rennie, Bryan. 2007. "Mircea Eliade and the Perception of the Sacred in the Profane: Intention, Reduction, and Cognitive Theory". *Temenos* 43 (1): 73–98. https://doi.org/10.33356/temenos.4625
Richards, Graham. 2000. "Britain on the Couch: The Popularization of Psychoanalysis in Britain 1914–1940". *Science in Context* 13 (2): 183–230. https://doi.org/10.1017/S0269889700003793
Richardson, Judith. 2003. *Possessions: The History and Uses of Haunting in the Hudson Valley*. Cambridge, MA: Harvard University Press.
Ricoeur, P. 1970. *Freud and Philosophy: An Essay on Interpretation*, translated by D. Savage. New Haven, CT: Yale University Press.
Rosenbaum, R. 2011. "Exploring the *Other* Dark Continent: Parallels between Psi Phenomena and the Psychotherapeutic Process". *Psychoanalytic Review* 98: 57–90. https://doi.org/10.1521/prev.2011.98.1.57
Rosenfeld, H. 1988. "The Psychopathology of Psychotic States: the Importance of Projective Identification in the Ego Structure and the Object Relations of the Psychotic Patient". In *Melanie Klein Today: Developments in Theory and Practice*, vol. 1, edited by E. B. Spillius, 117–137. London: Routledge.
Rosenthal, Lecia. 2010. "Fictions of Possession: Psychoanalysis and the Occult". In *Freud and Fundamentalism: The Psychical Politics of Knowledge*, edited by S. Gourgouris, 125–137. New York: Fordham University Press.
Rottenberg, Elizabeth. 2017. "What are the Chances? Psychoanalysis, Telepathy, and the Accident". *Paragraph* 40 (3): 310–328. https://doi.org/10.3366/para.2017.0237
Royle, Nicholas. 1995. *After Derrida*. Manchester: Manchester University Press.
Schimmel, Paul. 2014. *Sigmund Freud's Discovery of Psychoanalysis: Conquistador and Thinker*. New York: Routledge. https://doi.org/10.4324/9781315886770
Schmidt, Leigh Eric. 2003. "The Making of Modern Mysticism". *Journal of the American Academy of Religion* 71 (2): 273–302. https://doi.org/10.1093/jaar/71.2.273
Schore, Allan. N. 2011. "The Right Brain Implicit Self Lies at the Core of Psychoanalysis". *Psychoanalytic Dialogues* 21: 75–100.
——. 2012. *The Science and the Art of Psychotherapy*. New York: W. W. Norton. https://doi.org/10.1080/10481885.2011.545329
Schwartz, Joseph. 1995. "What Does the Physicist Know? Thraldom and Insecurity in the Relationship of Psychoanalysis to Physics". *Psychoanalytic Dialogues* 5: 45–62. https://doi.org/10.1080/10481889509539049
Shamdasani, Sonu. 2015. "S.W. and C.G. Jung: Mediumship, Psychiatry and Serial Exemplarity". *History of Psychiatry* 26 (3): 288–302. https://doi.org/10.1177/0957154X14562745

Smith, Jonathan Z. [1978] 1993. *Map is not Territory*. Chicago, IL: University of Chicago.
———. [1982] 1988. "Sacred Persistence: Toward a Redescription of Canon". In *Imagining Religion: From Babylon to Jonestown*. Chicago, IL: University of Chicago.
———. 2004. "Religion, Religions, Religious". In *Relating Religion: Essays in the Study of Religions*. Chicago, IL: University of Chicago.
Soffer-Dudek, Nir. 2015. "Overcoming O: Dewey and the Problem of Bion's Metaphysics". *Journal of the American Psychoanalytic Association* 63 (5): 937–945. https://doi.org/10.1177/0003065115604460
Solms, Mark. 1995. "Is the Brain More Real than the Mind?" *Psychoanalytic Psychotherapy* 9: 107–120. https://doi.org/10.1080/02668739500700121
———. 2013. "The Conscious Id". *Neuropsychoanalysis* 15 (1): 5–19. https://doi.org/10.1080/15294145.2013.10773711
———. 2016. "'The Unconscious' in Psychoanalysis and Neuroscience". In *The Unconscious: A Bridge between Psychoanalysis and Cognitive Neuroscience*, edited by Marianne Leuzinger-Bohleber, Simon Arnold and Mark Solms, 16–35. London: Routledge.
Spezzano, Charles, and Gerald J. Gargiulo, eds. 1997. *Soul on the Couch: Spirituality, Religion, and Morality in Contemporary Psychoanalysis*. Hillsdale, NJ: Analytic Press.
Spiro, Melford E. 1968. "Religion: Problems of Definition and Explanation". In *Anthropological Approaches to the Study of Religion*, edited by Michael Banton, 85–126. London: Tavistock Publications.
Starr, Karen E. 2008. *Repair of the Soul: Metaphors of Transformation in Jewish Mysticism and Psychoanalysis*. New York: Routledge.
Stoller, R. 2001. "Telepathic Dreams?" Edited by Elizabeth Lloyd Mayer. *Journal of the American Psychoanalytic Association* 49: 635–652 [Mayer's introduction is at 629–634].
Strieber, Whitley and Jeffrey J. Kripal. 2017. *The Super Natural: Why the Unexplained is Real*. New York: Tarcherperigree.
Suchet, Melanie. 2004. "Whose Mind is it Anyway?" *Studies in Gender and Sexuality* 5 (1): 259–287. https://doi.org/10.1080/15240650509349250
———. 2016. "Surrender, Transformation, and Transcendence". *Psychoanalytic Dialogues* 26: 747–760. https://doi.org/10.1080/10481885.2016.1235945
Sullivan, Barbara Stevens. 2010. *The Mystery of Analytical Work: Weavings from Jung and Bion*. London: Routledge
Taves, Ann. 2003. "Religious Experience and the Divisible Self: William James (and Frederic Myers) as Theorist(s) of Religion". *Journal of the American Academy of Religion* 71 (2): 303–326. https://doi.org/10.1093/jaar/71.2.303
———. 2009. "William James Revisited: Rereading *The Varieties of Religious Experience* in Transatlantic Perspective". *Zygon* 44 (2): 415–432. https://doi.org/10.1111/j.1467-9744.2009.01006.x
Taylor, Eugene. 1996a. "The New Jung Scholarship". *Psychoanalytic Review* 83 (4): 547–568.

———. 1996b. *William James on Consciousness Beyond the Margin*. Princeton, NJ: Princeton University Press.

———. 1999a. "William James and Sigmund Freud: 'The Future of Psychology belongs to Your Work'". *Psychological Science* 10 (6): 465–469. https://doi.org/10.1111/1467-9280.00190

———. 1999b. *Shadow Culture: Psychology and Spirituality in America*. Washington, DC: Counterpoint.

———. 2010. "William James and the Humanistic Implications of the Neuroscience Revolution: An Outrageous Hypothesis". *Journal of Humanistic Psychology* 50 (4): 410–429. https://doi.org/10.1177/0022167810376305

Tennes, Mary. 2007. "Beyond Intersubjectivity: The Transpersonal Dimension of the Psychoanalytic Encounter". *Contemporary Psychoanalysis* 43 (4): 505–525. https://doi.org/10.1080/00107530.2007.10745929

Treitel, Corinna. 2004. *A Science for the Soul: Occultism and the Genesis of the German Modern*. Baltimore, MD: Johns Hopkins University Press.

Van der Kolk, Bessel. 2015. *The Body Keeps the Score: Brain, Mind, and Body in the Healing of Trauma*. New York: Penguin Books.

White, Robert S. 2011. "Bion and Mysticism: The Western Tradition". *American Imago* 68 (2): 213–240. https://doi.org/10.1353/aim.2011.0027

Whitebook, Joel. 2017. *Freud: An Intellectual Biography*. New York: Cambridge University Press. https://doi.org/10.1017/9781139025119

Winnicott, D. W. 1974. "Fear of Breakdown". *International Review of Psycho-analysis* 1: 103–107.

———. [1960] 1990. *The Maturational Processes and the Facilitating Environment*. London: Karnac Books.

Wolffram, Heather. 2009. *The Stepchildren of Science: Psychical Research and Parapsychology in Germany, c.1870–1939*. Amsterdam: Rodopi.

Wooffitt, Robin. 2017. "Relational Psychoanalysis and Anomalous Communication: Continuities and Discontinuities in Psychoanalysis and Telepathy". *History of the Human Sciences* 30 (1): 118–137. https://doi.org/10.1177/0952695116684311

Wulff, David M. 2014. "Mystical Experiences". In *Varieties of Anomalous Experience: Examining the Scientific Evidence*, 2nd edition, edited by Etzel Cardeña, Steven Jay Lynn and Stanley Krippner, 369–408. Washington, DC: American Psychological Association. https://doi.org/10.1037/14258-013

Wuthnow, Robert. 1998. *After Heaven: Spirituality in America Since the 1950s*. Berkeley, CA: University of California Press. https://doi.org/10.1525/california/9780520213968.001.0001

Index

Adorno, Theodor 73, 77
   see also Horkheimer, Max and Theodor Adorno
American Society for Psychical Research (ASPR) 25
Applebaum, Jerome 112
Arden, Margaret 100
Arnold, Kenneth 129
Aron, Lew 67, 115
Asprem, Egil 3
attachment theory 148–149

Balint, Michael 66
   telepathic dreams 65, 108
Barad, Karen 111
Bass, Anthony 106
Bell's theorem 76
Beller, Maria 111, 113
Bender, Courtney 20
Bergson, Henri 41
Bernstein, Jay 141
Binswanger, Ludwig 9
Bion, Wilfred 82–84, 85, 86, 105, 136
Bion, Wilfred and James Grotstein 83–84, 86–87, 105, 115, 117
   alpha, beta elements 45, 86, 117, 120, 136–137
   "O" 83–84, 85–86, 104, 117, 120–121
Bohm, David 76, 77, 106
Bohr, Niels 113
Born, Max 113
Breuer, Josef see Freud, Sigmund
Britton, Ronald 64
Burkert, Walter 7

Caper, Robert 64
Carroll, Bret 33
Castoriadis, Cornelius 6
coincidentia oppositorum 58

Deutsch, Helen
   occult 68

Eckhart, Meister 132
Einstein, Albert 112, 113, 124
Eliade, Mircea 58–59, 85, 104, 115, 120, 126
Emerson, Ralph Waldo 45, 49, 105
ether metaphysics 41

Ferenczi, Sándor 59–60
Feuerbach, Ludwig
   The Essence of Christianity 143–144
Feynman, Richard 111
Fliess, Wilhelm 7
Fodor, Nandor see Freud, Sigmund
Forsyth, David see Freud, Sigmund
free association 25–26, 27
Freud, Sigmund 52, 86, 87, 130, 133–134, 152
   anti-Semitism 17–18
   archaic inheritance 7–8, 12, 14, 23
   Charcot, Jean-Martin 27
   collective unconscious 7, 8, 14, 150
   "The Dissection of the Psychical Personality" 24
   dreaming, dreams 79, 80, 109, 135
   drive theory 29, 72
   The Ego and the Id 24

Einstein, Albert 130
the Enlightenment 4, 5
evolutionary anthropology 8
"foreconscious" and "preconscious" 29
"Formulations on the Two Principles of Mental Functioning" 12–13
Forsyth, David 90–92
free association 25–26, 27
The Future of an Illusion 9, 10, 49, 90
Goetz, Bruno 18–19
Haizmann, Christoph 145–150, 151
Herr P. 90–92, 107, 109, 154
historical truth 68–69 *see also* material truth
hypnotism 25–26
the id 78
The Interpretation of Dreams 24, 29, 79
Janet, Pierre 36
Jews and trauma 150
Jung, Carl 10, 11, 12–14, 18
Leonardo da Vinci 73
material truth 68–69, 72
Moses and Monotheism 8, 68–69, 88
"A Note on the Unconscious in Psycho-analysis" 24, 28
the occult, occultism 27, 153–154, 155
oceanic feeling 16–17, 49–50, 52, 102, 127
Oedipus Rex 6–7
phylogenetic evolution 27
"pleasure-ego" and "reality-ego" 13
"Preliminary Communication" (with Josef Breuer) 25
primal crime 6
primal horde 8–9
theory of primary narcissism 70, 71, 72
Proceedings (journal of the Society for Psychical Research) 24, 25, 26, 28, 29
psychic reality 68, 69

psychoanalysis 1–2, 9, 24, 68, 89, 122–123, 153–155, 156–157
"The Psychotherapy of Hysteria" 18
The Question of a Weltanschauung 9–10
religion 1–2, 7–8, 9–10, 27, 94, 122, 155, 157
repression 23, 29, 36
Rolland, Roman 16–18, 49–50, 52, 127
science 9–10, 92–94
Society for Psychical Research (SPR) 24–25, 26, 28
Studies in Hysteria (with Josef Breuer) 25, 29, 30, 36
the subconscious and the unconscious 23–24, 28–29, 30
taboo 8
telepathic dreams 65–67, 109
telepathy 14, 26–27, 40, 88–89, 90, 93–94, 153–155, 157–157
the telephone 27–28
thought-transference (*Gedankenübertragung*) 14, 26, 67, 88, 153
Totem and Taboo 8, 88
trauma 150
the uncanny 56
the unconscious 1–2, 4–5, 9, 10, 12, 15, 22–24, 28–29, 30, 40, 78, 81, 93, 114, 153, 155
"The Unconscious" 24, 29
unconscious communication 27–28, 38, 40, 71, 88–89, 92–93, 94, 153, 155
unmediated consciousness 47
Vorsicht/Forsyth/Forsyte/foresight 91
Fuller, Robert 15, 115–116, 125

Gale, Richard 51
Ganzfeld experiment 100–102 *see also* Mayer, Elizabeth
Gargiulo, Gerald 103–104

Heisenberg, Werner 76
quantum physics 76, 77, 103, 112–114, 121
Gay, Peter
   Freud and telepathy 88
Gordon, Kerry 115
Greene, Brian
   parallel universes 77
Grotstein, James 76, 87, 88, 98–99, 121, 123, 135
   "angel" dream 79–80
   Bion, Wilfred 83–84
   dreams 79–81
   Gargiulo, Gerald 103
   Godhead 80–81, 84
   mystical and "Kabbalistic" themes in Freud 82
   "O" 82–83, 84, 85, 86
   psychoanalysis as a "religious" quest 117
   the unconscious 81–82, 87
Grotstein and Bion *see* Bion, Wilfred and James Grotstein

Habermas, Jürgen 118–119, 125
Haizmann, Christoph 145–150, 151
Hall, G. Stanley 1–2
Hamilton, Trevor 33, 37
Hanegraaff, Wouter 20, 119, 122
Harris, Adrienne 108
Hyman, Ray 162n2
Hegel, G.W. F. 73–74, 131
Heisenberg's uncertainty principle 77, 111
   indeterminacy 112
hierophany 58–59, 84, 85, 103, 104, 105, 120–121, 126 *see also* Eliade, Mircea
Hill, Peter 11
Hood, Ralph 11
Horkheimer, Max and Theodor Adorno 5
Husserl, Edmund 90
hypnotism 25–26

intersubjectivity 2–3, 59

Jackson, Shirley
   The Haunting of Hill House 136
James, William 4, 12, 14, 19, 39–57, 78, 105, 116, 123, 154
   A-region, B-region 45, 86
   American psychoanalysis 39
   conversion 96, 97
   dreams 56–57, 58
   Emerson, Ralph Waldo 45
   Hodgson, Richard 54–55
   metaphysical psychology 77, 115
   mother-sea 47, 105
   multiverse 47–48
   Myers, Frederic W. H. 39–40
   mystical experiences 58, 119
   Piper, Leonora 54, 55
   psychical and paranormal research 39
   radical empiricism 68
   Rankin, Henry W. 46–47
   religious feelings 89–90
   "Report on Mrs. Piper's Hodgson-Control" 54–55
   Society for Psychical Research (SPR) 25
   subconscious 28–29, 40, 44, 55
   subliminal consciousness 40, 53, 56, 58
   "A Suggestion about Mysticism" 55
   supraconscious 29
   supraliminal consciousness 56
   telepathic communication 40, 45
   trauma 63
   Trevor, J. 48–49, 50, 51–52, 56
   The Varieties of Religious Experience 42–43, 46, 48, 50, 53, 55, 56, 58
James and Myers *see* Myers, Frederic W. H. and William James
Janet, Pierre
   automatic writing 36
   Psychological Automatism 34–36
   the subconscious 34–36

Jaspers, Karl 125
Jung, Carl 10, 15, 120, 121
   analytical psychology 15
   Freud, Sigmund 12, 18
   "half-shadow" unconscious 14
   myths 12–14
   the occult 11
   psychotic regression 132
   quantum science 14
   synchronicity 14, 116
   telepathy 14
   "Two Kinds of Thinking" 12–14
   the unconscious 11, 12, 37

Kant, Immanuel 23
Kate 60–64, 65–67, 69, 75, 92, 106, 108, 109
Kirkpatrick, Lee 148–149
Kohut, Heinz
   cosmic narcissism 100
van der Kolk, Bessel 147
Kripal, Jeffrey 125–128, 131–132, 136, 143, 144, 151
   Eliade, Mircea 126
   Feuerbach, Ludwig 144
   Myers, Frederic W. H. and William James 124, 142, 143
   the paranormal as religious phenomenon 124–126
   Ramakrishna 133–134, 140, 141
   "religion of no religion" 39–40, 117
   "science mysticism" 104–105, 126
   Strieber, Whitley 128, 129–130, 140, 142
   telepathic communication 125–126
   "That Night" 133–134
   trauma 128

Laing, R. D. 75, 125, 130, 131, 132, 156
   Watkins, Jesse 131–132
Lev, Gideon 119–120
Loewald, Hans
   development of the mind 73–74
   dream interpretation 79
   Freud, Sigmund 69–72, 122
   "primordial experience" of infancy 74–75, 127
   psychic matrix 90, 100
   sublimation 73

Massignon, Louis 141
Mayer, Elizabeth 95–102, 104, 123, 126
   Ganzfeld experiment 100–102
   harp 95–96, 97, 99, 102
   James, William 96, 97, 102
   McCoy, Harold 95–96, 97
   quantum entanglement 102
   quantum physics 121
   Stoller, Robert 110–111
   telepathy 95
Merkur, Dan 42
   Bion, Wilfred 121
   Loewald, Hans 74
   "psychoanalytic mystics" 106
Mesmer, Anton 34
   magnetic fluids 41, 78
Myers, Frederic W. H. 30–34
   automatic writing 36
   Human Personality and its Survival of Bodily Death 39
   hypnotism 25–26
   Janet, Pierre 35–36
   Marshall, Annie 30–31
   multiplex mind 31, 37
   Piper, Leonora 31, 54
   post-mortem survival 31
   Society for Psychical Research (SPR) 25, 30
   the subconscious 30, 34, 36, 53
   subliminal consciousness, self 37–38, 40, 53
   "supernormal" capacities 26, 32, 38, 42
   "supraliminal" consciousness 37–38
   telepathic communication 26, 34, 38–39, 40

telepathy 33, 38, 42, 92
trauma 63
Myers, Frederic W. H. and William James 13, 68, 105, 121, 142
   cultural tradition of American spirituality 42
   ether metaphysics 41
   psychical and paranormal research 39
   relational ontology of science and spirituality 78
   spiritual psychology 41
   subconscious 24, 28–29, 41, 42
   telepathy 40, 94
   trauma 63
   unconscious 67
mystical psychoanalysis *see* psychoanalysis
mysticism and spirituality 19–20

New Age religions, thought 19–21, 95, 98, 114
Newtonian mechanics, physics 20

object relations theory 11
the occult 68
oceanic feeling 16–17, 49–50, 52
   unio mystica 16, 17, 71
"Odic" force 41
Oedipus Rex 6–7
Ogden, Thomas 62, 142, 147–148
   dreaming 134–137
   trauma 151
O'Shaughnessy, Edna 83

Palmer, Helen 106
parapsychoanalysis 94, 102–103, 11
Paul, Robert
   Oedipus Rex 6–7
   primal horde 9
Pauli, Wolfgang 113
de Peyer, Janine
   telepathy and quantum physics 99–100, 111, 113, 121

Piper, Leonora 31, 54, 55
Proudfoot, Wayne 47
psychoanalysis
   American 11, 15, 39, 102, 123
   mystical 9, 20, 39, 59, 78, 86, 102–103, 114, 116, 119, 122, 123, 125, 156
   "psychoanalytic physics" 106
   religion 1–2, 9, 122–123
   scientific or natural theory 9
Puységur, Marquis de 34
   magnetic fluid 41

quantum mechanics, physics, science, theory 14, 20, 21, 41, 75–78, 111–113, 116–117, 121

Reichenbach, Carl von 41
   "Odic" force 41
religion
   study of 1–2, 3, 10, 16, 122–123, 156
repression 23, 29
Richards, Graham 2
Richardson, Judith
   Hudson Valley 129
Ring, Kenneth 142
Rolland, Roman
   Freud, Sigmund 16–18, 49–50, 52
   oceanic feeling 16–17, 49–50, 52
Rosenthal, Lecia 90

Schmidt, Leigh 19
Schwartz, Joseph 111–112
Society for Psychical Research (SPR) 24–25, 26, 28, 43
spirit possession 32
Spiro, Melford E. 129
Stoller, Robert 107–110
   dreams 107
Strieber, Whitley 69, 151
   alien encounters 128–130, 138–140, 142, 145, 149, 150, 151
   the subconscious 30

subjectivity 73–74
Suchet, Melanie
　Cleo 106, 108, 109
　quantum physics 106, 121
supraconscious 29

Tadmor, Chaim 79
Taylor, Eugene 40
telepathic communications 21, 26, 41, 94, 106, 109, 123, 125
telepathic dreams 63, 64–65, 75–76
telepathic experience
　contemporary psychoanalysis 67
telepathy 3, 14, 26–27, 33, 38, 41, 42, 92, 99, 118, 153–155, 157–158
　see also Freud, Sigmund; Jung, Carl; Myers, Frederic W. H.
　Newtonian worldviews 95
　relational psychoanalysis 99
　science and modern rationality 3–4
　"supernormal" capacities 26
　thought-transference 14
trauma 63–64, 137, 139–142, 144, 150
　Abraham and Isaac 141
　Jesus 141

the uncanny 2–3, 56
the unconscious 1–2, 4–5, 9, 10, 11, 12, 22–24, 28–29, 30, 37, 40, 78, 81, 93, 114, 153, 155
　see also Freud, Sigmund; Jung, Carl
　collective unconscious 14
　drift 59, 67
　"half-shadow" unconscious 14
　the occult 11
　phylogenetic model 2
　religion 10
　repression 23, 29, 36
　the subconscious 23, 24
unconscious communication 41, 42, 63, 67, 68, 69, 76, 94, 116, 117, 125
　see also Freud, Sigmund
Underhill, Evelyn 119
unidentified flying objects (UFOs) 129, 130, 131

vitalism 41

Whitebook, Joel 9, 12
　unio maternalis 16
Winnicott, D. W. 134, 138
Wuthnow, Robert 3